Down to the Waterline

Down to the

SARA WARNER

Waterline

Boundaries, Nature, and the Law in Florida

The University of Georgia Press
Athens and London

© 2005 by the University of Georgia Press
Athens, Georgia 30602
All rights reserved

Designed by Sandra Strother Hudson
Set in 10/13 Galliard by G&S Typesetters, Inc.
Printed and bound by Maple-Vail
The recycled paper in this book meets the guidelines
for permanence and durability of the Committee
on Production Guidelines for Book Longevity of the
Council on Library Resources.

Printed in the United States of America
09 08 07 06 05 C 5 4 3 2 1

Library of Congress Cataloging-in-Publication Data

Warner, Sara, 1953–
Down to the waterline : boundaries, nature, and the law in
Florida / Sara Warner.
        p. cm.
Includes bibliographical references and index.
ISBN 0-8203-2703-4 (alk. paper)
1. Water boundaries—Florida.   2. Riparian areas—
Florida.   3. Watersheds—Florida.   4. Nature—Effect of
human beings on—Florida.   I. Title.
KFF446.W37 2005
346.75904'32—dc22
2004028034

British Library Cataloging-in-Publication Data available

For my father,

who showed me the amazing world.

Contents

Illustrations

Acknowledgments

MY SINCERE THANKS go to Ralph Berry, who encouraged me to write this book, helped me find its voice, and gave his much-sought-after attention to several careful readings. Ralph is one of those rare friends who knows what you risk in writing the book you really want to write.

My mentor and friend, Terry Wilkinson, taught me about the line. I suppose anyone who showed me a boundary I never knew existed would have placed on me the onus to redraw my world. Fortunately for me, Terry's ironic humor and vision make of most endeavors remarkable adventures, and this effort was no exception. His many valuable suggestions and corrections were served with a patience and wit seldom encountered in one's journeys.

My colleagues Rod Maddox and Joe Knetsch at the Bureau of Surveying and Mapping unfailingly lent their expertise and kindness to this undertaking, providing me the luxury of working with the most knowledgeable people in the United States on these issues. Dan Dearing, Anita Fodor, Bobby Jordan, Judy Johnson, Doug Woodward, and Scott Campbell performed what is to a writer that most wondrous of all deeds: each read my manuscript, made suggestions and corrections, and talked to me at length about it. Richard Malloy, Clay Hall, and Gene Callebs provided technical assistance and encouraged me in those bleak moments that are part of any long project.

I will always remember with much affection Professors Robert Silliman and Eugene Bianchi at Emory University, who gave great care and time to the dissertation from which this book emerged. Likewise, Emory's Graduate Institute of the Liberal Arts has earned an enduring place in my heart as "an oasis of calm in a troubled and turbulent universe," and I am grateful for the support I found there. Special thanks to Karen Cunningham, who prodded me at a key moment to write my dissertation.

My father, Henry Warner, read and corrected the manuscript as it developed, and continually hounded me for the next chapter. Because of the things he showed me about the world, the ideas in this book mattered to me. Without his interest and pride in me, this book would never have been attempted.

And thanks to Pete, who sees me through.

Introduction

THIS BOOK examines the broad shift in the American consciousness of the natural world by tracing the development of a centuries-old concept—the ordinary high water line. In the law of nearly all states, this line forms the boundary between publicly owned lands that lie beneath navigable waters and the adjoining uplands that are subject to private ownership. In Florida, because of the state's distinct topography, this boundary has been particularly controversial. It is this controversy that makes Florida's boundary such a telling case. For the ordinary high water line is not like other boundaries. It is a natural boundary that has been incorporated by our society into law. It differs from other boundaries in that it represents the dynamic forces of nature rather than the particular interests of humans.

Perhaps it is not surprising, then, that people have so little understanding of this line. Generally, we expect the law will reflect (only) human designs. And, it's also the case that few Americans have the opportunity to observe nature untransformed by human technology, so we don't readily identify the natural indicators of this boundary. Yet this boundary establishes the limit of some of the most valuable land in existence: in economic terms, waterfront real estate; in ecological terms, marshes and wetlands. With a steady flood of new residents and their demand for both waterfront property and clean water resources, the ordinary high water line boundary in Florida has come under increasing scrutiny, conflict, and challenge. But what this conflict reveals is not so much the battle over a rare commodity. Instead, what comes to light in these considerations is how this boundary acts as a marker of our awareness of and relationship with the natural world.

Even the wording of this simple statement hints at the way we have long conceived our species as somehow apart from the natural world—the notion that we must have *relations with* nature, that we are not of nature. Having grown up on Florida's Gulf Coast, I admit I have often wondered what it is we think we're doing when we build condos on top of the beaches, channelize some of the most biologically rich water sources in the state, or dredge and fill thousands of acres of marshes. Today, human technology is capable of overrunning the natural world, for better and for worse. But, in following out this case history, it has seemed to me it matters greatly where we locate our attention when we invoke the awesome capabilities of technology. Frequently in the past we have been focused on narrowly conceived goals without enough attention to consequences outside the project scope.

The legendary physicist, teacher, and science philosopher Richard Feynman often pointed out that some of the most important issues to humankind cannot be quantified and studied easily in science, and therefore are dismissed as unimportant: "Scientists take all those things that can be analyzed by observation, and thus the things called science are found out. But there are some things left out, for which the method does not work. This does not mean that those things are unimportant. They are, in fact, in many ways the most important. . . . They are humanitarian problems."[1]

This history of the ordinary high water line is in part a saga of its scientific development; but, more fundamentally, it is a case study of a humanitarian problem. The authority and cultural impact of science are themselves central to this story. Issues of language and the presentation of knowledge underlie many aspects of this inquiry. Radically different and irreconcilable viewpoints concerning science, law, and nature contribute to this analysis. Many voices shape the questions I articulate. My own position and interpretation of the situation, after many years of study, is elaborated. Rather than conceal or conflate these voices, positions, and interpretations, I have chosen to make plain their presence. I believe this presentation will allow readers to judge more readily the worth of my observations.

Over the course of this study, I have come to think of the ordinary high water line as a meditation on our place in nature. That this study also dwells on the scientific, legal, technical, and cultural histories of this boundary will, I hope, come to seem only the first step in understanding what this ancient concept might teach a modern age.

Down to the Waterline

But look! here come more crowds, pacing
straight for the water, and seemingly
bound for a dive. Strange! Nothing will
content them but the extremist limit of land.
HERMAN MELVILLE, *Moby Dick*

I   A Case of Conflict: Growth, Science, Tradition

ON A LEGAL HUNTING DAY in November 1994, four men followed their state-issued guidebook along Florida's Kissimmee River, exploring its marshy river swamp. Soon after daybreak, they were stopped by a deputized ranch hand who accused them of trespassing on private property. The men turned their airboats around and left, but that wasn't the end of the dispute. Arrested at their places of business in front of employees and clients, the hunters were soon facing trial for armed trespass, a felony that carries up to a five-year prison sentence. In response, the hunters filed a federal civil rights suit against the rancher, charging that he had commandeered thousands of acres of state property and was harassing citizens on public lands.[1]

This conflict between private property rights and public trust protection has many battlegrounds in American culture today. Perhaps nowhere do these battles ensue as readily as along public water bodies that, like the Kissimmee, form the confines of privately owned upland properties. During the European settlement of America, inland lakes and rivers provided ready transportation over vast reaches of wilderness and made exploration, agriculture, development, and commerce possible. Accordingly, American law recognized the importance of these geographic features, providing that navigable waters were "common highways, forever free" and vigorously defending the public's access to navigable waters.[2] Although few concepts are more fundamental in American thinking than that of private property rights, American society, from its beginning, upheld the notion that navigable waterways could not come under the purview of private ownership.[3] Especially notable is the development of law pertaining to navigable freshwaters. Under English common law, the test for publicly owned waters was whether the waters were tidally influenced.[4] This tidal test of public ownership sufficed for an island such as Great Britain, surrounded as it is by tidal waters; but the tidal influence test did nothing to protect the thousands of miles of navigable inland lakes and streams in America.[5] Thus, during the early nineteenth century, American law developed the concept of public ownership of navigable freshwaters, augmenting Britain's tidal influence test with the navigability test.[6]

When Florida became a state in 1845, the beds and shores of all navigable water bodies within its bounds passed to the state as sovereignty lands. These lands comprise part of a public trust, which the state, as the sovereign, is charged with protecting.[7] These sovereignty lands are the "property of the states, or of the people of the states in their united or sovereign capacity, and are held, not for purposes of sale or conversion into other values, or reduction into several or individual ownership, but for the use of all the people."[8] The English common law that Florida adopted at statehood located the boundary of sovereignty lands at the ordinary high watermark.[9] This mark became the basis of Florida's water boundaries, both tidal and nontidal. But the law concerning tidal water boundaries and the law concerning nontidal water boundaries developed at different times. This discrepancy arose because Britain's law addressed only tidal waters, and the body of law addressing nontidal waters grew up only as settlement began to intensify around the inland, fresh waters of the state. (Compared to Florida's coastal development, relatively little settlement of Florida's interior took place until the mid-twentieth century.) Eventually, the tidal water boundary came to be called the mean high water line, while the boundary on nontidal waters came to be called the ordinary high water line—also referred to as the OHWL. These boundaries, however, were both defined from the same mark, and the same concept, that has been used for centuries to protect navigable waters and their shores for public use.

So, in Florida today, as in many other states, the legal boundary between navigable freshwater lakes and streams and the privately owned uplands bordering them is the ordinary high water line.[10] The history of this concept, its interpretation and development in society and in the law, and the controversies surrounding this boundary in Florida are the overt subject of this book. But the particular situation of this boundary in Florida stands as a case study of the broader theme: how human relations with the natural world are changing in a technological age.

The present-day concept—ordinary high water line—has evolved from many centuries of law taken from other nations and languages and addressing vastly different topographies. A natural consequence of this long and particular development is that the terminology of this concept—as well as that of many other, related, scientific concepts—has evolved, and the criteria establishing the limits of the concept have been clarified. As it turns out, the issues of language comprise an important aspect of our current understanding of the ordinary high water line, or OHWL. So, as with any history, it is important not to assume that the precision of present-day terms was part of the understanding of those concepts in the past.

OHWL legal cases exemplify an increasingly vitriolic battle over the balance between property rights and public interest. In the instance of the four hunters arrested for trespass on the Kissimmee River, the rancher's case depended on proving that the men were on private property—not state-owned sovereignty lands. When the state cadastral surveyor appeared at the courthouse on the day of the trial to testify that the location where the hunters had been accosted was below the ordinary high water line (that is, on state land), charges were abruptly dropped. This isolated case might mean little in terms of the conflict between private and public interests were it not for the fact that similar cases have been prosecuted for years. Even though many of these cases were resolved with plea bargains or lesser charges, the injury of arrest and the expense of defending oneself had, by 1994, taken a toll on many an unwary sportsman. After the charges were dropped, Earth Justice Legal Defense Fund attorney David Guest—a former special projects litigator in the attorney general's office—called for the attorney general's office to reopen any case in which an individual had been prosecuted for trespass on disputed lands in the Kissimmee River area. In a subsequent letter to the state attorney in Orlando, Assistant Attorney

General Jonathan Glogau wrote that any future disputes of trespass should be prosecuted only if deemed necessary after consultation with the state cadastral surveyor:

> It has been brought to our attention that a situation exists in central Florida where members of the public can be arrested for trespassing on lands that constitute sovereignty submerged lands. . . . These arrests are made by local sheriffs or private security forces deputized by the local sheriff. It then falls upon your office . . . to determine whether to prosecute such a case. A decision to prosecute necessarily involves a determination by your office that the defendant was on private land.
>
> The question of whether particular lands are state owned public lands is one which can only be decided by [authorized personnel of] the staff of the Trustees. . . . We believe that when a situation as described arises, the state cadastral surveyor is that authorized official and he should be contacted for a determination. . . . Only after a determination by that official that the location is not on land owned by the state should a prosecution be instigated.[11]

Yet the issues are far from resolved. On the other side of the line, owners cite the expense of protecting their property from trespassers, who they say destroy property and even injure or poach livestock and wildlife.

In fact, cases involving trespass arrests are merely the tip of the OHWL iceberg. Characterizing such cases as part of "a broad effort by large landowners . . . to parlay public land into private property," Guest notes that the trespass disputes are not really about whether a crime has been committed, but whether the owners' land claims are valid.[12] On the other side, landowners charge that the state is attempting to enlarge its claim of sovereignty land. The owners say they have paid taxes on the disputed property for years and have deeds proving their ownership. Mike Rosen, executive director of the Florida Legal Foundation, whose mission is supporting landowners against "excessive regulation or confiscation by governmental agencies," has characterized the state's actions as an attempt to confiscate private property without compensation. "What [the state is] really after are the farmers and the ranchers and the people who are trying to develop property," Rosen said. "What [they] really want to do is avoid having to pay people for a regulatory taking of their wetlands. [The state is] going to claim that their wetlands are really sovereignty lands."[13]

At the heart of this conflict is a fundamental change in the way we think about nature. Since the passage in 1965 of the federal Water Quality Act, there has been a tremendous increase in the number of federal and state environmental laws. These laws have limited environmentally damaging practices of farmers, businesses, industry, and private citizens. These environmental laws emerge from a changing understanding of our relationship with nature, and they express the will of most people to protect the natural processes on which our lives depend. However, opposition to environmental laws remains substantial. Some people believe the environment is best protected by individual landowners or through the local action of farm bureaus or business councils. Still others believe that environmental problems have been greatly exaggerated; they point to the fact that we have gotten along for hundreds of years without these laws. Some people express the opinion that nature takes care of environmental problems; other people believe that technological solutions can mitigate any damage.[14] A primary factor in the opposition to environmental laws, however, is the economic impact of such laws. In many instances, protecting the environment requires a rethinking of ingrained practices, retooling, and redefining goals—both in business and in personal conduct.

Environmental laws are themselves, then, frequently the target in public interest versus private rights battles. In 1995, a rash of "takings" bills in state legislatures and in the U.S. Congress sought to require compensation from the government for *any* limitation on the use of private property. On the surface such a requirement doesn't seem anything out of the ordinary. The Fifth Amendment to the Constitution, in fact, provides that: "No person shall be deprived of life, liberty, or property without due process of law; nor shall private property be taken for public use without just compensation." Critics of the radical new legislation, however, have charged that the takings bills are used by large corporations and others to avoid environmental laws. As Scott Harsbarge, attorney general of Massachusetts, pointed out: "These bills would put a chilling effect on the efforts of conscientious government officials to enforce environmental laws previously enacted by Congress." Thirty-three state attorneys general signed a letter to Congress cautioning that the bills would "greatly increase the costs of government . . . with no corresponding benefits."[15] The *Tampa Tribune* of March 9, 1995, opined (somewhat less diplomatically) that the takings legislation was designed to allow a few large landowners to profit at the expense of the citizens of the state: "[the legislation] is the brainchild of a select group of wealthy landowners and big-time developers. Their aim is obvious. Destroy the state's growth regulations so they can build whatever they want, wherever they want, regardless of the consequences for others." Takings legislation might historically be regarded as a tool to protect individuals from undue governmental interference in the possession and use of private property. But its critics suggest that, by making environmental laws too costly to enforce, the more recent bills would allow powerful individuals enormous gain while sacrificing the public well-being.

The growth of environmental law, as well as the opposition to it, indicates a broad change in later twentieth-century American culture—a change in our awareness of, and relation to, the natural world. As our understanding of the natural world becomes more complex, we tend to see ourselves as *part of*—not *apart from*—nature; we begin to recognize that human efforts to control and direct natural processes rarely take adequate account of the complexity of these processes; we learn that we cannot ignore the unintended results of the changes we initiate. This new awareness, however, runs counter to the interests of groups that traditionally have been able to exploit natural resources with little or no oversight or regulation. In this atmosphere of tension and fundamental disagreement, the ordinary high water line emerges as a dividing line not only between public lands and private property, but between conflicting views of the natural world.

The Conditions of Conflict

With so much at stake in ordinary high water line controversies, the greatest surprise to many people is that these boundaries are—in many cases—not already established. Unfortunately, when Florida received title, in 1845, to all navigable water bodies within its bounds, these water bodies were not listed, mapped, or otherwise identified. Even today, the extent of the state's ownership has not been specified. Because of limited resources, the state only conducts OHWL determinations on a case-by-case basis when a question of public interest arises. And, although there have been efforts for some years to have funds appropriated for a sovereignty lands inventory, to date no such funding exists. Adding to the complications, most landowners and many local and state officials do not understand land-water boundaries and often have expectations not borne out by the law or the criteria governing ordinary high water line determinations. Why so little concerning so much has still not been settled in Florida's development remains the abiding question of the ordinary high water line. As with most such questions, the answer begins in the past.

Over the past several decades, three general, interrelated changes have contributed to an increase in the conflicts and litigation concerning the ordinary high water line. First, the increase in populations inhabiting and using the lands along water bodies has led to what might be called a natural increase in conflicts. In 1988, the Southwest Florida Water Management

District estimated that Florida was attracting one thousand new residents a day. With expanding demand for waterfront property, those land values have escalated, making any policy decision concerning these properties one in which the stakes are high.[16] At the same time, the high demand for waterfront property encourages development of land that had previously been used for farming or ranching, and the change to the more intense use of the waterfront for residential or recreational purposes triggers oversight of these activities. Sovereignty land questions frequently arise in these situations, sometimes necessitating a boundary (OHWL) determination. Often, though, the state can provide a "safe line" to riparian owners based on previous surveys and hydrology records. While safe lines are not boundary lines, they can be used to provide landowners more quickly the information they need to proceed with development plans. Sometimes, however, a landowner expresses concern that the state is taking his property or charges the state with interference in private property rights. In these cases, litigation may ensue.

This growth in Florida's population has also created demands on water resources that are more diverse than ever before. Policies addressing water resources must balance the interests and demands of many different groups of people, while protecting the resource itself.[17] This situation can lead to resentment among groups, such as farmers and ranchers, who traditionally constituted a clear majority but who are now being challenged by newcomers with other priorities. For example, many more people now use water bodies for recreation, and the courts have found this use to be one worthy of protection. Since the early 1980s, the trend in both state and federal court decisions to protect recreational uses of water bodies has increased the number and type of water bodies subject to public use.[18] Landowners may then challenge public use of such lakes and streams, claiming them as private property. If these water bodies are subsequently declared by the courts to be navigable, and therefore public, then they may be declared sovereignty lands (depending on the state statutes). At this point the ordinary high water line may come into question as well, if the boundary between the sovereignty lands and the uplands is implicated in the dispute. Establishing this boundary for any given water body frequently produces conflict. Thus, changes in water use by a growing population also contribute to increased controversy over the OHWL.

Second, changes in the nation's awareness of and approach to environmental problems generally have affected controversies concerning the ordinary high water line. In Florida, one of the most dramatic examples of this change and its effect is the Kissimmee River channelization and subsequent restoration. During the 1950s, it was becoming increasingly clear to a few water managers, scientists, and citizens that a century of efforts to drain Florida's Everglades was a misguided disaster.[19] At that time, however, water management policy was established primarily by navigation and flood control goals, and the era of structural control of Florida waters was entering its heyday. The endeavor to make rivers and lakes manageable during floods often led to their channelization and damming and to the construction of canals, levees, and locks to replace naturally flowing rivers. People tended to perceive the wetlands and marshes adjacent to such natural water bodies as problem areas to be drained, filled, and made useful. There was little awareness of the importance of marsh areas to flood control or water quality. In the late 1950s it was proposed that the U.S. Army Corps of Engineers channelize the entire Kissimmee River, a one-hundred-mile meandering river that formed the heart of the Everglades hydrologic source. This project came about partly as a result of the 1928 hurricane, in which thousands of people lost their lives in the Lake Okeechobee area, and partly in response to cattlemen's requests that the vast floodplains and river swamps of the Kissimmee be made safe year-round for grazing. Although there were already a few voices urging a more coordinated management of drainage and flood-control projects—a management based on understanding the hydrologic link between the drainage activities and the floods—in the 1960s the Kissimmee River was channelized. Completion of the project was touted as an unprecedented engineering feat. It was also, almost simultaneously, condemned as an ecological disaster. A group of environmental scientists from several Florida universities went before the legislature in 1972 to explain the importance of marshes to Florida's capability to sustain life.[20] Although a completed Army Corps project of this magnitude had never before been undone, the decision was made in Florida to restore the Kissimmee River to its meandering, uncontained condition. This effort meant that the state must acquire a corridor of land along the river for reflooding. But, in order to proceed with many of the acquisitions, it became necessary to establish the ordinary high water line so that the state could determine what it already owned. During the course of these proceedings, which stretched over three decades, the method of establishing the ordinary high water line—and the use of the OHWL as a title boundary—was challenged not only by landowners in conflict with the state, but by surveyors, realtors, land title companies, and others.

Third, as the concept of the ordinary high water line has evolved, the importance of natural indicators as determinants of this line has grown. In

America, the concept of the OHWL developed primarily as a legal concept from its foundation in common law and was assumed to be an obvious line. Although the physical evidence of the line has always been the basis for determining its location, our understanding of the contribution that natural indicators make has become more complex. This changed understanding reflects not only the general trend toward environmental awareness (in the courts as well as in the culture at large) but the growth of the environmental sciences themselves. Early cases establishing criteria for locating the OHWL tended to describe the landscape in the general categories of a line that was "always manifest."[21] In 1851, in *Howard v. Ingersoll*, the U.S. Supreme Court stated that the line would be found "where the action of the water has permanently marked itself upon the soil" and stated further that the boundary needed "no scientific exploration to find."[22] But the *Howard* case dealt with a treaty boundary on a steep-bank type of river, and its observations weren't applicable to other cases in which the topography and dynamics of the water bodies differed.[23]

In Florida, the court in the 1927 case of *Martin v. Busch* recognized that Florida's particular flat topography contributed to the formation of water bodies with low, vegetated banks. Disputes over boundaries of these flat-banked-type water bodies usually have at stake a substantial area of land, a factor that in itself motivates a closer look at their margins. As Guest has pointed out, controversies "rarely erupt over the boundaries of [steep-banked] waters because the steepness of the banks leaves only a narrow zone for argument."[24] On the other hand, where the "water margins are very flat and shallow, small fluctuations in water level translate to large lateral changes in the location of the water's edge."[25] With such water bodies, a rise or fall of a foot or so in water level can change the shoreline by hundreds of feet, and these valuable lands become the subject of much contention.

As the OHWL question arose on these kinds of water bodies, the courts began seeing more complex analyses of the water's margin. The shift from submerged to upland species of vegetation became an important indicator, and this type of evidence began to emerge in the testimony of natural scientists coming before the court as expert witnesses. In a 1990 article, Richard Hamann and Jeff Wade explained the factors leading to the courts' increasing reliance on scientific testimony. "Normally, Florida lakes and rivers are characterized by gradual transition from water-tolerant species near the edge of the water body, to those less tolerant of water on nearby uplands," they wrote.[26] "In many situations, a clear dividing line is not apparent to an untrained observer, necessitating careful analysis of the plant communities. In these situations, the depth and breadth of scientific documentation is important in supporting a particular placement of OHWL based on vegetation."[27] By the late 1970s, ordinary high water line cases frequently involved the "battle of the experts," in which each side presented its version of the scientific evidence.[28] Over the course of time, several issues have contributed to the involvement of the environmental sciences in determining the water boundary. But, the involvement of these scientists has challenged long-standing ideas and customs concerning surveying and title law generally and led to an increase in the conflicts surrounding OHWL determinations.

In 1988, the Board of Professional Land Surveyors attempted to adopt rules pertaining to the determination of the ordinary high water line. Its rules proposed changes to the state's methods of locating the OHWL that some of its most powerful clients (mining companies, large farming and ranching conglomerates, waterfront developers, and others) had been seeking. The Trustees of the Internal Improvement Fund—which is comprised of the governor and cabinet, who are charged with preserving the public trust in sovereignty lands—challenged the board's rule making, stating that the proposed rules violated Florida law and attempted to institute standards that the board did not have the authority to establish. In the final order, the hearing officer agreed that the board had exceeded its authority in most of its proposals.[29] Among the rejected proposals were definitions that would have reclassified thousands of acres of sovereignty lands as privately owned uplands. Supporters of the board's proposed rules claimed that the state's method of determining sovereignty lands' boundaries was an unduly complicated "scientific approach" that required surveyors to understand data from fields beyond their areas of expertise. In the official publication of the Shoreline Owners and Residents Association, one author wrote:

> The Trustees' proposal . . . utilizes a process very similar to that used for wetlands regulation. . . . It is very difficult to understand how such a process could be undertaken by a land surveyor unless he happens also to be a botanist, hydrologist and soils engineer.[30]

Clearly, for some, the emphasis on scientific evidence in establishing ordinary high water boundaries amounted to a crisis of authority in the surveying profession.

Another factor that frequently involves scientific evidence in sovereignty land disputes is the question of navigability.[31] To establish a water body as sovereign in character, it must be determined that the water body was navigable or capable of becoming navigable at the time of statehood, since only lands underlying navigable water bodies passed to the state as sovereignty lands. Water bodies that do not pass this historical navigability test are not subject to sovereignty land claims by the state. If a water body is navigable today this tends to indicate that it was navigable at the time of statehood, since waters are, for the most part, less navigable today than in 1845. But sometimes water bodies have been so altered as to damage their navigability, and their present-day condition obscures the fact that they were navigable water bodies at the time of statehood. In Florida today, after more than a century of drainage and artificial manipulation of water bodies, determining the condition of a water body at the time of statehood often requires scientific, as well as historical, investigation.

In the 1997 case of *Trustees v. Lykes Bros., Inc.*, the navigability of Fisheating Creek at the time of statehood was the primary question before the jury.[32] Fisheating Creek courses through an area of the state that remains remote even today—an area that was largely unsettled frontier at the time of statehood. When a dispute about the creek's ownership arose, it was not clear what historical evidence would be available to demonstrate its navigability. In the trial, the defendant, Lykes, argued that Fisheating Creek was not a navigable water body but a series of "pothole lakes" connected by a stream only during heavy rains. For that reason, Lykes maintained, the creek was private property—not sovereignty lands. The state countered that the creek was still navigable and had certainly been so at the time of statehood before its navigability had been damaged by flood control projects. To support its claim, the state presented historical, hydrologic, and photographic evidence. The research team documented man-made changes to the watershed areas north and west of the creek that deprived it of what had been its normal flow. The team uncovered records of military expeditions on the creek from the Seminole Wars and postal records of trading posts indicating use of the creek. In addition, witnesses presented evidence of a canoe-building enterprise among the Indians living along the shores. Early government surveys also played a key role in shaping the jury's picture of the creek in its natural condition at the time of statehood. In holding for the state, the jury forewoman stated that the historical evidence presented by the state had been key in the jury's decision.

Even in cases in which there has been little artificial alteration of the water body, physical evidence of the water line is often correlated with long-term records of water levels and other scientific data in determining where the OHWL is. When long-term water level records for a water body are not available, scientific information (vegetation, soils, and so forth) may substitute for the missing data. Guest points out how vegetative patterns can help establish the water profile : "[S]cientific research in recent decades has revealed that vegetation patterns correspond closely to normal hydrologic regimes. These vegetative surrogates can provide a reliable substitute for long-term average hydrologic data, and are consistently found in bands corresponding to the reach of water during different hydrologic regimes."[33] Increasingly too, aerial photography is being used in ordinary high water line surveys of large areas. Advances in our understanding of hydrology, geology, botany, and soils science have become crucial to interpreting the hydrologic regimes indicated in aerial maps.[34] In effect, the involvement of science in locating the OHWL gives the natural world a legal standing it has not had in the past, and this changing status itself contributes to much of the conflict between private property rights and public trust protection.

The population explosion in Florida, our changing understanding of our relations with the natural world, and the increased participation of the sciences in determining boundaries have exacerbated tensions surrounding the ordinary high water line in recent years. But the fundamental issues of this discord have been matters of discussion, opposition, and law for thousands of years.

The Sovereign Authority

The practice of preserving the lands beneath navigable water bodies for public use embodies a long and rich history. Sovereignty lands come under the purview of the Public Trust Doctrine, one of the oldest bodies of law still in use today. The Public Trust Doctrine comes to us from the sixth century Institutes of Justinian and the accompanying Digest, which, during the reign of Emperor Justinian, codified Roman civil law (circa 529–35 C.E.).[35] These institutes were themselves, however, based on the Institutes and Journal of Gaius, a second-century Roman jurist who codified the natural law of Greek philosophers.[36]

The importance of these institutes to the concept of the ordinary high water line derives from the guarantee these laws provided for the public use of the shore of the sea or bank of the river. Book 2 of the Institutes specifies the public nature of rivers, ports, and seashore:

> And truly by natural right, these be common to all: the air, running water, and the sea, and hence the shores of the sea. Also all rivers and ports are public. . . . And by the law of nations the use of the shore is also public, and in the same manner as the sea itself.[37]

The protection of the shore for public use is profoundly connected to the OHWL concept: the use of a low or average water mark as the legal boundary between public and private property would not include the shore. It is because ordinary high water periodically and regularly covers the shore that its mark includes the shore. Low or average water stages do not typically cover the shore. The adoption of the ordinary high watermark, then, as a boundary between public and private property, includes the shore in the lands protected for public use. Today, attempts to circumvent the designation of the shore as public often take the form of redefining the ordinary high water line as an average or low water boundary, but the public trust law adopted in Florida traces its origins to the ancient Roman law protecting the shore. Some version of this law eventually passed into the jurisprudence of all Western European nations and was adopted into English common law after the Magna Carta.[38]

Two basic changes occurred in the English adaptation of the Roman law. First, under the English common law, only waters influenced by tides were deemed navigable; thus, the public use of freshwater rivers and lakes was lost.[39] English law, nevertheless, remains pertinent to the development of the OHWL (which, in Florida, as in most other states, determines the boundary of freshwaters). The procedure for locating the boundary of a navigable freshwater body (that is, for establishing the OHWL) is today distinct from the procedure for locating the boundary of a tidal water body (the Mean High Water Line).[40] However, the criteria defining the OHWL—particularly our notion of *ordinary high*—come directly from the English common law concepts of tidal water boundaries. Second, whereas Roman law considered the waters and shores incapable of ownership (*res nullius*), English common law tended to put what was capable of private ownership into private hands.[41] In 1867, in *Cobb v. Davenport*, the British court noted:

> The policy of the common law is to assign to everything capable of ownership a certain and determinate owner, and for the preservation of peace, and the security of society, to mark, by certain indicia, not only the boundaries of such separate ownership, but the line of demarcation between rights which are held by the public in common, and private rights.[42]

Thus, it was not out of the question for the title to tidal lands underlying British navigable waters to be vested in private hands. But, as David Slade of the National Public Trust Study explains, English law still provided for the public's right to use privately owned tidal lands by dividing the title to these lands into two parts—one dominant and the other subservient. The dominant title dealt with the public rights of use and was called the *jus publicum*. This title was held by the sovereign and was not to be conveyed into private ownership. The subservient title to tidal lands addressed the private proprietary rights in the use of sovereign lands and was called the *jus privatum*. This private title was also held by the king unless conveyed into private ownership.[43] This distinction of title interests in public lands is still made today. Even when the *jus privatum* has been conveyed, however—say, for example for the building of a dock on navigable waters—the *jus publicum* remains intact, protecting the public use of those waters.

Establishing a high water line as the public/private boundary (as opposed to a low water line or average water line) provides for the public status of the shore—that area that is exposed during low water and submerged during high water. Simply stated, a water boundary describes where the water ends and the land begins. But, since continuous change characterizes natural water bodies, establishing their boundaries requires more precise criteria. Some of the changes water bodies undergo occur regularly (daily tides, seasonal highs and lows), while other changes occur irregularly (droughts) and/or catastrophically (floods). In defining the boundary then, a key question is at what stage of the tide (diurnal, semi-diurnal) or seasonal cycle do we mark the line? In Roman law, the public shore of the sea was determined by how far the "greatest wave extended itself in winter."[44] The English law defined the shore to be "the flux and reflux of the sea at ordinary tides," introducing the concept of "ordinary" into the formula for determining the extent of the shore.[45] When the American Revolution took place, "the people of each state became themselves sovereign," holding the "absolute right to all their navigable waters, and the soils under them for their own common use."[46] Although English law provided the basis for colonial law, after the Revolution, English law was not controlling in the states.[47] Instead, each colony had the right to modify the common law to better fit the uses and physical characteristics of its own shorelands. In practice, most of the thirteen original states defined the extent of their public trust shorelands to be the mean high tide line, in accordance with the 1854 English case *Attorney General v. Chambers*.[48] In this case the "medium high tide between the springs and the neaps" was considered "as bounding the right of the Crown."[49] The importance of this formula is that it further defined and limited the concept of an ordinary high watermark.[50] Because spring tides occur on the full and new moons (not, as the name would indicate, in the spring), they have higher highs and lower lows than tides measured at other times. This phenomenon occurs because during the full and new moons the gravitational pulls of the moon and sun combine to produce extreme tides. Neap tides are those that occur at the first and third quarters of the moon, when the gravitational pull of the moon and the sun form a ninety-degree angle.

Thus, neap tides have lower highs and higher lows than tides measured at other times. By adopting the boundary for tidal shorelands at the reach of the medium high tide between these extreme spring tides and more moderate neap tides, the original states laid the groundwork of the ordinary high water line concept.

In addition, the thirteen original states passed on several common principles important to public trust doctrine to the new states that later joined the Union. These general principles were usually enacted through a state's legislature. Slade identifies these broad principles as holding that each state:

—Has public trust interests, rights and responsibilities in its navigable waters, the lands beneath these waters, and the living resources therein;

—Has the authority to define the boundary limits of the lands and waters held in public trust;

—Has the authority to recognize and convey private proprietary rights (the *jus privatum*) in its trust lands, and thus diminish the public's rights therein, with the corollary responsibility not to substantially impair the public's use and enjoyment of the remaining trust lands, waters and living resources;

—Has a trustee's duty and responsibility to preserve and continuously assure the public's ability to fully use and enjoy public trust lands and waters for certain trust uses; but

—Does not have the power to abdicate its role of trustee of the public's *jus publicum* rights, although in certain limited cases the State can terminate the *jus publicum* in small parcels of trust land.[51]

But, as the rights of the original states inured to the new states under the Equal Footing Doctrine, a confusion of language arose around the issue of navigability that would confound courts for two centuries.[52] Under English common law, no waters were "deemed navigable except those in which the tide ebbs and flows."[53] The conflation of the two terms, *navigable* and *tidal,* in England, reflected the situation that "no rivers above the ebb and flow of the tide were significant with respect to navigation."[54] America, however, contained "thousands of miles of public navigable water, including lakes and rivers in which there is no tide."[55] Early on, American courts tended to follow the English law in defining navigable waters as tidal waters. This practice was explained in the 1851 Supreme Court decision of *The Propeller Genessee Chief:*

At the time the Constitution of the United States was adopted, . . . the definition [of navigable waters] which had been adopted in England was only proper here. In the old thirteen States the far greater part of the navigable waters are tidewaters. And in the States which were at that period in any degree commercial . . . every public river was tide-water to the head of navigation.[56]

Over time, however, in following the British practice in America, the public character of many lakes and rivers was lost. In 1845 Congress had passed an act extending the federal regulatory jurisdiction to cases involving interstate (or interterritorial) trade via commercial vessels of twenty tons or more operating on the navigable freshwaters of the United States. In the 1870 case of *The Daniel Ball* the Supreme Court stated unequivocally that the English common law could not be the determining test for navigability of waters:

> The doctrine of the common law as to the navigability of waters has no application in this country. Here the ebb and flow of the tide do not constitute the usual test, as in England, or any test at all of the navigability of waters. . . . The test by which to determine the navigability of our rivers is found in their navigable capacity. Those rivers are public navigable rivers in law which are navigable in fact.[57]

In 1876, however, in the case of *Barney v. Keokuk,* the U.S. Supreme Court noted that regarding title questions—as opposed to regulatory (admiralty) questions, the federal law "remained in confusion as to whether land beneath 'navigable waters' meant land beneath tidewaters only, or land beneath waters that were actually navigable":[58]

> The confusion of navigable with tide water, found in the monuments of common law, long prevailed in this country, notwithstanding the broad differences existing between the extent and topography of the British island and that of the American continent. It had the influence for two generations of excluding the admiralty jurisdiction from our great rivers and inland seas; and under the like influence it laid the foundation in many States of doctrines with regard to the ownership of the soil in navigable waters above tide-water at variance with sound principles of public policy.[59]

The Court concluded that "all waters are deemed navigable which are really so" and emphasized that the "proprietorship of the beds and shores of such waters" properly belonged "to the States by their inherent sovereignty."[60] In 1892 in *Illinois Central Railroad v. State of Illinois,* the Court clarified the federal title question by holding that the lands beneath the Great Lakes are subject to the same doctrine of sovereignty and ownership as are lands beneath tidal waters, unmistakably making navigability the controlling test of title to freshwaters. In addition, the Court clarified that the title a state holds to lands under navigable waters "is different in character from the title of the state to lands intended for sale. It is a title held in trust for the people of the state."[61] By 1988 the Supreme Court held that it had come to be recognized "as the 'settled law of this country' that the lands under navigable freshwater lakes and rivers were within the public trust given the new States upon their entry into the Union."[62]

The federal navigability test, then, became one defining model of state sovereignty lands, providing as it did a description of the lands and waters falling within the states' trust under the Equal Footing Doctrine. This federal test for title purposes derives from the Supreme Court's definition of navigability in *The Daniel Ball,* which clearly stated that those waters are navigable in law that are navigable in fact.[63] The case further established three key elements: The water body (1) need only be *susceptible* to navigation (whether or not it has actually been used for navigation is not defining); (2) must be susceptible of use in commerce by any customary mode of trade or travel;[64] and, (3) must be susceptible to navigation in its natural and ordinary condition. One more element of the test was added in 1971 in *Utah v. United States,* which determined that navigability for title purposes must have existed at the time the state entered the Union.[65] But the use of the federal title test and/or its similarity to state tests determining sovereignty lands has led to some confusion. The federal role in state sovereignty lands has been widely interpreted as that of grantor of those lands to the state at the time of statehood. But the federal government was essentially only the trustee of these lands beneath navigable waters. When a state formed and was accepted into the Union, it acquired the navigable waters within its bounds by virtue of its sovereignty, and not as the result of a grant from the federal government. In 1914 the Minnesota Supreme Court declared that the "United States government never owned the soil under public waters, and its patent to the shore land does not pass title to the land under the water. This belonged to the states, and if the riparian owner has acquired it at all it is by the favor or concession of the state."[66]

State navigability tests may be equivalent to, broader than, or narrower than the federal test.[67] In 1889, the Florida Supreme Court in *Bucki v. Cone* held that a water body is navigable if it is a "stream of sufficient capacity and volume of water to float to market the products of the country," and added that it is "not essential . . . that the stream should be continuously, at all seasons of the year, in a state suited for such flotage."[68] The court further noted that log floating provided sufficient evidence to prove navigability. In 1909, in *Broward v. Mabry,* the Florida court, similarly to the federal test, concluded that *"capacity* for navigation, not usage for that purpose,"* was sufficient to establish navigability.[69] This distinction of capacity as opposed to actual use has helped ensure that streams that were navigable-in-fact at the time of statehood remain in the public trust. Without this distinction, the state could find itself in the position of needing to prove actual use of streams in areas that were not even settled at the time of statehood. In some cases today, the state's ownership of a stream is challenged on the issue of navigability when, in fact, twentieth-century drainage projects have diminished the stream's flow significantly. (Such avulsive, man-made changes in water bodies do not generally alter their status as sovereignty lands, even if the change results in non-navigability.) In these cases the state can sustain its ownership claim if it can show that the stream was navigable at the time of statehood (1845) and *could have been used* for commerce.[70]

The federal title test was not the only model operating to define sovereignty lands. Other models are apparent, for instance, in the public trust protection afforded the "great ponds" in several New England states. In Massachusetts, state law established the sovereignty of ponds greater than ten acres in size "from a period reaching back almost to the first settlement of the colony, [treating] great ponds as a character nearly resembling tidewaters, the enjoyment of which for fishing and fowling and other uses was common to all, and the title in which and the lands under them was not the subject of private property, unless by special grant from the legislature."[71] Likewise in Vermont and New Hampshire, state law classed ponds of more than ten acres as public ponds.[72]

In general, state courts sorted out the issue of navigability on freshwaters much earlier than did the federal courts and accorded those waters public trust protection. In *Putting the Public Trust Doctrine to Work,* the authors note that Pennsylvania "discarded the English common law years before Congress passed the Act of 1845," with the case of *Carson v. Blazer:*

> In 1803, a farmer on the shores of the Susquehanna River asserted exclusive rights of fishing in the river adjacent to his land. This assertion led to "force and arms" against a fellow townsman who insisted that he, as a member of the public, had an equal right to seine for shad as did the riparian farmer. The disagreement, which raised the complex legal issues of bottomland ownership, was fought all the way to the Pennsylvania Supreme Court. In 1810, the court stated: "This [ebb-and-flow] definition may be very proper in England, where there is no river of considerable importance as to navigation, which has not a flow of the tide; but it would be highly unreasonable when applied to our large rivers

such as the Ohio, Allegheny, Delaware, Schuylkill, or Susquehanna and its branches."[73]

Although today three states continue to use the English common law definition of navigable waters, on the whole, the Public Trust Doctrine has emerged in state law in accordance with a state's particular topographic features and its views of public interest.[74] Either by statute or case law, every state has defined "navigable waters" and established the public's right to use those waters; and, in most cases, states have seen fit to include navigable freshwaters in the public trust.

In Florida, dozens of acts in the laws of territorial Florida (prior to 1845) and in the laws of Florida (after 1845) establish the public's right to use navigable waters and prohibit the obstruction of such waters. In the 1823 Act for Ascertaining Aims and Titles to Land in the Territory of Florida, section 12 provided that "all the navigable rivers and waters in the Districts of East and West Florida, shall be, and forever remain, public highways."[75] The 1827 Act to Keep from Unlawful Obstruction the Navigable Streams in the Territory of Florida stated that any person erecting a "dam, bridge, hedge, seine, drag or other stoppage, whereby the navigation of boats drawing five feet water, or the passage of fish may be obstructed" would be charged forty dollars, and the obstruction would be removed as a nuisance. It further stipulated that the felling of trees in navigable waters would cost the offender five dollars per tree if the trees were not removed within twenty-four hours.[76] An 1833 act, Declaring Cold Water Creek in Escambia County, a Navigable Stream, stated that all bridges, impediments, or obstructions would be treated as common nuisances and be removed except those bridges that did "not obstruct the free navigation of said creek, for boats drawing three feet water, or for rafts of timber or lumber of every description."[77]

The flexible nature of the public trust doctrine has helped ensure a tradition of public lands protection through many generations and in widely varying situations. Some commentators have observed, however, that the courts' use of the doctrine has not followed a course of continuous progress toward protection, but has waned and waxed over the years.[78] Like any dynamic theory of common law, the doctrine reflects the prevailing sense of justice and public policy at the time of its application. At any given time, the court's reading of the law provides insight into how things stood with regard to public lands as Florida developed, and its rulings voice a crucial part of the dialogue concerning sovereignty lands. Often, cases in which the court upheld sovereignty lands protection triggered powerful legislation that sought to balance the court's effect. At other times, when the court upheld private claims against the public trust, the effect has been to point out to the people of Florida where and how the law has failed to protect sovereignty lands. In this way, the court's rulings often helped provide the incentive and guidance to formalize the public trust doctrine. The strengthening of public trust laws became particularly important as Florida developed into one of the most densely populated states in the nation. For in the early days of Florida's statehood, the urgent needs driving land policy established a mind-set geared not toward public lands protection but toward public lands disposal. This mind-set persisted well into the twentieth century and, even today, figures greatly in litigation pertaining to the ordinary high water line.

The Early Mind-set

When Florida became a state in 1845, the new state's administrators faced vastly different problems than we encounter today. With population estimates for the twenty-first century pushing 15 million,[79] and with thousands of newcomers flocking to the state each week, it is difficult to remember that Florida's government once sought settlers. But, in actuality, Florida's population boom and its resulting "land crisis" are relatively recent developments.[80] As a child growing up in Panama City, Florida, during the 1950s, I can recall, for example, that when my mother would take my sister and me for a picnic on Panama City Beach (a five-mile trip from where we lived), we had to gas up the car beforehand. At that time there were *no* gas stations, convenience stores, motels, condominiums, RV parks, strip malls, or houses on the beach. There was nothing but sea oats and sand dunes. By the early 1970s all of these "improvements" were there, overrunning the unspoiled natural beauty I remember.

In 1845, despite three centuries of attempts by European and American governments to encourage settlement and twenty-four years as a U.S. territory, only about 70,000 non-native people were living in Florida.[81] (Although admission to statehood required 80,000 people, some historians believe the number of non-native settlers living in Florida in 1845 was less than that number, perhaps substantially less.)[82] Most of these settlers lived in the northern panhandle of the state, where navigable waterways, a few roads, and two local railroads provided the only means of internal transportation available.

Numerous acts in Florida's early laws demonstrate that navigable waterways were crucial to the (European) settlement of Florida. These acts prevented obstructions, established ferries, provided guidelines for bridges, and erected lighthouses. The 1839 Resolution Respecting Suwannee and Santa Fe Rivers in the territorial laws bears witness to the link between navigable waters and the effort to attract settlers:

> Whereas the increase of population would be accelerated, the value of said lands and the agricultural prosperity of that region of country greatly advanced by suitable improvements in the navigation of said rivers, of which improvements the said rivers are deemed highly susceptible. That our Delegate in Congress, be hereby requested to procure the passage of a law appropriating thirty thousand dollars, to be applied to the improvements of the navigation of said rivers.[83]

Attempts to settle the central and southern regions of the state also depended heavily on navigable water routes. But, here, delays ensued from the Seminole Wars. In *Laws of Florida*, no. 14, resolution (1846), the "Preamble and Resolutions for Clearing out the Oclawaha River" indicate difficulties beyond those of maintaining the navigable channels:

> Congress has heretofore appropriated the sum of $10,000 for the purpose of clearing out obstructions in the Oclawaha river [near present-day Ocala]. . . . And Whereas the whole of said appropriation, on account of the dangers of the Indian wars, could not be applied to the purposes for which it was made, . . . And Whereas said river, if rendered navigable, would afford great facilities for the transportation of the U.S. mail, and be productive of the rapid growth and settlement of the surrounding country, and thereby greatly expedite and extend the sale of the U.S. land bordering on said river. . . . Request to have the said appropriation applied to the purposes for which it was originally intended.[84]

Although the early laws sought to protect navigable waters as part of Florida's public trust, from the beginning these sovereignty lands were inextricably linked with the duty of attracting "growth and settlement."

When the drafters of Florida's Constitution met in 1838, they acknowledged the importance of funding development:

> A liberal system of internal improvements, being essential to the development of the resources of the country, shall be encouraged by the Government of this State, and it shall be the duty of the General Assembly, as soon as practicable, to ascertain by law, proper objects of improvements in relation to roads, canals and navigable streams, and to provide for a suitable application of such funds as may be appropriated for such improvements.[85]

Less than three years later, the U.S. Congress passed an act granting 500,000 acres of land to each state upon its admission to the Union for the purposes of internal improvement. The title to these lands passed to the state on lists of selected surveyed lands that were approved by the commissioner of the general land office and the secretary of the interior of the United States.[86] These lands were to be sold by the state, with the proceeds "faithfully applied to objects of internal improvement . . . namely: roads, railways, bridges, canals and improvement of water courses, and drainage of swamps."[87] Additionally, Florida received nearly 1 million acres in federal land grants to benefit public education, as well as various other grants amounting to some 100,000 acres.[88] The grants of educational lands, internal improvement lands, and sovereignty lands (lands beneath navigable waters to the ordinary high watermark, and tidelands) all inured to the new state in 1845.

But, even before the state could develop the means to benefit from these substantial assets, Congress passed the Swamp and Overflowed Lands Act of 1850, granting to states all of the unsold swamp and overflowed lands within their borders. As survey historian Joe Knetsch has observed, the exact criteria for determining these lands was somewhat problematic: in "basic terms, land that was wet and unfit for cultivation during the major part of the year was to be considered swamp and overflowed."[89] But these lands were clearly distinct from sovereignty lands in two ways: swamp and overflowed lands were intended to be sold—not held in trust for public use—and they were located above the ordinary high watermark of navigable waters. Under the swamp and overflowed lands grant, Florida received patents to some 22 million acres, a number which gives some indication of Florida's terrain a century and a half ago.

In 1855 the Internal Improvement Fund was created and placed under the control of a board of trustees comprised of the governor, comptroller, treasurer, the secretary of agriculture, and registrar of state lands. W. Turner Wallis, in his 1960 analysis of Florida's Public Land Management Agency, explained the formation and purpose of the fund:

> Referring to the provision in the 1838 Constitution calling for "a liberal system of internal improvements," the Legislature created a special fund to be used exclusively for promoting this end. Into this "Internal Improvement Fund" were placed all internal improvement lands and all swamp and overflowed lands available to the state, together with all monies accruing from the sale or disposition of such lands. The responsibility for administering the fund was irrevocably vested in the same five cabinet members formerly sitting on the first Board of Internal Improvement, to be known thenceforth as the Trustees of the Internal Improvement Fund.[90]

The trustees' new duties were twofold: "first, to obtain and hold title to state lands, and second to use these lands for the promotion of a system of internal improvements."[91] Railroad and canal projects approved by this board were generously funded—sometimes more generously than the value of lands underwriting the projects would allow. Lands granted for public education, however, were not administered with the Internal Improvement Fund and eventually came under the direction of the State Board of Education.

This arrangement left the trustees of the Internal Improvement Fund with responsibility for three large land groups: internal improvement lands, swamp and overflowed lands, and sovereignty lands. The first two of these groups were public lands subject to sale and to private ownership in fee simple absolute. They were intended from the outset as negotiable assets. Sovereignty lands, on the other hand, were intended to be held by the state in trust for the use and benefit of all people. Preoccupied as they were, however, with developing the state's population and infrastructure, the trustees showed little interest in sovereignty lands administration; the millions of acres of saleable lands were a much more promising source of revenue.

During this time, sovereignty lands issues only occasionally came to the fore, and Florida case law proceeded slowly to sort through the state's position on sovereignty lands boundaries. The prevailing approach to sovereignty lands administration as the new state got under way is perhaps best conveyed by the 1856 Riparian Rights Act, which granted riparian owners the right to fill and use submerged (sovereignty) lands in order to promote growth and commerce:

> Whereas, It is for the benefit of Commerce that wharves be built and Warehouses erected for facilitating the landing and storage of goods; and whereas, the State being the proprietor of all submerged lands and water privileges, within its boundaries, which prevents the riparian owners from improving their waterlots: Therefore, Section 1. *Be it enacted by the Senate and House of Representatives of the State of Florida in General Assembly convened,* That the State of Florida for the considerations above mentioned, divest themselves of all right, title and interest to all lands covered by water, lying in front of any tract of land owned by a citizen of the United States, . . . for public purposes, lying upon any navigable stream, or Bay of the Sea, or Harbor, as far as to the edge of the channel, and hereby vest the full title to the same in and unto the riparian proprietors, giving them the full right and privilege to build wharves into streams or waters of the Bay or Harbor as far as may be necessary to effect the purposes de-

scribed, and to fill up from the shore, bank or beach, as far as may be desired, not obstructing the channel, but leaving full space for the requirements of Commerce.[92]

Although the act seems to have cleared the way for projects today's developers would quickly pursue, Wallis points out that there "is no evidence that this right was very extensively exercised during the period following enactment of the law. The requirements of commerce did not necessitate a dock or warehouse at every turn in the coastline or bend in the river, and the expense of artificially filling submerged land was excessive in view of the benefits to be derived."[93] It is also the case that the 1856 act contained a flaw. Although it seems to have been the intention of the legislature to make the proffered rights widely available, in fact, language in section 2 of the act restricted the grant to "those persons and body corporate owning lands actually bounded by, and extending to *low* watermark, on such navigable streams, Bays and Harbors."[94] But only in certain rare cases would private ownership extend to low water, and the burden of proof to such title would be considerable.[95] It seems likely that the legislature simply erred in wording the act, since, if the low water stipulation had been strictly adhered to, very little commerce would have resulted.

Whether or not the low watermark was its intended boundary criterion, section 2 of the 1856 Riparian Rights Act provided the subject of Florida's first public trust case restricting the power of the state to alienate sovereignty land. The Riparian Rights Act had been widely interpreted as actually changing the boundary of sovereignty lands from the ordinary high water line to the edge of the channel of navigable waters. In 1859, however, in *Geiger v. Filor,* the court found that sovereignty submerged land "belonged to no one, or rather, to the public at large" and could not be alienated by the sovereign (in this case the state), which held the land in trust for public use. Rather than rule on the legality of the Riparian Rights Act itself, though, the court simply stated that the act supplied no benefits to the claimant before the court, since his title did not extend to low water.[96] By interpreting section 2 literally, the court probably did limit the initial impact of the Riparian Rights Act to some degree.

However, confusion surrounding sovereignty land boundaries persisted. As Norwood Gay has pointed out in "The High Water Mark: Boundary between Public and Private Lands," subsequent courts seemed reluctant to interpret the act as strictly as the *Geiger* court had done:

> The court in *Rivas v. Solary* [1881] did not seem worried about the not-so subtle distinction between *high* and *low* water marks. In *Alden v. Pinney* [1868], the

court found it immaterial on the facts in the case to inquire whether the act embraced the owner to the line of ordinary high tides; it apparently was not concerned that the words of the statute itself plainly precluded the possibility. The court in *Sullivan v. Moreno* [1882] would evidently have been willing to listen to the plaintiff if he could have shown ownership to *either* high or low water mark, which he was unable to do.[97]

These cases indicate that, although Florida's sovereignty lands extended to the ordinary high watermark, little understanding of or concern for the distinction between the ordinary high and ordinary low watermark was brought about in the court's early rulings. (And, with regard to these boundaries, the court's language probably reflected the vagueness of the concepts in the culture at large.) In 1893, in *State v. Black River Phosphate Co.*, the court refused to interpret the meaning of "low watermark" beyond saying that the lands in question were "washed by the flow of [the creek's] . . . waters at their ordinary stage and [extended] down to such waters at such stage."[98] As Gay points out, "This [reading of the term] does not sound as though the court had in mind what would be referred to today as the low water mark, and serves to point up the generalities in which the early courts were wont to talk with regard to tidal boundaries."[99]

State v. Black River Phosphate did, however, clarify certain aspects of the Riparian Rights Act. The case concerned a phosphate company that had claimed the "right to mine the bed of a river down to the navigation channel on the theory that the Act had divested the State of ownership down to that point."[100] Refusing the assumption, as the *Geiger* court had, that the act had divested the state of ownership below the OHWL, the court indicated that interpretation of the act must comply with the public trust doctrine. Thus, the navigable waters, "including the shore or spaces between high and low water marks, were the property of the State or of the people of the State in their united or sovereign capacity, and were held not for the purpose of sale or conversion into other values, or reduction into several or individual ownership, but for the use and enjoyment of the same by all the people of the State."[101] Riparian owners, the court held, only perfected their rights to submerged lands by actually making improvements that provided a public benefit.[102] The court reasoned that because the state had the authority to construct warehouses or deposit fill up to the navigation channel, the state could authorize private parties to do the same.[103] In retreating from the extravagant language of the Riparian Rights Act, the *Black River Phosphate* court reasserted the public trust character of sovereignty lands, holding that the wholesale divestiture of a category of sovereignty land by shifting the boundary waterward was not permitted.

These early Florida cases, then, involved the ordinary high water line only in a general way—as part of sorting out the public trust issue raised by the Riparian Rights Act. Defining what would constitute the OHWL on a water body that had no tidal influence or, for that matter, locating the line for any given water body does not seem to have been part of the court's concern during the nineteenth century.

Although the public trust doctrine continued to gain strength in early twentieth century case law (primarily under the guidance of Chief Justice J. B. Whitfield), the state's vicissitudes during the latter part of the nineteenth century had placed sovereignty lands ever more at risk. By the 1880s, the trustees of the Internal Improvement Fund had expended more than 9 million acres of internal improvement lands for the construction of railroads. As Wallis has observed, these grants, along with federal grants from the public domain, amounted to "a full third of all the land area in the state, an average of about 10,000 acres for each mile of railroad constructed." [104] Mark Derr gives this account of the board's actions:

> [T]he trustees determined to offer the land as collateral for bonds offered by various antebellum railroad and canal companies, who managed to lay 531 miles of track and several scores of ditches to link lakes and rivers before the Civil War. The policy of the Internal Improvement Fund trustees violated the Swamp Lands Act's requirement that the wetlands be diked and drained for human settlement, but the board justified its favoritism toward corporations by arguing that transportation would open the interior of the state to homesteaders. [105]

But in the devastation following the Civil War, the railroads defaulted on their loans. Uneasy bondholders resolved to block the board—now controlled by so-called Radical Republicans—from using the land to underwrite any further development projects until their claims were satisfied with either money or land. To meet these obligations, the board took over the defaulting railroads and sold them at public auction, canceling bonds amounting to $2,872,700 with the proceeds. But the land fund was still unable to meet interest payments on the outstanding amount—just more than $700,000. In the post–Civil War climate, millions of acres of internal improvement lands had been deeded to wealthy northerners at vastly reduced prices. In one such act, the republican board sold over 1 million acres to the New York and Florida Improvement Company for ten cents an acre. This scandal was just one of many such acts that continually led bondholders to appeal to the courts. In 1876 after more than a decade of "carpetbag" rule, voters returned a democratic administration to the state government. But the state was badly crippled by the staggering debts and impoverished treasury left behind by the radicals.

"By the time Democrat William Bloxham became governor in January 1881," historians Charlton W. Tebeau and Ruby Leach Carson explain, "the Internal Improvement land carried a debt of a million dollars, on which the interest was seven percent."[106] It was hoped that the fund could be replenished by selling a large body of the swamp and overflowed land, even at a cut-rate price. But the two governors before Bloxham had tried this strategy to no avail. This failure, together with the dire need to pull the state into solvency, encouraged the state to offer high incentives to prospective buyers. In this climate the state negotiated the Disston Drainage Contract.

Less than a month into his administration, Governor Bloxham brought before the trustees of the Internal Improvement Fund an offer from Hamilton Disston, son of a Philadelphia manufacturer, who proposed "the drainage and reclamation of the lands overflowed by the waters of and adjacent to Lake Okeechobee and the Kissimmee River."[107] In the proposal, Disston and his associates agreed to drain 12 million acres of submerged lands in south and central Florida in exchange for half of what they drained—6 million acres.[108] The problem with the Disston drainage deal was that the state's creditors were unwilling to go along. They petitioned the federal court in New York, which had jurisdiction in the case, for title to all the internal improvement lands—some 14 million acres—as settlement of their claims. Rather than see the drainage deal stalled, or blocked altogether, Disston offered to buy 4 million acres for $1 million. The trustees unanimously approved, for now the Internal Improvement Fund's million-dollar debt could be retired and the title cleared on the remaining internal improvement lands. Bloxham and the board celebrated their agreement with Disston and hurried to make new deals for development of the now unencumbered state lands.

The Disston deal initiated a period of intense focus by the trustees on drainage and land reclamation. But, as Wallis notes, by the end of the century, the trustees were running out of internal improvement lands.

As the Twentieth Century began, the State of Florida found itself virtually without public assets. The vast acreages patented to the state since 1850 under the Swamp and Overflowed Land Act had been bartered, often ill advisedly, for several hundred miles of precious railroad, a few navigation improvements, and one very significant land reclamation enterprise.[109]

Then, in 1904, the state received a federal patent to the nearly 3 million acres of land in the southern tip of the Florida peninsula known as the Everglades. With this tract the state's reclamation activities continued in full swing, and the trustees were assigned the additional title of the Board of Drainage Commissioners. The trustees set aside sizeable tracts for water storage purposes and conveyed hundreds of thousands of acres to private companies as recompense for various waterway improvements. But, as in the past, it seems much of the land was sold at token prices for reclamation.[110]

With the removal of the last large tract from the public land rolls, the trustees' attention began to shift to other possibilities for revenue. The railroads had by this time achieved the aim of bringing people to south Florida, and the cities of Miami and West Palm Beach were bustling. With the popularity of waterfront properties growing rapidly, interest in filling shallow bay bottoms and other sovereignty lands now emerged.[111] Sovereignty lands had thus far escaped the burden of other public lands because of their public trust protection. But now, as the only substantial lands remaining under the trustees' control, sovereignty lands came under increasing pressure to generate revenue.

In the meantime, the Florida Supreme Court continued to assert "limitations upon the power of the legislature to pass to private ownership the submerged lands under navigable waters."[112] In the 1908 case of *State ex rel. Ellis v. Gerbing,* Gerbing had marked off parts of the bed of the Amelia River for an oyster project and, claiming exclusive right to use the bed of the salt marsh, asserted that neither the state nor the federal governments had claimed the marshes of a navigable stream.[113] In overturning the lower court decision, Justice Whitfield explained the situation of swamp and overflowed lands adjoining navigable waters. Because lands under navigable waters inured to the state as sovereignty lands at the time of statehood in 1845, no parts of navigable waters were conveyed to the state under the Swamp and Overflowed Lands Act of 1850. Therefore, the court held, deeds conveying swamp and overflowed lands could not convey any part of the beds of navigable waters. Furthermore, the court pointed out, the trustees did not hold title to sovereignty lands and therefore lacked the power to convey them. The court also clarified that the extension of survey lines over the beds of navigable waters cannot and does not alter the inherent public character of navigable waters.

In 1909, in the *Broward v. Mabry* decision, the court warned again that the "trustees of the internal improvement fund, who have the disposal of the swamp and overflowed lands of the state, have no authority to convey the title to lands under navigable waters that properly belong to the sovereignty of the state."[114] That same year the legislature countered with the passage of chapter 5943: "An Act to Provide for the Sale of Lands That are now or May Hereafter Be, Vested in the Trustees of the Internal Improvement Fund of the State of Florida." In the 1912 case of *Symmes v. Prairie Pebble Phosphate Co.*, Justice Whitfield reasserted the public character of sovereignty lands:

> navigable waters in the state and the lands under such waters, including the shore or spaces between ordinary high and low water marks, are the property of the state or of the people of the state in their united or sovereign capacity. Such lands are not held for purposes of sale or conversion into other values, or for the reduction into several or individual ownership, but for the use of all the people of the state.

The *Symmes* court also stated that a plaintiff making a claim for injury to property located in the beds of navigable waters of the state, "must show the lawfulness of the ownership asserted, since the acquisition of such property is not within the common right, but depends upon proper legislation and authorized appropriate action duly taken thereunder."

Then, in 1913, the legislature enacted a law providing the trustees with the authority they had never before had—the authority to dispose of certain sovereignty lands. The law provided that, in Dade and Palm Beach Counties only, all sovereignty lands covered by less than three feet of water at high tide and separated from the mainland by a channel five feet deep at high tide (that is, low, submerged islands and sandbars) were vested in the trustees for disposition.[115] The 1856 Riparian Rights Act, as construed by the courts, had allowed the upland owner to perfect title to submerged lands only after certain improvements benefiting the public had been completed. With the passage of the 1913 law, those submerged lands in Dade and Palm Beach Counties meeting the criteria of the law could now be sold outright to anyone. Unvested individuals could, under this law, acquire title in fee simple to submerged lands without meeting any requirement for filling, bulkheading, or improvements. These parcels could then be developed as choice residential property or resold for speculative purposes. In 1917, with the passage of chapter 7304, the law was broadened to apply statewide. Now, acquiring submerged lands was no longer restricted to the riparian owner; anyone could buy certain types of sovereignty lands. As Gay points out,

The 1917 act meant that the upland owner could get title to lands below high water mark in two ways: (1) by filling in and bulkheading, or (2) by buying from the trustees; while the non-upland owner could purchase directly from the trustees, thus apparently cutting off the rights of any upland owner to obtain title to the submerged lands in front of his property by filling and bulkheading.[116]

But if the trustees seemed eager to divest the state of sovereignty lands, the court continued focusing on the state's public trust duties. In 1919 in *Brickell v. Trammel*, Whitfield wrote that the lawmaking power of the state

> may grant to riparian proprietors owning to high-water mark on the navigable waters of the state easements in the lands below high-water mark contiguous to the riparian holdings, for the purpose of constructing there-on facilities for reaching navigable water that may be opposite or in front of the uplands, with rights of action to protect the easements granted . . . , provided such facilities do not materially impair the rights of the public in the navigable waters. . . . But such granted easements and rights give no title to islands or to lands below high-water mark.

Whitfield also reaffirmed the *Black River Phosphate* court's reasoning with regard to the 1856 Riparian Rights Act, stating that for the "act to be operative to the riparian owner, the owner must hold title to the *low* water mark."[117] By interpreting the 1856 law to apply only to riparian owners with title to the low watermark—a construction severely limiting the law's applicability—the Whitfield court sounded a clear note against the chorus that seemed ready to dispose of sovereignty lands. But the *Brickell* ruling was not the final word by any means.

The State's Dilemma: Public Trust and Waterfront Development

In 1921 the legislature responded by passing chapter 8537, commonly known as the Butler Act, which supplied the legal basis for sovereignty landfills that the flawed 1856 act had probably been meant to provide. By making the grant applicable to those persons owning lands to the *high* watermark and making it retroactive to 1856, the Butler Act brought the law into closer agreement with the popular interpretation of the 1856 act and clarified the "judicial inconsistencies and overgeneralizations with regard to just what water mark it was that set the 1856 act in operation."[118] But, the act contained several important safeguards as far as the public trust was concerned. Sections 6 and 7 of the act stipulated that the law did not apply to nontidal lakes or to public beaches. And, where many had interpreted the 1856 act as an outright shifting of the sovereignty lands boundary waterward to the channel,[119] the Butler Act concurred with the court's opinion that the grant only applied in cases where permanent improvements had been made—specifically by filling from the high watermark out to the channel. However, the law clearly stated that it was "for the benefit of the State of Florida that water front property be improved and developed,"[120] and among the purposes for which sovereignty lands might be filled, the act included the construction of dwellings—an element some commentators saw as founding a new emphasis on the development of residential property.[121] With the 1917 law providing nonriparian owners the right to negotiate for sovereignty lands, and the Butler Act supplying riparian owners an unregulated right to fill from shore to channel, the legal basis for sovereignty land development was in place just as the Florida boom began.[122] "It was during this period of the early 1920's," Wallis and Ney C. Landrum note, "that the submerged land 'fill' firmly established itself on the Florida scene."[123] The boom was curbed temporarily, however, by the downturn in national economic conditions, which for a time slowed the rate of bay fill for residential purposes.[124]

Then, in 1924, the court seemed to reverse its direction in the case of *State ex rel. Buford v. City of Tampa*. The case involved a series of legislative acts that granted to the city of Tampa "certain lands and middle ground and overflowed lands in the Hillsborough river and in Sparkman Bay and in Hillsborough Bay for a period of 1,000 years, for the purpose of commerce, navigation, and municipal docks and terminals for such purposes." Further, the grants specified that the improvements be made within twenty-five years and that the city would be allowed to widen, deepen, and extend the channels and to "fill in, build up, have, possess, use, and own shoals, shallows, and middle ground or flats and all overflow lands therein."[125] In 1924, the city entered into a contract to sell to D. P. Davis all the city's right, title, and interest in a sizeable tract of land consisting almost entirely of tidelands and riverbed. The property was to be developed into a "high-class residential subdivision" using extensive dredging and filling and the construction of a concrete bulkhead. At that point, the attorney general stepped in, seeking to stop the sale.

In reviewing the case, the court distinguished constitutional law from common law, pointing out that Florida's Constitution in no way forbade the legislature from disposing of submerged lands, nor did it declare any trust in the state in its tidewaters, nor the submerged lands that might overflow at high tide. "Whatever trust was imposed," the court asserted, "was that of the common law which the state through its Legislature assumed, and the state accepted." [126] Justice Ellis, writing for the majority, further stated that the declared policy of the state was that "it is for the state's benefit that water front property be improved and benefited." For the first time the court seemed ready to retreat from its previous reading of the public trust doctrine as the established law of the land. Yet, the opinion itself seems full of ambivalence. In support of the court's holding for the defendant, Ellis quotes the legislative acts granting the land to the city of Tampa. But the citations can be read to support a decision for either party. "*Subject to any inalienable trust* under which it holds such lands," the grant said, the state divests itself of "*all right, title, and interest*" to the lands.[127] Then, as if this contradiction in terms were not sufficient doublespeak for one case, the court provided this ambiguous comment:

> This court has never held that the state could not by act of the Legislature divest itself of the title to such lands, and counsel's criticism to the contrary did not so hold in Broward v. Mabry. . . . The court in that case said:
>> "The trust in which the title to the lands under navigable waters is held is governmental in its nature, and cannot be wholly alienated by the states." [128]

Then, referring to the Butler Act and the 1856 Riparian Rights Act, the court upheld the legislative grants and declared the bulkheading and fill of the mudflats within appropriate limits. Reading the majority opinion, one is left to wonder exactly what the authors of these documents had in mind when writing the words "inalienable" and "trust."

In his dissenting opinion, Justice Whitfield defined two classes of public lands: sovereignty lands and ordinary public lands; "the nature and uses of the two classes being materially different." Then, in contradistinction to the majority opinion, which had taken up the defendants' description of the mudflats as "valueless for any purpose," Whitfield declared such lands "of great value to the public for the purposes of commerce, navigation, and fishery. Their improvement by individuals," he asserted, "when permitted, is incidental or subordinate to the public use and right. Therefore the title and the control of them are vested in the sovereign for the benefit of the whole people." [129] Whitfield went on to warn that grants of title to sovereignty lands should be made by "definitely worded statutes duly enacted for appropriate purposes" and that they should be construed "with reference to the nature of the state's title, and with due regard for the rights of the whole people of the state . . . to the end that such public rights may be . . . fully conserved." [130] Then, summing up his disagreement with the majority, Whitfield wrote:

If it be assumed that a duly enacted statute may, by vesting title in a city or otherwise, authorize the city to grant in fee-simple title, to an individual for private development and sale as a residential subdivision, a large body of tidelands and a considerable portion of the bed of a navigable river and bay adjacent to the city, aggregating "approximately 600 acres," the lands to be filled in to main navigable waters, and without provision for access by the public to the navigable waters from the lands granted, *no such statute is shown in this case.*[131]

Whitfield's admonition to lawmakers and trustees to be explicit in their actions concerning sovereignty lands might well have arisen from his frustration with the majority opinion. For the tension between the state's trust responsibility and its policy of encouraging waterfront development seemed to result from the same failure to clarify the full implications of such concepts as public rights, trust, divest, and title.

Over the next several decades, numerous laws were passed to allow for the sale of sovereignty lands;[132] and, with broad powers to convey submerged lands placed in the trustees' hands, Florida's sovereignty lands now became "highly-prized negotiable assets."[133] Notable, however, in all this legislation is the absence of any detail concerning the location of the ordinary high water line. Essentially, these laws continued to manipulate the title to sovereignty lands without addressing the issue of where exactly the line might be. For the next forty years the policies concerning sovereignty lands focused on issues of title and extending title boundaries beyond the ordinary high water line. What much of the case law and the legislation seemed to take for granted was that the OHWL was an obvious line, and there was little hint of the trouble to come.

Needing "No Scientific Exploration to Find"

In the meantime, the Florida Supreme Court considered two cases, both in 1927, that were to become cornerstones of Florida's OHWL law: *Martin v. Busch* and *Tilden v. Smith*. These cases not only defined and clarified the concepts inherent in the ordinary high water line, they brought to light the problems of *locating* the OHWL on Florida water bodies. In *Martin v. Busch,* the bill of complaint sought to remove a cloud of title on property, a part of which lay in the former bed of Lake Okeechobee that had been exposed during the state's drainage operations. The complainant's claim of ownership derived from a chain of title originating in the 1850 swamp and overflowed lands grant from Congress to the state. In sorting out the case, Chief Justice Whitfield began by explaining, as he had done nineteen years before in *State ex rel. Ellis v. Gerbing,* that swamp and overflowed lands deeds could not convey sovereignty lands. He went on to assert that the state owned the beds of all navigable lakes to ordinary high watermark—including the shores and any tidelands, and, even though drainage operations caused the waters of the lake to recede, "as such lands were sovereignty lands when covered by the waters of the navigable lake, they remained sovereignty lands when the water receded."[134] The court declared that the state cannot divest itself of sovereignty lands without the express intent to do so through the proper agency. The court also held that it was the state's responsibility to establish the official boundary between sovereignty lands under navigable water and the uplands.

In considering the issues, the court then addressed the problems of determining the ordinary high water line on low, flat-banked water bodies whose swampy margins can make a difficult job of locating the shore—let alone the OHWL.

> In flat territory or because of peculiar conditions, there may be little if any shore to navigable waters, or the elevation may be slight and the water at the outer edges may be shallow and affected by vegetable growth or other conditions, and the line of ordinary high-water mark may be difficult of accurate ascertainment; but, when the duty of determining the line of high-water mark is imposed or assumed, the best evidence attainable and the best methods available should be utilized in determining and establishing the line of true ordinary high-water mark. . . . Marks upon the ground or upon local objects that are more or less permanent may be considered in connection with competent testimony and other evidence in determining the true line of ordinary high-water mark.[135]

Earth Justice attorney Guest points out that the language describing the procedure for determining the OHWL begins with a technique in *Howard v. Ingersoll,* which stated that "where the bank is fairly marked by water, that water level will show at all places where the line is."[136] This technique involves using the elevation of marks indicating the OHWL to locate the boundary in areas without clear marks. "On lakes," Guest explains, "the elevation of the marks provides an ordinary high water elevation that can be surveyed into the swamp by using a transit and level, rather than finding the water's edge at the exact moment the water is at the water mark." For the first time, though, the Florida court also provided guidelines for establishing the OHWL of the flat-bank type of water bodies often found in Florida—water bodies without a clear bank. And, although it went without comment at the time, the method suggested by the court constituted a point of departure from the idea that the OHWL would be an obvious boundary needing "no scientific exploration to find."[137]

In *Tilden,* the complainants sought to enjoin the defendant from lowering the waters of Lake Johns, which, because of unusually heavy rains, had overflowed the defendant's property (as well as some of his neighbors'), causing damage to citrus groves, a golf course, and houses, and killing pine trees and other natural growth. The complainants, who were situated on somewhat higher ground (literally, if not figuratively), were enjoying certain benefits to their groves and did not desire to see the lake returned to its usual level. Justice Brown, writing for the court, noted that the appellants seemed to hold the position that

> a riparian proprietor on a pond or lake has no right to attempt to lower the level of the lake under any circumstances, no matter how unusual and unnatural the existing level may be. He may not endeavor to restore it to the usual or natural level. Appellants contend that whatever the level of the water happens to be, if caused by a natural cause such as rainfall, that is the natural level or at least the level intended by the statute. . . . But neither the statute nor the common-law rule will bear any such strained construction. The law gives no man a vested right in a flood or a freshet, or conditions created thereby.[138]

In clarifying the concept of ordinary, the court noted that it is "well settled that government patents of lands bounded by navigable waters convey titles to the *ordinary* high-water mark of such waters, and not to high-water mark temporarily existing during flood or freshet or unusually high tides."[139] The court stated further that the ordinary level of the lake could not be inferred from unusually dry or wet years but must be obtained "under fairly normal or average weather conditions."[140]

Perhaps most important though, the *Tilden* court highlighted the importance of vegetation indicators to Florida's OHWL determinations. In coming to its conclusions, the court considered evidence of water-killed trees as proof that the present stage of the lake was abnormally high. Several mature orange groves of as many as eight hundred trees up to twenty years old were killed by the high water. In addition, the defendant, Smith, argued that a survey he had had done in 1915 showed that the water level had not been in its present (flooded) condition for many years. For this argument Smith pointed out that trees near the lake at the time of the survey were approximately thirty-five years old and that in recent years the high elevation of the lake had killed hundreds of these trees.

The court also quoted extensively from a Minnesota Supreme Court rul-

ing that stated that in the case of freshwater rivers and lakes the high watermark could be ascertained "where the presence and action of the water
are so common and usual, and so long continued in all ordinary years, as
to mark upon the soil of the bed a character distinct from that of the banks,
in respect to vegetation, as well as respects the nature of the soil itself." The
Minnesota court ruling went on to describe the situation of the high water mark with regard to two different bank configurations:

> "High water mark" means what its language imports—a water mark. It is co-
> ordinate with the limit of the bed of the water; and that only is to be considered
> the bed which the water occupies sufficiently long and continuously to wrest it
> from vegetation, and destroy its value for agricultural purposes. Ordinarily the
> slope of the bank and the character of its soil are such that the water impresses a
> distinct character on the soil as well as on the vegetation. In some places, how-
> ever, where the banks are low and flat, the water does not impress on the soil any
> well-defined line of demarcation between the bed and the banks.
>
> In such cases the effect of the water upon vegetation must be the principal test
> in determining the location of high-water mark as a line between the riparian
> owner and the public. It is the point up to which the presence and action of the
> water is so continuous as to destroy the value of the land for agricultural pur-
> poses by preventing the growth of vegetation, constituting what may be termed
> an ordinary agricultural crop.[141]

The Minnesota case thus indicated that the OHWL may be located by the
physical indicators showing the usual, common, continuous presence and
action of water. Where banks are steep, the impact of water may produce
a clear mark on the soil and banks. But in low-bank areas a "well defined
line of demarcation" may not be found, and, here, the "effect of the water
upon vegetation" becomes the "principal test." The *Tilden* court concluded from this case that in "ascertaining the normal level and average
high-water mark of a lake, evidence may be introduced as to the character
of the vegetation upon its banks."[142]

The *Tilden* ruling not only established these important foundations in
Florida's OHWL case law, it also opened the door to a more comprehensive acknowledgment of the natural world. Although there is a clear emphasis in early case law on the idea that an "obvious mark" will distinguish
the ordinary high water line, *Tilden* recognized that in certain cases we
might not find anything so distinct. In its discussion of the low-bank
areas, the court noted that the presence of the water would *prevent* the
growth of vegetation. But the court then qualified this statement by its reference to agricultural crops. The agricultural crops test contains the seed

of an important idea—one that would become a controversial aspect of OHWL determinations much later. By specifying *agricultural* crops as the test for OHWL, the court indicated some awareness that the low-bank margins of water bodies are frequently thickly vegetated; in other words, the continuous presence and action of the water does *not* leave a mark above which is vegetated and below which is barren. It leaves a mark above which *some types* of vegetation are present and below which *some types* of vegetation are absent. This implication was not made explicit, but the court's tacit acknowledgment that water affects different types of plants in different ways prepared the ground for further investigation.[143] Thus, in establishing guidelines for locating Florida's OHWL, the *Martin* and *Tilden* rulings opened the way for the very scientific exploration the *Howard* court, some eighty years before, had said was not needed.

The Emerging Battle Line

By midcentury, the vulnerability of sovereignty lands in Florida had expressed itself in an explosion of bay fills. In 1941 the legislature passed chapter 253, vesting in the trustees the "administration, management, control, supervision, conservation and protection of all land and products on, under, or growing out of, or connected with, lands owned by . . . the State of Florida." [144] The statute described the trustees' authority to sell submerged lands and islands "upon such prices and terms as they shall see fit," the only requirement being that the sale be advertised. "With the general economic upswing," Wallis and Landrum wrote in 1958, "the unparalleled increases in Florida's population, the real estate boom and the premium values attached to waterfront homesites, it was indeed inevitable that the bay fill should be the developer's response to this conducive situation. Legal authority was abundant; regulations were lax; and Florida history provided forceful testimony to the feasibility and lucrativeness of filling bay bottoms." [145] The absence of a consistent management plan by which the trustees could allow appropriate private improvements while protecting sovereignty lands had now become glaring.

In 1951—for perhaps the first time in more than a century—the legislature acted to strengthen the protection of sovereignty lands. In effect, the law enacted that year repealed the 1917 law that provided for the sale of lands in the bays, but specifically excluded Dade and Palm Beach Counties. Although the 1951 law confirmed the authority of the trustees to institute more stringent control over sovereignty lands, it failed to remedy the legal inconsistencies of the various conflicting laws still in force. In 1957, the legislature passed chapter 57-362, Laws of Florida, which became known as the Bulkhead Law. This law expressly repealed chapter 271.01 (the 1917 statute) as well as "all laws and parts of laws in conflict herewith." Titles granted to lands already filled were confirmed, but further filling was restricted and required a permit. The heart of the bill, however, was section 253.122, Power to fix bulkheads, which provided for the establishment of bulkhead lines by local governing bodies. The lines, which were subject to the formal approval of the trustees, set the outward limit "beyond which a further extension creating or filling of land or islands outward into the waters of the county shall be deemed an interference with the servitude in favor of commerce and navigation with which the navigable waters of this state are inalienably impressed." The law further stipulated the responsibility of the local governing body to fix a bulkhead line upon the written application of any riparian owner in the event such a line had not been established in that vicinity, and it specified that a drawing showing the location of the bulkhead line be promptly filed in the public records. Individual applications to purchase submerged land within an approved bulkhead line were required as well as a separate application to fill the land purchased.

Writing from the Office of the Trustees of the Internal Improvement Fund the year after passage of the Bulkhead Law, Wallis and Landrum commented:

> With the enactment of the bulkhead law, the Trustees received the unequivocal responsibility for upholding the public interest in sovereign lands; but the law provided, too, a means by which this formidable responsibility can be discharged. . . . The device of placing the initial responsibility for the establishment of a bulkhead line in local hands would serve the double purpose of satisfying local needs while relieving the Trustees' staff of a task which would be virtually overpowering if attempted for the entire state. . . . Chapter 57-362, for the first time in Florida's sovereignty land history, goes beyond the arbitrary issue of the right to fill or not to fill, and provides through its bulkhead line requirement a *scientific means* for resolving the problem.[146]

The authors recommended that the local authorities responsible for fixing the bulkhead lines coordinate with engineering, surveying, and other professionals. These professionals, Wallis and Landrum felt, could provide the expertise critical to identifying a suitable bulkhead line—one which would separate "desirable from undesirable bay fills." But, it was important that engineers and surveyors "familiarize themselves thoroughly with what is to be accomplished." Fixing a bulkhead line such as that contemplated by chapter 57-362, the authors observed, went far beyond determining the line most advantageous to a single client's interest. "All too often," they wrote, "the principal considerations in designing bay fills are the expense of filling, the acreage to be filled, the number of waterfront lots available and the anticipated income from the project." Instead, it was the duty of those professionals charged with establishing the bulkhead lines to consider the effects a "permitted bay fill would have on public navigation, sanitation and public health, wildlife and its habitats, tidal movements and currents, erosion and shoaling, public access, and the like."[147] Because the trustees of the Internal Improvement Fund lacked the staff and resources to scrutinize every bulkhead line, Wallis and Landrum noted, they necessarily relied on the professional engineers and surveyors who planned the projects and prepared the applications. "In a word," the authors concluded, "the responsibility of upholding the public interest in sovereignty land management is shared from a practical standpoint by each member of the engineering and surveying professions. This is a considerable responsibility."[148]

The passage of the bulkhead laws ushered in a new emphasis on precision in locating the ordinary high water line. Once the upland owner had to buy the property between the ordinary high water line and the bulkhead line in order to fill it, the accurate setting of the OHWL became important in a way it had not previously been. Even more fundamentally, however, the bulkhead laws expressed the stirrings of a change in the political will of Floridians, for these laws represented a real departure from the spirit and policy of the Riparian Rights Acts of 1856 and 1921. In 1965, Justice Ervin, in his dissenting opinion in a case involving a bulkhead line, wrote:

> The [Bulkhead] law was enacted in response to an aroused public interest and alarm concerning the great number, promiscuity and adverse effects of fills already made in coastal offshore waters of the state and the anticipation of even greater filling of this nature in the absence of any statute regulating indiscriminate filling. The Legislature recognized that unregulated and uncontrolled filling of submerged lands threatened the economy of the state and its growing communities, impaired the scenic beauty and utility of our coastal lands and waters and adversely affected the enjoyment and utilization of these areas by our citizens and visitors to a degree inimical to the public welfare.[149]

Of course, Floridians' "aroused public interest and alarm" over bay fills was only one expression of the broad-based environmental movement surging through the nation. In 1949 Aldo Leopold had seemed a rather lone voice when he wrote of a land ethic that enlarged the boundaries of the community to include "soils, waters, plants, and animals, or collectively, the land. A thing is right," he said, "when it tends to preserve the integrity, beauty, and stability of the biotic community. It is wrong when it tends otherwise."[150] But as the 1960s got under way, many more voices joined in calling for a holistic approach to the natural world and began urgently warning of the environmental degradation our newfound technological power now made possible.[151] No longer was it sufficient merely to conserve or preserve "natural resources." Only a fundamental reassessment of our relations with the natural world would prevent our destroying the very processes we relied on for life itself.

In Florida, holders of this environmental ethic found themselves squaring off against bulkhead applicants at the ordinary high water line. The Bulkhead Law had made the trustees responsible for considering "the conservation of natural resources" when making sales of submerged lands. This provision, as Gay pointed out in 1966, seemingly would preclude any further questions about whether the property owner could fill submerged lands out to the bulkhead line—at least concerning the conservation issue. But this was not the case.[152] Because a separate, local permit was required actually to fill acquired submerged lands, property owners were not assured that they could, in fact, use property they had purchased. Local conservation interests often raised objections when the landowners applied for the fill permit, citing the importance of submerged lands to birds and marine species and the public's right to enjoy the natural surroundings. This situation, Gay noted, "puts the private purchaser of submerged lands in an extremely vulnerable position, because he is not really certain what he has bought until he makes application to the local group for a fill permit." On one side of the debate, landowners contended that once the submerged land was sold by the trustees, the purchaser should be able to exercise full property rights in the land, "any question of the greater public interest in conservation of natural resources as opposed to private rights having been already resolved by [the trustees'] approval of the sale." Conservationists and environmentalists, on the other side, flatly opposed dredging and filling submerged lands, saying that these activities destroyed the ecological balance in nature and pointing out that mudflats, salt marshes, mangrove swamps, and shallow bottoms are among the most productive lands on earth. Some local permitting agencies, under pressure to provide specifics of what would and would not receive a permit, attempted to solve the dilemma by passing special legislation detailing such criteria. But increasingly it seemed that "more serious thought and planning should be put into the original, or revised, setting of local bulkhead lines," Gay wrote in 1965, "making the line coincide with the high water mark in those areas where it is desired to preserve the bottom lands for conservation purposes."[153] Yet this suggestion met with opposition from the landowners. Gay continued:

> The conclusion is inescapable, however, that all attempts by whatever means to balance public interests on one side of the high water mark against private interests on the other will leave some people frustrated and dissatisfied. It cannot be too strongly urged that all those concerned with weighing these opposing values utilize every bit of factual, objective information of which they can avail themselves. As Dr. Robert Ingle of the Florida State Board of Conservation has pointed out: "If the problem of conservation versus private development is not solved on the fact level, it gets down to the emotional level, and there the whole picture becomes distorted."
>
> . . . Whether the people want the high water mark raised as a barrier to preserve their public lands from private encroachment, or whether they want it lowered as an inducement to private development, they should make their views known.[154]

In 1968 the citizens of Florida did make their views known. They ratified a new constitution. In article 10, section 11, the Florida Constitution "elevated the public trust doctrine to the stature of a constitutional mandate . . . [holding] that the State was trustee rather than proprietor of navigable waters and that acts in breach of that trust were judicially voidable."[155] The new constitution stated that the title to lands under navigable waters that had not been alienated was to be held in trust for all people. It further stipulated that the "[s]ale or private use of portions of such lands may be authorized by law, but *only when not contrary* to the public interest." In 1970, this language was amended to read: "Sale of such lands may be authorized by law, but *only when in* the public interest" (emphasis added). With this mandate from the citizens of Florida to protect sovereignty lands, the accurate determination of boundaries between publicly owned trust lands and private uplands had never been more critical—or more embattled. The method of locating the ordinary high water line for any given water body now came to the forefront of the fracas. What no one could have guessed was that at that very moment the unprecedented engineering feat of channelizing the Kissimmee River was about to bring into focus the controversies surrounding Florida's OHWL.

2 The Kissimmee River Story: Empire and Ecology

IN 1989, I WAS COMMUTING every week from Tallahas-
see, Florida, to Atlanta, Georgia, in order to complete course work for my
doctorate at Emory University. One day as I was speeding along the
Florida-Georgia Parkway, racing to get to class, I heard a story on National
Public Radio (NPR) about Florida's Kissimmee River. In spite of the facts
that I am a third-generation Floridian and that, as I now know, the Kissimmee forms the hydrologic heart of my state, I had never heard of the river.
It occurred to me that my unawareness spoke volumes to the question of
how we commit ecological devastations, guilty merely of never looking up
from the hectic pace of our so-called "lives." Like most Floridians, I rarely
contemplated where the water comes from when I turn on the tap.

The story I heard that day was compelling, and even though it is a story that, still at the time of this writing, is not finished, it changed forever the way I see the landscape of Florida. According to NPR's report, the one-hundred-mile-long river had been "straightened"—channelized—in the 1960s by the Army Corps of Engineers. Then, in the early 1970s, the decision had been made to undo the work, "restore" the river—even though no one was exactly sure what that could mean. But funding stalled. Political will wavered. Years went by. Now in 1989, NPR said, the restoration was finally about to begin. Support had been galvanized by the crisis in the Everglades, an ecosystem unique in the world and one that was dying of dehydration. Listening to the radio that day, I realized that I couldn't picture what had happened. What did it mean to "ditch" a one-hundred-mile-long river? Then to put it back in its "natural" condition? Did we do such things simply because we could? Perhaps there had been good reasons. Or perhaps there had been an unawareness as ordinary as my own unawareness of the river had been. I decided to find out.

River Talk

Florida shares important characteristics with the areas of the world in which the great deserts have formed. It lies in the same "latitudinal belt" as the great deserts, and its subtropical climate produces wet and dry seasons similar to those that prevail in the great deserts.[1] Although these seasons typically form a pattern of rainy summers and dry winters, within this pattern there are often years of extremes, and both flooding and drought are common. In most places in the world, this climate has produced a tropical savannah, characterized by a long dry season, which severely limits the support of life.[2] That Florida did not develop a tropical savannah ecosystem is due to the unique conditions of its evolution. In 1973, a group of scientists described the Florida ecosystem's protective function:

> The natural ecosystem literally developed the ability to sustain a highly diverse and productive aquatic and upland ecosystem where, but for the water conserving mechanisms of that ecosystem, an arid and harsh tropical savannah would exist. The importance to man of this water storage ability, developed over thousands of years by living components of the ecosystem, cannot be overestimated.[3]

What no one seems to have understood until recently was how intricate were the links between the south Florida ecosystem and the Kissimmee River.

The Kissimmee River came into being a long time ago, with the formation of the Florida peninsula landmass, which lies between latitudes 24°

and 31°30′N and longitudes 80° and 87°30′W. Underlying the peninsula is the Floridan Plateau, a long, narrow bed of rock dividing the Atlantic Ocean from the Gulf of Mexico. Over millions of years the Floridan Plateau developed its present landmass through the actions of climate and ocean. During the Pleistocene epoch, each glacial advance caused the waters around the developing plateau to recede and also drove a great variety of animals onto the peninsula. When the glaciers withdrew, vast areas of the Florida peninsula were again flooded. This cycle continued until the Recent epoch when a warmer climate sent the glaciers into a more sustained retreat.[4] It was during this period that the large deserts across the world were formed. In Florida, however, shells and bones of creatures as well as minerals precipitated from ocean currents formed layers of highly porous rock. The very rock that shapes Florida's surface contributes to water storage, forming underground reservoirs that may hold well over 1 quadrillion gallons of water.[5]

The word *Kissimmee* is a Calusa Indian word meaning "long water." The Kissimmee River ran through the heart of the Florida peninsula in a region known as the Central Highlands and was part of a large watershed area, the Kissimmee River Basin.[6] For thousands of years before the U.S. Army Corps of Engineers completed its channelization project, wet season water flowed through this "inland sea," gliding down a nearly imperceptible slope from the Upper Kissimmee Chain of Lakes southward some ninety miles to Lake Okeechobee. From there it spilled over the south lip of the shallow lake into the forty-mile-wide "river of grass"—the northernmost portion of the Everglades. The gentle slope of the river's course meant that the water flowed slowly southward in a broad sheet, allowing ample time for the water to percolate into the soil and to be taken up by the floodplain vegetation. In 1973, a special project report on efforts to prevent the eutrophication of Lake Okeechobee explained that because of this flatness of the Floridan Plateau, "natural drainage in the Kissimmee Valley was principally downward into the deep sandy soils. In the uplands of the valley, the ground water table fluctuated several feet between wet and dry seasons. In the floodplain and other low areas, ground water was stable and near the land surface during both wet and dry seasons and during all but the longest drought." Here, water was stored that, "during dry season and drought, was available as base flow from the shallow aquifer into surface waters and lowland marshes."[7] This capacity for water storage resulted in the formation of countless lakes, marshes, wet prairies, and ponds that prevented desertlike conditions from prevailing.

The winding turns of the natural Kissimmee River took shape as rainfall and the varied topography of the river basin caused water levels to rise and fall, triggering erosion and deposition along the river's edge. Over many centuries of this process, the broad, flat floodplain formed, dotted with lakes and ponds that remained when the river's course shifted. When inundated from river overflow, this floodplain formed wetlands up to three miles wide.[8] The organic soils characteristic of these wetlands acted as a huge sponge to absorb and conserve wet season rains. Thus, the wetlands and their water-absorbing soils made water available during the yearly dry season as well as during scorching droughts that occur under natural conditions in the region about one year out of six.[9] Wetlands vegetation also acted to filter sediments and other nutrients from the water entering the river, ensuring a high water quality. In addition, the marshes provided the habitat for billions of freshwater shrimp and other small fish and invertebrates, which were a primary food source for wading birds and river fish species. With the natural fluctuations of the water levels, the marshes were continually "communicating" with the river. This dynamic interaction of rising and falling water with the various communities in these wetland ecosystems resulted in a high diversity of plants, animals, and habitats.[10]

Thus, prior to channelization, the Kissimmee floodplain abounded with white ibis, great blue herons, snowy egrets, Louisiana herons, glossy ibis, sandhill cranes, and many other wading birds. According to Louis Toth, a biologist with the South Florida Water Management District, some 25,000 waterfowl typically used the basin during the winter months. More than thirty-nine species of fish were supported by the river and floodplain, and "despite extremely limited access for fishermen," in the mid-twentieth century, "the historic Kissimmee River had a nationally renowned largemouth bass fishery." Broadleaf marsh, shrub, and prairie wetland communities comprised a "mosaic of hundreds of distinct patches of intermingled vegetation types" living in the Kissimmee floodplain.[11] Water was the all-important element in the formation of the Florida peninsula ecosystems. Ebbing and flowing over the centuries, water became something like the language of the various communities that depended on its rhythms, its variations, and its unique capacity to carry the nutrients of their cultures. Water was meaning, and what it meant was life.

It was this formation on which all life depended—the wide, flat floodplain between open water and uplands—that would one day test our understanding of the ordinary high water line, and would help make clear why the erasure of this line became an unacceptable human transgression.

From the Head of the River

In March 1990, I went to see what had become of the Kissimmee River—what was now Canal 38. Driving south on U.S. 27 out of Ocala through the early spring green, I began to notice a battle-worn look about the Florida landscape. What I remembered from a trip twenty years before was lush orange groves stretching as far as the eye could see, broken only by the topaz sky glittering in one of the hundreds of lakes that dot the area—and the intoxicating scent of orange blossoms. I had told my husband that if the orange trees were blooming, it would be like heaven. This wasn't heaven. This looked more like the wrath of an angry god descending on people who had too long ignored his warnings. What had happened? Where there were still groves, dead leaves and too-orange fruit hung from the branches, and the stench of decaying citrus permeated the crisp air. But most of the groves had already been bulldozed—from the looks of it more than a year before—pushed into piles and burned. For Sale signs littered both sides of the highway, but it didn't look like there were going to be any buyers. When we stopped at a restaurant midday somewhere around Clermont, we overheard two grove owners—a couple in their mid-thirties—consulting with their county agent at the next table. I noticed the woman didn't eat her lunch.

At Lake Wales we headed east through the sand hills and pine flatwoods that make up the Kissimmee Prairie west of the river. Few people live in this part of Florida, and that surprised me. Over the years, hearing the Chamber of Commerce boast that "2000 people a week now move to the south Florida area," I thought every square inch below Ocala—really the entire peninsula of Florida—was populated. But the environment along state road 60 to the river seemed distinctly hostile to human habitation. Tight clusters of high and low spots made the idea of working the ground with a tractor unappealing. Palmettos and scrub pines claimed broad areas, with only an occasional "cracker home"—a tar-paper shack or rusting metal trailer—to break the landscape. Then, suddenly there'd be a cattle ranch, with picture-perfect pastures stretching into the skyline.

We drove on to the point on state road 60 where the Kissimmee River flows out of Lake Kissimmee. It's here that the Army Corps put the first set of locks. Looking north from the lock toward the lake, one can see the river fan into a wide panorama of sparkling blue water and marsh grasses in which the banks of the river are indiscernible. Here, clumps of grasses growing in the river merge with the marshland, blending so subtly into a solid bank that the eye can't tell what's river, what's land. The old cabins along the shore are raised high on stilts in silent acknowledgment of the river's patterns. South of the lock, a straight channel, three hundred feet wide and thirty feet deep, has been cut, and here the river meanders no more. Spoil piles of sand and mud, dredged from the river, form a barrier on the west bank. Behind the barrier the land is low and wet, full of marsh vegetation. Mature wax myrtles grow on the spoil bank. I walked along the spoil bank, trying to understand what had happened here. I stopped to talk to some fishermen, but they were from out of state, so they didn't know much about what is now called Canal 38. When I asked them about the fish, they said, "No luck."

I talked to two men from Palm Beach County. One of them knew a lot about the canal. He told me they were "in a bad way" down in Palm Beach because water from the Kissimmee wasn't being let through the locks. Lake Okeechobee at the south end of the river, he said, was too low, and all their tributaries and "catchments" in the Palm Beach area were dry. He pointed over the canal's east bank, across a broad, flat pasture to a line of trees about a mile away. That used to be the riverbank, he said. After a while the lock keeper noticed me taking pictures. He came down and took the padlock off the big chain-link gate and invited me in to watch a boat pass through the locks. As the water rushed into the hold between the locks, I stood on the platform above, watching the two boatmen steady themselves with ropes that hung down alongside the gate wall. I noticed the drop in water level from the lakeside into the canal. It looked to be at least five feet.

The Dream of Florida

The story of the Kissimmee River's conversion to Canal 38 is, in many ways, like a modern-day biblical narrative. It's a composite work, put together over many years from separate—often competing— traditions, some oral and primitive, others literate, official, scientific. Thus, one finds the river's history in many voices, speaking through various documents, from travel guides to legislation, and in the dialects of journalists, historians, engineers, state-agency scientists, politicians, real-estate developers, local farmers and hunters, university professors. In still other ways, the story of the Kissimmee River is a fable of modern science itself. For it is a tale, above all else, of the human claim to control nature—a claim arising, as Carolyn Merchant tells us, with the seventeenth-century mechanistic view of nature that came to dominate political, economic, and social philosophy for the next three hundred years.[12] But the story of the river is overlaid by another story: the building of Florida. This is a story of destiny.

In this story the dominant vision sees a Florida yet to be built, teeming with great hordes of people populating huge cities, swelling state budgets, constructing great commercial enterprises, spreading over the peninsula like God's chosen ones. The authors of Florida's development from wilderness to modern state achieved success—they realized their vision. Part of what this success means is that their story dominates all the other stories one might tell of Florida. But as present-day readers looking back, as readers of the Kissimmee River, we can tell that there are things these authors didn't notice. Like those biblical characters who missed signs, they were too busy to see anything but their chosen course; so, even when it was the road to damnation, they persisted in that course. Although the moral of such tales can by now be guessed, we probably will not know for a long time what kind of story we are authoring with this river. For too often there is a voice that most of the authors of Florida's story don't hear. I think of it as the voice of the river.

After my first day on the river, I spent the evening reading histories of the area, and I found out that the alterations of the Kissimmee didn't start with the project that converted it to Canal 38 in the 1960s. That was when alterations finally ended. Although the U.S. Army Corps of Engineers finally succeeded in ditching the Kissimmee, their project was merely "the final, crowning glory," as Mark Derr says, of a 150-year war on the ecosystems of south Florida.[13] The war began in earnest in 1881 with the state's negotiation of the Disston Drainage Contract, in which the northern industrialist Hamilton Disston promised to drain 12 million acres of submerged lands in south and central Florida in exchange for half of what he drained. "In order to render these lands fit for cultivation," Nelson Manfred Blake writes, "[Disston and his] associates pledged themselves to lower the level of Lake Okeechobee, to deepen and straighten the channel of the Kissimmee River, and to cut canals and ditches to connect Lake Okeechobee with the Caloosahatchee River on the west, the St. Lucie River on the east, and the Miami and other rivers on the southeast."[14] By deepening the Kissimmee and cutting off its bends, the river would be confined to its "natural" banks.[15] Derr comments on the deal:

> In effect, Disston was to drain the upper Everglades and create passage through Lake Okeechobee from the Atlantic to Gulf of Mexico, thereby fulfilling two dreams of Florida schemers to create waterways and land. The final configuration of south Florida's maze of canals, dikes, and channelized rivers generally follows this blueprint, but it took nearly a century and more than $500 million to accomplish.[16]

When the state's creditors tried to sour the drainage deal, Disston bought 4 million acres outright, bailing the state out of its million-dollar Internal Improvement Fund debt.

The *New York Times* heralded the Disston land deal as the largest land purchase by an individual in the world. Disston was to be allowed to select his 4 million acres after making his first payment of $200,000. The selections for the first 3.5 million acres were to be in parcels of at least 10,000 acres, with the last 500,000 acres in smaller tracts. The blocks Disston selected formed a triangle across central Florida, running along the Gulf of Mexico from Marco Island north for two hundred miles to above Tampa Bay, then cutting across to a point above Titusville before angling back down toward Marco.[17] "The significance of his influence cannot be overstated," wrote historian Kathryn Abbey. "It is difficult to see how the peninsula could have flowered as it did without some initial push of this kind."[18]

But not everyone was happy about the deal. Some people felt Bloxham had sold the land too cheaply, and, in fact, higher offers had been rejected in consideration of Disston's immediate cash and the desire to close the drainage deal. Even more critical were those observers who argued that "much of the land included in the purchase and drainage area was neither swamp nor submerged, but was piney woods and dry prairie, a region of saw-toothed palmetto, scrub cattle, and scattered settlers."[19] It seemed as if, in its rush to bail out the Internal Improvement Fund, the state had neither assessed the value of the purchase area for timber and agriculture, nor considered homesteaders with legitimate titles to portions of the land.[20] Instead, such critics argued, the state had sold inhabitable uplands and agricultural lands at swamp prices.

The 1850 federal Swamp and Overflowed Lands Act had specified swamp and overflowed lands as those lands covered by non-navigable waters during all or a portion of the year so as to render them unfit for usual purposes of cultivation unless drained or ditched. Such lands were distinguished from submerged lands, which are below ordinary high water mark of navigable waters in the state, and also from tide lands, which were designated sovereignty lands. But many of the huge tracts treated in the Disston purchase as swamp and overflowed lands were comprised of tightly clustered high and low spots. How could parcels as large as 10,000 acres fail to include *some* high land—that is, lands not fulfilling the swamp and overflowed lands criteria?

With the end of the Seminole War and the forced removal of indigenous people from the prairies north and west of Lake Okeechobee, cattlemen from north Florida had moved their herds south into the Kissimmee Valley. In the 1870s, following the Civil War, more settlers had come, lured by cheap land for orange groves and open-range cattle ranches. "Squatters," who were without any money to buy land, also came into the region and established small farms. These people protested the Disston land sale, and the state responded by recognizing legitimate titles and offering to sell squatters their claims for one dollar an acre.[21] To appease Disston, the state planned to credit these sales and claims to his account. But, according to some accounts, Disston refused to cooperate in this settlement, wanting instead to settle the country with people he and his sales agents had chosen for their economic and social standing.

By 1883, as part of the fulfillment of the drainage contract, Disston's engineers began reporting to the state's trustees that they had lowered the lakes forming the upper Kissimmee River by between two-and-a-half and eight feet and Lake Okeechobee by one-and-a-half feet.[22] However, Lamar Johnson, in *Beyond the Fourth Generation,* notes that the limited rainfall records of the period indicate that a dry cycle may have been responsible for some of the lower water levels that Disston's engineers claimed. "For the next several years," Johnson writes, the engineers "continued to enlarge the original channels that they had hurriedly partially excavated." Johnson began his career as a youth on the first canal dredge off of Lake Okeechobee, worked with F. C. Elliot, Florida's chief drainage engineer during the drainage heyday and finished his long and distinguished career with the South Florida Water Management District before writing his memoirs of south Florida's development. At the end of a painful chapter detailing the trustees' mismanagement of Florida's public trust lands, Johnson writes that it is "difficult to understand why the people of that (Disston's) generation did not realize what was happening, when they lived so close to the land and the weather."[23] If we have learned anything from the past, though, perhaps it is that the seemingly unlimited scope of human vision can make it very difficult to see what we are closest to.

In 1893, Disston was "caught short of cash by the Panic [on Wall Street]," Allen Morris reports in *The Florida Handbook.* "The dredges stopped working and the steamboats quit running. 'The boss was out of money.'"[24] If it is difficult today to assess the overall effect of Disston's drainage efforts in Florida, it seems that was equally the case only a few years after his dredges fell silent. Disston's canals were hailed as the impetus to the settlement of the vast Florida frontier; they were criticized as being virtually ineffectual, some critics claiming that drought—not the canals—had lowered the water levels and drained the lands. In an 1899 report, Henry Jervey, captain of the Corps of Engineers, gave extremely low water as the chief obstacle to the navigation of the Kissimmee River. But he also noted the "'cut-offs' across some of the worst bends of the river" had "on the whole been a benefit to navigation, providing straighter and safer channels." He went on to say, however, that the "work done has been on a very small scale. The depths in the several channels at the time of this examination . . . vary from 1.8 to 30 feet, being generally from 3 to 5 feet."[25] Yet, even this comment is difficult to put into context given that some 1,218 tons of merchandise valued at $151,316 were shipped on the Kissimmee in 1898. Disston was never to return to Florida, however. Shortly after the panic of 1893, according to one account, he "attended the theater one evening in his native Philadelphia, went home, filled a tub in his bathroom, sat down in the water and shot himself in the head."[26] Other, less sensational accounts of Disston's death reported that he died of a heart attack.[27] In any case, Disston's death ended an important chapter in Florida history, but it did not extinguish the dream of Florida.

The second day on the river, I rented a boat from a Disney-like resort called River Ranch, which is located about a mile below the river's first set of locks on the west bank. It was a weird place. Most of it looked two-dimensional, like a movie set. But the marina seemed to predate the rest of the resort. It had a nice old bar and grill and the only boats for hire within fifty miles. It was a cool, sunny morning, just the kind of day to be out on the water. As I brought my boat from the marina canal into the main channel, I saw two herons fishing on the east bank. I turned north and ran up to the lock I had explored on foot the day before. I wanted to see how far the spoil piles I'd been walking on extended downstream. About half a mile below the lock I spotted an opening in the spoil bank. Idling the motor, I nosed the boat into the break, maneuvering through a narrow opening in the hyacinths and marsh weeds.

The contrast between the area behind the spoil pile and the channeled river was striking. Behind the bank, vegetation flourished. In fact, after fifty yards or so in either direction, there was nowhere to go. The hyacinths and marsh grass took over the shallow water, threatening to bind the boat's propeller. I headed back down the main channel, past the resort. Every so often there would be similar breaks in the spoil pile, and these seemed to be the favored fishing spots. Several parties in bass boats and a lone gallinule tried their luck among the weeds, but I didn't see any fish caught either day we were there.

I kept wondering what this river *should* look like. Disston had planned to cut off the river's bends and confine the river to its natural banks. But what would that mean? The bends were its natural banks. What idea of a river might Disston have had that prevented him from seeing *this* river? Probably an idea he had grown up with, and Disston—being from the northeast—would have had a very different idea of a river. The Kissimmee, like many Florida rivers, had flowed through wide, flat-banked sections with sprawling marshes. Many of the rivers Disston would have encountered prior to his Florida experience would be of the steep-bank variety— rivers confined to channels by well-defined banks. Disston had basically set out to "fix" the Kissimmee River—to make it like "regular" rivers. This kind of landscape prejudice is a good example of why it is dangerous to allow development by people who don't have long experience with the local ecology—or bioregion, as Jim Dodge calls it.[28] Such developers can lack a "sense of place" and sufficient ties to the area to plan developments that respect the integrity of natural processes in that place. Of course, in Disston's day the people who would've met this "local" criterion were mostly indigenous Indians—not given to large-scale drainage projects to attract new settlers. Also in Disston's day respect for the integrity of natural processes was a responsibility to which the majority of industrialists had not yet awakened.

Farther down channel, where the west bank rose to over twenty feet high, I tied up the boat and climbed out. Making use of a cow trail, I scrambled up the steep bank to the top. Here it leveled out into a road, high grassland, half a mile wide and stretching for miles along the channel. It was hard to imagine this had ever been wetland. Crossing the open ground to the trees, I discovered they were only a narrow band of trees. Behind them, another steep, high bank turned out to be a roadbed, with a one-lane sand trail, running parallel with the channel. Beyond the roadbed was an even wider area of open ground, spanning roughly a mile to dense pine forest. From high up on the roadbed, I could see that this second huge tract was low and wet, with mostly marsh vegetation growing on it. This seemed puzzling indeed. If channeling the river had been to "reclaim" such land, why was this tract still marshy? The plateau I'd just crossed was high and dry. Were these deviations in the land their natural dimpled character? It occurred to me that I might be standing on a gigantic spoil pile, but the magnitude boggled the mind.

I tried to decide what effect restoring the river would have on this ground. It was certain people would lose land they'd been given access to by the channelization of the river. At the time I knew nothing about the public trust doctrine, ordinary high water lines, or sovereignty lands. I couldn't imagine why ranchers would be willing to go along with the restoration project—at least, I couldn't imagine it without a grand-scale buyout at taxpayer expense. I headed back toward the boat. Standing on the bank overlooking the channel, with several miles of clear view, it struck me that the only animal I could see was a cow over on the east bank. I kept thinking of a passage I'd read the night before:

> In Disston's day the river trip yielded vistas of uncut verdure, from the river banks bordered with ferns, willows, cat-tails and custard apples, to lonely and distant oak hammocks, cypress swamps and islands of cabbage palm trees. Great wading birds stood motionless among the lily pads and the saw grass, watching for fish, or poised for flight. Wild game was everywhere.[29]

It was hard to imagine.

I did see two big alligators on the river that day, and that seemed like a hopeful sign. Alligators eat snails, fish, ducks, raccoons, and turtles, so it seemed likely that at least some of these species must be thriving. Alligators are also a keystone species in subtropical, wetland ecosystems, providing important services to other wetland inhabitants. Alligators dig deep depressions that hold fresh water during dry periods. These "gator holes" provide a home for aquatic species that are themselves crucial to the food supply of birds and other animals. Gator nesting mounds also serve as nest sites for herons and egrets; and, as alligators move from their holes to their nesting mounds, they help keep waterways open. Because alligators eat gar, a fish that preys on other fish, they also play an important role in maintaining populations of bass and bream.[30] Seeing the alligators made it seem possible that the ecosystem could be revived.

But as I was bringing the boat back in, I noticed several people watching a young alligator about three feet long that had come into the marina. The gator seemed right at home around boats and people—too much at home—and I wondered if he'd already learned to look for a handout here. Alligator attacks on humans in Florida have been on the rise over the last decade, and many people feel that, since gators were placed on the endangered species list, gator populations have made too strong a comeback. These critics have argued that gators should no longer be protected. Usually, though, there is no mention in this argument of the two thousand people pouring into south Florida every week, encroaching steadily on the gators' habitat, or of the fact that people feed the gators, and that that action in a gator's mind comes to be represented by a simple equation:

people = food.

It was getting late. I packed up and headed for home. But driving north, back through those ruined groves in Lake and Polk Counties, past the restaurant where I'd seen the worried grove owners, I kept thinking about that young alligator. Somehow the two things seemed connected—all those dead orange trees with their mottled fruit hanging down, rotting amid the towering irrigation sprinklers and For Sale signs, and that young gator cruising through the pleasure boats, holding his head high up out of the water as if to get a better look at the woman in pink shorts eating french fries on the dock, the two boys with cane poles chasing after him on the bank, the old man waving everyone over to see the gator. There seemed to be a connection. But at the time I just thought, No, that doesn't make any sense.

Parting the Waters

In the early 1880s, Disston had dredged the Kissimmee River to make it navigable, at least for the smaller steamboats, but this effort was not an overwhelming success. In an 1883 visit by President Chester A. Arthur to promote Disston's colonies, the party's steamboat ran aground in the Kissimmee River. The river was dredged again in the early 1890s to permit passage of side-wheel and stern-wheel steamers. On December 29, 1899, the *Kissimmee Valley Gazette* described the river:

> in its narrowness, the rampant growth of water plants along its low banks, in the unbroken flatness of the landscape, in the variety and quality of its bird life, in the labyrinth of by-channels and cutoffs, and dead rivers that beset its sluggish course, and above all in the appalling, incredible bewildering crookedness of its serpentine body. There are bends where it has taken nearly an hour's steaming to reach a spot less than 100 yards ahead of the bow. On either side, as far as the eye can reach lies the prairie dotted with small hammocks. Occasionally, the bank rises a few feet to a ridge or hammock and here the steamers make a landing.[31]

Then, for a time, a thriving commerce in passengers and freight—including furs, citrus fruit, and sugarcane—brought prosperity to landings all along the Kissimmee—Grape Hammock, Rattlesnake Hammock, Alligator Bluff, and Mary Belle among them. In 1902 a federal navigation project authorized dredging of the Kissimmee to provide a channel three feet deep and thirty feet wide; it further provided for maintenance of the river to remove fallen trees and keep sand bars passable.[32] Derr notes that in spite of occasional objections (such as those recorded by Florida naturalist

Charles Torrey Simpson in 1923), few people were disturbed by the continuing efforts to channelize wild Florida rivers. "Rather," Derr says,

> the drive was for more reclamation and settlement. The desire for profit played
> the lead in these efforts, but accompanying it, among many developers, was a
> sense of righteousness, an unwavering faith in the efficacy of their undertakings.
> They sought to control . . . every aspect of development, from the basic town
> plan to the character and financial resources of colonists. A new society was being ripped out of the Florida "wilderness." [33]

It is important to remember, however, that in south Florida, water was everywhere, there seemed no end of water, and people were eager to find ways to send the water seaward in the quickest possible route. Channelization of natural rivers and canal building not only drained the land, but they also seemed to provide another benefit—one that was rapidly becoming a top priority: flood control. Hurricanes and floods had long been part of the natural occurrences on the south Florida peninsula. With the state's intensive efforts to drain the Everglades and attract settlement to the area came now the problem of how to protect the state's new citizens from recurring natural disasters.

During the last years of the nineteenth century it had become evident that private contracts were perhaps not the best means to achieve the ambitious drainage goals for the Everglades and central Florida. By the turn of the century, the idea that a more coordinated effort could be directed by a public agency began driving the creation of such entities as the Board of Drainage Commissioners, the Everglades Drainage District, the Florida Everglades Engineering Commission, and the Okeechobee Flood Control District. Work to drain the Everglades progressed slowly through the 1920s, financed by a succession of bond issues, but came to a halt in the later 1920s when the Florida land boom collapsed and the Depression got under way. By 1931, the Everglades Drainage District had defaulted on its bonds.[34] At the same time that drainage efforts were stalling out, a series of devastating hurricanes and floods swept across the south-central region of Florida, causing widespread loss of life and property. Flood Control District records describe the situation:

> Although some 440 miles of canals had been completed and $18,000,000 expended, only the Caloosahatchee and St. Lucie Canals provided satisfactory outlets from Lake Okeechobee to the sea. The other canals lacked the slope necessary to reduce the Lake level appreciably. . . . It also became apparent that canals alone did not afford sufficient protection from overflow during unusual weather.[35]

In 1926 a devastating hurricane swept the southern third of the penin-sula, killing over two hundred people and causing tremendous property damage. This storm galvanized public pressure for federal intervention in Florida's flood control problems. But federal plans had hardly begun to ad-dress the catastrophe when the hurricane of 1928 struck. Winds sweeping in from the Palm Beach area across shallow Lake Okeechobee sent a wall of water crashing into the town of Moore Haven on the lake's western shore. More than 2,400 people drowned. These disasters marked the en-try of the federal government—via its U.S. Army Corps of Engineers—into Florida's water control activities. Federal interest had hitherto been limited primarily to navigation projects, but following President Hoover's personal inspection of the devastated regions around Lake Okeechobee, the army engineers drafted a new plan providing for the construction of floodway channels, control gates, and major levees along Okeechobee's shores. Construction began in 1930 and by 1937—after an expenditure of some $16 million—the project was virtually complete.[36] These federal projects not only provided the first comprehensive flood control in Florida, they also provided a boost to the state's bogged-down Everglades recla-mation effort. Canals and channels built to carry off floodwaters also drained land.

In June 1936 the National Flood Control Act was adopted by Congress, establishing the policy that the federal government "should improve or participate in the improvement of navigable waters or their tributaries for flood control purposes if the benefits to whomsoever they may accrue are in excess of the estimated cost, and if the lives and social security of the people are otherwise adversely affected."[37] But even as the federal flood control works were being built, the complex nature of Florida revealed it-self further with the onset of a drought. A 1954 retrospective report from the Central and Southern Florida Flood Control District (CSFFCD) en-titled *Five Years of Progress: 1949–1954* gives this account:

> The successive extreme dry spells of 1931 through 1945 resulted in lowered ground water levels and the threat of serious salt-water intrusion into the mu-nicipal wells of Miami and other coastal cities. When the water level fell in the Everglades area, salt water from the ocean rose in the wells upon which cities de-pended. Here was an important relation between the areas around Lake Okee-chobee and the other water resources of the region which had been overlooked in earlier efforts to drain the interior.
>
> Furthermore, land which formerly was regularly flooded was now actually vanishing before the eyes of anxious owners. The peaty, organic soils of the Ever-

glades were drying out and shrinking at a clearly-visible rate. Thousands of acres caught fire and the muck itself was consumed and lost forever. . . .

The situation grew worse as Florida recovered from the depression and experienced the economic stimulation of the arrival of World War II. High agricultural prices and demand encouraged the opening of vast acreages of land. A great strain was placed on the water resources of the area by the drainage and irrigation works which continued to expand, *since the improvement of raw land in Florida does not tend to hold water in the soil, but increases the run-off into streams and lakes.*[38]

This report gives an agonizingly clear picture of the difficulties Florida's water managers have always had to deal with. Activities in pursuit of isolated drainage or other goals often cause severe, unforeseen problems such as saltwater intrusion or uncontrollable fires. Yet, all too often, economic demand rather than comprehensive study and understanding drives the state's water project goals. To make matters worse, water managers who have tried to understand Florida's complex nature—who have sounded a call for more comprehensive planning based on scientific study, have frequently found themselves at cross-purposes with agricultural (and other) interests. That agricultural practices in Florida have long been in conflict with sound ecological principles is evident in the district's nonsensical but perfectly ordinary statement (italicized above) that the "improvement" of land destroys the soil's capacity to hold water.

Of course, the sins of water management in this century have been the sins of modernity itself: the delusion that if technology has failed us it was only because we did not have enough of it, and the confidence that because our goals were technologically attainable they must be worth pursuing.[39] In 1947 the long drought ended. A hurricane followed by two severe tropical storms flooded 3 million acres of land in central and south Florida, and the waters lingered for many months. Thousands of cows died, and the Corps of Engineers estimated the damage at more than $59 million. "The pendulum of nature made a complete swing in 1947," the CSFFCD report continues. "It finally became apparent that the *whole problem* of proper water supply and control had been aggravated by *uncoordinated efforts at improved drainage*" (emphasis added). What is remarkable in water management records is the candor with which these scientists and administrators readily admit the mistakes of the past; what is dismaying is the assurance at every turn that now the answers are clear. Nevertheless, in 1947 water management was taking an important step in the ongoing journey to discover Florida. It had recognized that (at least some of) Florida's parts were connected, that addressing problems piecemeal resulted in more problems. The report declared, "The devastation of this new tragedy made imperative a new approach to water control in central and southern Florida."[40] What would the new approach be?

Five Years of Progress, which reviews the district's own creation, contains all the confessions appropriate to a new beginning: "By this time [1947] it became clear that 'drainage' of the Everglades had come to a bad end." The long drought and its resulting problems of saltwater intrusion and dehydration of the glades had convinced the district engineers and managers that "water conservation was just as much or more a necessary function of any plan as drainage." It had also become apparent that "the very structures designed to drain certain areas and protect them in time of flood were also depriving them of necessary moisture during other periods." In its natural condition the Kissimmee River basin had drained into Lake Okeechobee and thence into the Everglades. With the drainage project in place, the basin's water had been diverted to the Atlantic Ocean and to the Gulf of Mexico, preventing the Everglades from receiving any water but its own rainfall. This diversion the district now seemed to view as a mistake since the basin's contribution to the glades was crucial to providing the "moisture necessary for the preservation of the very soil and for the maintenance of the underground water tables which prevented saltwater intrusion." Even with these stark acknowledgments that things were so much worse than they had been before, the thought apparently occurred to no one that we might be better off to learn more about nature's ways before setting out to change them. The document goes on enumerating the difficulties a new approach must address: With the expansion of the Everglades Agricultural Area, more land was being put into cultivation and less land was available as a "dumping ground" for excess water during floods. Prolonged dry periods had proved the need to store surplus water for use during the dry seasons. Individual landowners, and dozens of small drainage districts had effected drainage programs without coordinating their efforts. In sizing up the situation, the district concluded that "Nature had been disrupted. In turn, man had not *sufficiently* planned to restore the balance" (emphasis added). All the evidence, it seemed, "pointed in only one direction—that of formulating one master plan, involving all levels of activity, into which everything would fit. Out of that realization came the Central and Southern Florida Flood Control Project."[41]

What it came down to was that the "new approach" would simply be a more coordinated and energized version of the old approach. Apparently, this singular new component—that of *coordinating* efforts to produce flood control and water conservation—seemed sufficient to solve the tremendous disasters earlier drainage operations had only exacerbated. The direction of this logic seems to have pervaded the atmosphere: in public hearings to discuss the project, the Corps of Engineers determined that in the public's opinion the "problem was too large and complex for the capabilities of either state or local agencies acting alone." Although no plan would please everyone, a comprehensive plan that would "embrace the whole area, satisfy the major needs as expressed by the various agencies, be beneficial to the greatest number and to the largest portion of the area, and be effectuated by the Federal Government, with local cooperation, seemed to offer the best solution."[42]

In 1948, Congress authorized the Central and Southern Florida Flood Control Project, a master plan to control once and for all the flow of water through central and southern Florida. The plan called for the largest earth-moving job entered into by the Corps of Engineers since the Panama Canal was dug. To carry out this ambitious project the Central and Southern Florida Flood Control District (CSFFCD) was created. Derr, writing in 1989, says of this creation that it was the

> forerunner of the state's water management districts and the agency that would oversee one of the most comprehensive and environmentally ruinous water control projects in the nation's history. Conceived to correct through more engineering the damage wrought by haphazard, piecemeal canal and levee building around Lake Okeechobee and the Everglades, the project engulfed the Kissimmee River and the marshes at the headwaters of the St. Johns River. When completed, the project had nearly destroyed the ecological viability of a third of the peninsula.[43]

It is difficult for some of us today not to see the huge projects of the 1940s and '50s as the epitome of our hubris regarding the natural world. But reading the record one mostly sees people working to solve problems in the best of faith. One can also see the paradigm of technology within which these people were working. And looking back, one can see what they can't see—that it will fail them.

If any one document can exemplify the peculiar mixture of humility and arrogance characterizing Florida's water projects in the mid-twentieth century it is House document no. 643, in which the engineers of the flood control project summarized its overall purpose.

> In its natural state the part of central and southern Florida considered in this report was a vast wilderness of water, forest, prairie, and marshland. The forces of

nature had combined to establish a fine balance which supported the vegetable, animal and human life that prevailed and resulted in building up the land to the condition in which white man first found it. A large part of this land, the Everglades, was still in a formative stage when its development began. The inherent fertility of the area and its resources made its development and use inevitable. This development, however, resulted in physical changes which altered the natural balance between water and soil, and much of the development was undertaken without any real knowledge of the area or of the hazards involved. The parched prairies and burning mucklands of the Everglades in 1945, the flooding of thousands of acres of farms and communities in 1947, and the intrusion of salt water into lands and water supplies of the east coast are basically the results of altering the balance of natural forces. The basic problem of this area is, therefore, to restore the natural balance between soil and water . . . insofar as possible by establishing protective works, controls, and procedures for conservation and use of water and land.

The acknowledgment of nature's perfect balance, of the destruction wrought by human ignorance, of the apocalyptic consequences of human meddling surely could not have issued from an attitude of disdain for the natural world. On the other hand, the conception of *restoring* a balance wrought over thousands of years using the very engineering and technology that had so rapidly destroyed that balance may seem the height of hubris—or naïveté. Probably closer to the truth is that such actions indicate a faith in nature even deeper than the faith in technology: nature was simple, healthy, strong; it would rebound. Today we have learned to doubt this proposition. With the growing evidence of how quickly technology may overwhelm natural ways, we now live with the possibility that we may exhaust natural systems we depend upon or change their course so fundamentally that we can't survive the world of our own making. But this is a recent realization, and not widespread.

In 1948 the decision to channelize the Kissimmee River was not unanimous, however. William R. Barada of the Florida Conservation Foundation, writing in 1977 about the channelization, described the "way it was":

> The battle over the Kissimmee River began long before it was gutted by Canal-38. The project, proposed in 1948, was vigorously opposed by the Florida Game and Fresh Water Fish Commission, the Federal Fish and Wildlife Service and a number of conservation organizations. At that time, however, the opposition to such projects consisted almost entirely of arguments against the destruction of a wild and beautiful river.[44]

But ditching the Kissimmee was promoted in the name of flood control, and conservationists lost the battle. (Barada insists that in spite of all the talk of flood control, the primary purpose of the program was "drainage, with only minor flood control benefits because the floodplains, marshes and swamps [in the Kissimmee River Valley] were unoccupied.")[45] The U.S. Army Corps of Engineers' comprehensive plan for central and south Florida was presented to Congress in 1948 and authorized for construction in 1954. In an October 8, 1956, general memorandum issued by the corps, the plan for flood control and water conservation in the Kissimmee River watershed was detailed. The memorandum stated that "prolonged seasonal rainfall, coupled with inadequate secondary drainage canals and limited outlet capacity, results in almost yearly flooding of large areas in Kissimmee River basin." The corps cited damage to pasturelands and the expense farmers incurred from having to provide cattle with supplemental feeding during times when flooded pastures were not available for use. A Florida Game and Fresh Water Fish Commission (GFC) report, *Recommended Program for Kissimmee River Basin,* responding to the corps plan, agreed that, "Consequently, annual damages are relatively high as a result of long-duration flooding." The GFC document went on to enumerate recent floods and concluded that "future flood damages are expected to be much greater in view of the expanding agricultural economy in the central Florida area."[46] Thus, the corps plan for "facility improvement of the Kissimmee River basin" was supported.

The GFC report provides insight into the conditions and assumptions guiding such decisions in the late 1950s. Clearly, it was a time when "agricultural interests" constituted a majority—or at least an uncontested—slice of the political pie. Reading the report, it is hard to keep in mind that the GFC's charge is the protection of fish and wildlife, so prevalent is the concern for "agricultural interests." But what, specifically, does this phrase refer to? I think it is safe to assume (and Barada's comments support the assumption) that the phrase "agricultural interests" does not refer to the protection of human life; but one probably would assume that it includes the loss of livestock. However, the documents make no mention of any loss of livestock. What "agricultural interests" actually seems to refer to is a narrowly conceived economic factor—the loss incurred by ranchers (who depended on access to the floodplain) due to the cost of supplemental feed when the plain is flooded.

Then there is the prediction of greater flood damages in view of "the expanding agricultural economy" in the area. This means further development of the area is expected, and there is no mention of limiting further agricultural activities on the floodplain. Yet, the corps report had described the "annual floods" as being the result of "seasonal rainfall." This sounds more like the natural, seasonal fluctuation of a river in flat terrain than it does an unpredictable flood. Why do people rely on floodplains not to flood? Of course, the assumption here is that human beings can control natural forces. The fact that storms, hurricanes, and heavy seasonal rains are inherent to the very being of Florida is not completely missing; but these routine occurrences are treated as faults in the natural beauty of the state—flaws to be "improved" by human ingenuity. The GFC program, for example, agrees with the corps assessment that "seasonal rainfall, coupled with inadequate secondary drainage canals and limited outlet capacity" causes flooding in the Kissimmee Valley; and they add, "The region is subject to tropical hurricanes which normally occur during the rainy season. Those hurricanes bring intense rainfall which often aggravates a flood situation already serious from heavy seasonal rainfall." [47] Then, the GFC program goes on to assume with the corps that technological intervention is the appropriate response to these natural events:

> An adequate system of water control for the agricultural areas in the Kissimmee River basin would provide (1) protection of lands adjacent to the headwater lakes and along the Kissimmee River from frequent and prolonged flooding, (2) maintenance of adequate water levels in the lakes and drainage canals to enable maintenance of more desirable ground-water levels and (3) means for storing water for agricultural use during dry seasons. [48]

A corollary to the assumption that humans can control natural forces is the assumption that we have full control over the changes we initiate in natural systems. But the unforeseen consequences of converting the Kissimmee River into Canal 38 (C-38) included the devastation of some of the state's most productive ecological systems and, as one result, the pollution and depletion of the south Florida water supply. In the Kissimmee River Basin, more than 138,000 acres were drained at a cost of $31.6 million to taxpayers. The drainage of the floodplain soon resulted in more farmers, cattlemen, and developers moving into the former river margins. And, with the resulting proliferation of private drainage ditches, the waters of unprotected wetlands continued to be drained into the flood control channels to be shunted out to the oceans. [49]

What the GFC document and many others from this period reveal is the absence of a public ethic regarding the environment as crucially important to all life. Since the GFC is the agency charged with managing the wildlife "resources" of the state, they clearly feel obligated to point out in their report aspects of the corps' plan that are not in the best interest of wildlife. Yet, throughout, the GFC argument is constrained by the pressure of what they refer to as "other interests." Here again, a ranking of priorities permeates the reasoning in these documents. Human economic interests are at the top of the hierarchy; nonhuman survival interests are at the bottom. Thus, the GFC Recommended Program recommends that all interests must be considered—including those of wildlife. But an unspoken acknowledgment that economic interests will prevail haunts the argument:

> Interests other than agricultural must also be considered. These include navigation, recreation, and the fish and wildlife resource and its users. All aspects must be given due recognition and proper consideration in order to present a plan acceptable to the majority of the involved public.[50]

I imagine I can see, half-erased in the margins, the GFC director's remarks to the program's authors: *This isn't about ducks—bring the human interest more forward, make it sound reasonable.* What the GFC authors didn't have for their argument, what the state policymakers and the public didn't have to help them make decisions—what nobody had then—was the broad recognition that these separate interests had much more in common than they thought. More basic than all the various concerns of special interest groups is that they all depend on a functioning ecosystem to support life. Without that, interests are meaningless. The simple fact of our dependence on natural life-support systems is still not widely understood. But the Kissimmee River has taught us much.

In the early 1960s, though, the dredges went to work, and between 1962 and 1970 the one-hundred-mile-long meandering river with its expansive floodplain was confined to a fifty-mile-long, thirty-foot-deep, three-hundred-foot-wide canal. Six water control structures with tieback levees were constructed along the length of the canal, transforming the former river into five stair-step impoundment pools.[51] A 1965 story in the *Miami Herald* gives this account:

> I have just returned from south central Florida and the death-bed of an old friend. Although it has been definitely established that the death will be a boon to something called "progress," the sight was a most depressing one.
>
> The about-to-be-deceased is a river, the Kissimmee River that wound for nearly 100 miles down to Lake Okeechobee. It twisted from a couple of lakes

near Kissimmee, across great marshbanks, past cypress heads and live oak and cabbage palm hammocks.

Now under the assault of great, floating suction dredges and draglines—seemingly enough of them to build another Panama Canal—a straight-gut canal is being chopped through it, cutting its length in little more than half.

It is the more depressing to those who love their rivers *au naturel* because this sort of thing has become a rapidly increasing pattern in a state where wooded streams once were a major natural asset.[52]

Barada describes dredge spoil, amounting to some 70 million cubic yards, piled on either side of the ditch, covering 6,000 acres of former marshland. Some 43,000 acres of wetlands, which had produced rich habitats for fish and wildlife, were completely destroyed, virtually eliminating the complex food web that the floodplain had supported. Over 90 percent of the waterfowl populations throughout the river valley were lost. Bald eagle territories were reduced by 74 percent, and wading bird use of the basin declined dramatically.[53] The only "wetlands" remaining were approximately 13,000 acres of "man-made, static-water pools created behind five locks and dams which control the flow of water in the Kissimmee Ditch."[54] And biologist Louis Toth reported a vastly reduced diversity over the entire floodplain, with "broad expanses of relatively homogenous plant communities" replacing the prechannelization mosaic.[55]

Reading the descriptions, I remembered the two stretches of open ground I had seen in my explorations south of the first lock. The first stretch, nearest the canal, had been high and dry, with a mixture of shells and sand heaped into mounds that dotted the area nearest the canal. The second stretch, lying farther inland off the canal, had been lower and wet, and full of weeds. Given the massive amounts of dredge spoil Barada described, it was now plain that the high plateau I had been standing on was a spoil pile. One of the things that's hard to accept about postmodern life is that once we've made changes in a natural system, we can no longer tell what natural is. The meaning of a river is different when it's dammed. And we've made so many changes without any understanding of the processes we were disrupting.

Barada's description verified the intuitions I'd had about the wildlife on the river. "The fish, birds and other wildlife which thrived in the Lower Basin have all but disappeared and visitors now describe the area as a biological desert." From an airplane, Barada pointed out, you could still see the former path of the river. But the old river was dead, Barada said, "robbed of its life-supporting flow of fresh water by Canal-38, an ugly, wide, deep ditch that slices through the center of the valley and cuts across loops of the meandering channel."

It was soon discovered that the man-made pools and the canal acted as anaerobic sediment traps, accumulating and concentrating the pollutants and detritus in runoff water from upland pastures and agricultural lands. GFC studies revealed little or no dissolved oxygen in C-38 at depths below ten feet. Anaerobic decomposition of organic material in bottom water produces hydrogen sulfide gas, which is the smell of rotten eggs, and which is lethal to most aquatic life. Postchannelization sampling of the canal documented a low density and diversity of benthic invertebrate communities and domination by taxa tolerant of a degraded habitat "characteristic of a reservoir rather than riverine environment."[56] Because the water levels of the canal were now kept stable, Toth reported, the food supplies of fish contained in the channel were reduced since the "import of floodplain invertebrates which used to occur in the pre-channelization system" was no longer possible. Loss of the floodplain also meant the devastation of nursery or breeding areas of many important fish species.[57] And, with the floodplains drained, floodplain wetlands could no longer filter sediments and associated nutrients from the river. When flood control gates were opened, Barada pointed out, "the slug of unconsolidated muck accumulated in the Ditch" flushed straight into Lake Okeechobee, the "liquid heart" of the south Florida water supply.

More ironic still, even the agricultural interests that had been given such high priority were not served. Benefits from "improved" (dried out) marshlands failed to materialize. Both the Department of Agriculture and the Kissimmee Valley ranchers stated that the best grazing land for cattle was *marsh vegetation*. Pat Wilson, head of the Florida Cattlemen's Association, told Barada that "during the dry season, marshes are the best forage available, even more so than an improved pangola pasture." With the marshes dead, winter cattle forage had to be provided by expensive supplemental feeding, or seeding, fertilization, and irrigation.

The cattlemen's story illustrates a point that is sometimes difficult to keep in mind—how little we understood about ecological systems before the 1960s. The cattlemen and agricultural agents had known for years that marsh vegetation was the best grazing for their cattle. It wasn't the ditching of the Kissimmee River that taught them that. What almost no one seems to have expected was that drying up the marshes would change them, would alter their life-producing qualities. The common viewpoint had been that the only trouble with marshes was they were too wet to use, they flooded. The solution was to dry them up. An example of this thinking is provided by an October 4, 1957, memorandum from the district Division of Planning and Research director to the executive director of the Flood Control District, which describes previous unsuccessful attempts to solve the cattlemen's problems:

> The Florida cattleman has two basic and very real problems, a shortage of winter grazing due to frosts and lack of winter rainfall, and the extremely low average soil fertility. For years cattlemen along the river have relied upon the Kissimmee marsh to furnish a large portion of the required forage during winter months. Also, the majority of the flood plain has a *peat or peaty muck soil* with the inherent fertility lacking in the upland prairie or flatwood soils and as a result, furnishes *at least as much forage per acre annually as upland native range* **in spite of the fact that it is under water the majority of the time.**
>
> **Because of these advantages, there have been a number of attempts to control the water and introduce improved grasses on the flood plain.** Of the approximately 4,350 acres of lowland on which development has been attempted, only 600 acres appear even partially successful in controlling high water, and agricultural technicians in the area doubt that even these have been economical. **This rather large scale attempted development under adverse conditions serves to point up the value which the cattlemen place upon the flood plain and its potential usefulness when the river is brought under control.**[58]

It's hard for us to realize today how anyone could overlook the illogic of getting rid of the water that provides the benefits. One thing that's important to notice is that this illogic is partially masked by the metaphor of control. It's an old and powerful figure of speech—a way of speaking mechanistically about nature in the manner of Francis Bacon in the seventeenth century. And, it's the metaphor that lulled Floridians while the natural life support systems of the Kissimmee Valley were devastated.

With the Kissimmee ditched, groundwater tables were lowered in the valley and uplands dried out more quickly in dry season. Irrigation of citrus and other crops became necessary, resulting in an enormous waste of fresh water during the winter—the time when it's needed most in south Florida. Thus, a low-cost, natural energy system was replaced with an expensive, artificial system that consumes nonrenewable fuels and wastes fresh water. Realizing these impacts, I couldn't help wondering if such widespread repercussions had reached the miles of devastated groves I'd passed on my way to visit C-38.

The Times They Are A-Changin'

By the 1960s, a new public awareness of the natural world began making itself felt throughout the country. Especially apparent was the public concern over the devastation produced by dredge and fill operations in the nation's navigable waters. In 1970, John W. Bellinger told the Southeastern Association of Game and Fish Commissioners that federal permitting of dredge and fill activities had always been a matter of "formality." But, he said, in 1958 public concern brought about the Fish and Wildlife Coordination Act, which required the Army Corps of Engineers to consider the impact on fish and wildlife populations when evaluating dredge and fill applications.[59] Soon after the act was passed, the corps, for the first time in the nation's history, denied a dredge and fill permit because of the project's harmful ecological effects. The denial was challenged, and in 1970, in *Zabel v. Russell*—a case originating in Pinellas County, Florida—the Fifth U.S. Circuit Court of Appeals upheld the right of the corps "to deny a permit for works detrimental to the environment." Public concern, Bellinger said, over the "irrevocable alteration of our Nation's coastal areas" had resulted in such legislation as the National Estuary Act of 1968 and the National Environmental Policy Act of 1969, which required federal agencies to cooperate in any evaluation of major federal actions affecting the quality of the environment. On May 19, 1970, at the Jacksonville, Florida, District, the Corps of Engineers announced that they were "no longer concerned only with the impact a proposed project would have on navigation and would now give greater consideration to effects on the environment and natural resources."[60] That same year saw passage of the Water Quality Improvement Act, which requires applicants for Army Corps dredge and fill permits to include a certificate from the appropriate state water pollution control agency assuring that the proposed project will not violate water quality standards.

"There is a great awakening, both in Florida and in the rest of the Nation," Bellinger told the Game and Fish Commissioners in 1970, "to the seriousness of maintaining a quality environment." He continued:

> Concerned private citizens are becoming environmentally educated and are swelling the ranks of our alert conservation groups. As a result, it will become increasingly more difficult for state and federal agencies to waive or ignore their duties in enforcing laws protecting our natural resources. Special interests that previously enjoyed immunity to exploit publicly-owned resources are now being taken to court. . . . We no longer can afford to sit back and hide behind the worn cliché of "more research is needed." What is needed instead is more action.[61]

Bellinger went on to discuss zoning laws and to recommend that coastal zoning be reconceived based on bioecological systems, thereby protecting the future of shoreline areas. He talked about scientific studies comparing the silt deposition in the bottoms of dredged and undredged waters, which concluded that the sediments in dredged canals provide unsuitable substrates for benthic communities. This conclusion, Bellinger felt, provided an explanation for the "paucity of sport or commercial species" (of fish and other aquatic life) in such dredged areas.[62] But it was the new grassroots awareness that Bellinger described as the environmental education of "concerned private citizens" that provided the impetus of a major shift in the political will to protect the environment of Florida. For the groundswell served notice to agencies and legislators alike that Floridians considered environmental quality a matter of the highest public interest—not some luxury we could ill afford.

Correspondence from archived dredge-and-fill permit applications of that period bear out Bellinger's remarks. One 1971 letter from a citizen in Winter Haven, Florida, to the Board of Trustees of the Internal Improvement Trust Fund reveals his concern about environmental impact from a proposed drainage project:

> Having lived in this area for fifty years I would like to register a protest against the proposal by the Ridge Cattle Company to ditch and drain an area along the shore of Lake Hatchineha in Polk County. The Kissimmee Valley already has too many problems brought on by man-made "improvements" made in the desire to utilize low acres for agriculture and homes. The increase in nutrients from sewage and fertilizers used and the loss of wetland that would result from this project would further compound the damage already done.[63]

Here the author's inclusion of quotation marks around the word *improvements* not only points out that such usage constitutes a misnomer but also signals an outdated notion of progress.

In 1968 Floridians passed a new constitution, which included article 10, section 11 providing that sovereignty land may be sold and used for private use, but only when to do so would not be against public interest:

> The title to lands under navigable waters, within the boundaries of the state, which have not been alienated, including beaches below mean high water lines, is held by the state, by virtue of its sovereignty, in trust for all the people. Sale or private use of portions of such lands may be authorized by law, but only when not contrary to the public interest.[64]

In 1970 the last sentence was repealed and replaced with the more stringent requirement that sales of sovereignty lands must be *in* the public interest:

> Sale of such lands may be authorized by law, but only when in the public interest. Private use of portions of such lands may be authorized by law, but only when not contrary to the public interest.[65]

This mandate from the people of Florida is frequently overlooked even today in portrayals of the conflicts between public protection and private property rights. Newspaper accounts typically pit state officials against landowners, farmers, or businesses in what may be termed an "investigation," "claim," or "state land-grab." The opening paragraphs of these accounts establish the drama of the conflict by characterizing the state as a relentless force threatening the ownership rights of these hapless individuals. Buried in the middle of the article there will be the mention of what provoked the state's action: a citizen complaint. What such accounts fail to acknowledge is that the authority of state agencies is derived directly from the will of the state's citizens, not only as it is reflected in the state's laws but in the direct voice of the citizens themselves. Every case I have worked on or read about in the years I have worked at the Division of State Lands (which is charged with protecting all sovereignty lands) has been initiated by a call from a concerned citizen. I often wonder when reading the newspapers how the headlines would read if the agencies *failed* to respond to the complaints that initiate their actions.

In 1967 Attorney General Earl Faircloth advised the Board of Trustees of the Internal Improvement Trust Fund (BOT) that he would propose a moratorium on the further sale of submerged lands and reclaimed lake bottoms, observing that "we seem anxious to sell public land when it should be just the opposite." The moratorium, he said, would "give the Legislature an opportunity to establish sound, clear, consistent and comprehensive policies to assure the highest and best use of all state-owned lands, including submerged lands and reclaimed lake bottoms, in the public interest."[66]

However, the impulse toward environmental protection was not expressed solely as a grassroots political movement. By the late 1960s, interest in life sciences had spawned new curricula in the nation's universities, and over the next two decades new professional fields emerged that reflected the public's growing concern for the environment. One researcher, tracing the development of conservation biology programs in U.S. academic institutions, noted that programs addressing conservation themes tended in the beginning to be ensconced in such existing departments as natural resources or were components of interdisciplinary programs.[67] "Only a decade has passed since conservation biology became an identifiable and proliferating element at universities in the United States," states the 1997 introduction to the Center for Conservation Biology Network. "Recent theoretical and applied developments in science are offering insights and new directions, particularly in the areas of landscape ecology, ecosystem management and restoration, and sustainable development."[68] In the late 1960s and early 1970s, however, environmental research in Florida was being conducted in such programs as the University of Miami's Division of Applied Ecology in its Center for Urban and Regional Studies and in various branches of the biology department at the University of Florida.

In 1972, a group of these scientists gathered to address the Florida cabinet.[69] In his opening address, Arthur R. Marshall, ecologist at the University of Miami, broke with the tradition of staid language and cautious recommendations that had typified reports of agency scientists. Yet, he nevertheless sought to assure his audience that he and his colleagues were no radical fringe element. In the first words of his address he declared the group's intention:

> Despite the stringent nature of our statements, my colleagues and I are on a conservative mission—to try to restore some of the lost values of the Kissimmee basin and, in association with that, to try to prevent an Apopka-like collapse of Lake Okeechobee. Since the basin has been gutted and the Lake is already highly enriched, that is not going to be an easy task.[70]

Marshall went on to say that since 1957, Florida had had a "liberal education in the over-enrichment of fresh waters" and to describe the now critical concern for the south Florida drinking water supply. "Clearly," he said, "it is conservative to protect our waters, the most vital of all natural resources; it would be radical to do otherwise." Marshall discussed the regional scope of the problem, pointing out that the canalization of the lower Kissimmee River had "drained 65% or more of the valley's marshes, greatly reducing their fish and wildlife populations and nearly obliterating their ability to reduce the passage of nutrients to Lake Okeechobee." Furthermore, the canal accelerated Lake Okeechobee's problems because it served "as a pipe in speeding the flow of wastes accumulated in the upper lakes to Okeechobee."[71] But even this devastation was not the full extent of the damage the canal had caused:

That Canal, like all drainage canals in south Florida, struck another hard blow. It opened up former marshlands for extensive real estate development, generating wastes where we can least tolerate them and elevating land prices so markedly that the public can consider land purchases only because failure to do so will jeopardize prime water supplies. This element is clarion-clear in the case of the Kissimmee Canal. The FCD [Flood Control District] estimates that it can purchase the lands to be re-flooded in four of their proposed sub-impoundments along the Kissimmee Canal for about $4 million—about $400 per acre. To buy the fifth impoundment—in the vicinity of River Ranch Acres development— will cost about $18 million or about $4000 per acre.

This is a particularly important issue in the future of the lower Kissimmee Valley, for whatever re-flooding we accomplish now will likely fix the limits of marshland development, whether or not we find later we need more marsh. By that time all adjacent lands will have been opened up to $4000 per acre development—all the way down the valley—forever.[72]

Marshall's far-sighted vision of the problems of restoration came at a time when many policymakers were struggling to understand what was causing the fundamental problem of eutrophication. The idea of restoration—of putting the river back the way it was—had barely been conceived, much less the problems to be dealt with should restoration be attempted. Yet Marshall's warnings about rising land values were borne out over the next two decades, as policymakers struggled to find a course that would restore the ecological balance of the devastated Kissimmee-Okeechobee Basin.

Marshall's colleagues also addressed the cabinet that December day in 1972. Hydrologist James H. Hartwell described the streamflow characteristics of a natural stream and of those that had been canalized. He emphasized the importance of a river's meanderings to the development of wetland areas and characterized the impact of wetland losses. Biochemist David S. Anthony explained the eutrophication process, observing that we had "quite simply not even come close to paying the costs of growth over the years."[73] Microbiologist John V. Betz described the dangers to public health devolving from eutrophication:

When a lake becomes grossly polluted through the process known as cultural eutrophication, its waters become unfit for human consumption. . . . It becomes enriched in disease-producing bacteria and viruses which must be killed or removed before the water is safe to drink. These include the bacteria of typhoid, dysentery, food poisoning, and many others. There may be viruses which cause aseptic meningitis, rashes, myocarditis, diarrhea, paralytic polio, respiratory infections, hepatitis, and several other exotic diseases.

Betz went on to say that although the knowledge of the process of eu-trophication was only now becoming widespread, "our knowledge of the hazards of the array of organisms, toxins, and chemicals I have described is . . . even more tardy, less sophisticated. We expose ourselves to them in a wide aura of ignorance."[74] Ecologist Aerial Lugo detailed the impor-tance of marshes to water quality because of their ability to remove nutri-ents and heavy metals through the process of photosynthesis and to accel-erate the sedimentation of suspended materials in floodwaters.[75] "Since the Kissimmee River basin contains, or can be made to again contain, many thousands of acres populated by marshes, their value to society is very ob-vious."[76] Lugo went on to explain that "[n]atural ecological systems are centers of biological activity whose main product is the support of life on earth. . . . To maximize this life-support role is to maximize the value of the system to society."[77]

It is important to remember that the scientists addressing the Florida cabinet in 1972 were not rehearsing familiar phrases to a group of policy-makers already versed in the concepts of ecosystems—marsh or otherwise. These men and women came before the state's top leaders as before a group of freshmen students—that is to say, teaching in earnest. What they were seeking to reverse was not only the channelization of one of Florida's most important rivers; they sought to reverse the course of Western think-ing about marshes, and more fundamentally about what nature is to us. Compare, for example, the language in the 1924 case of *State ex rel. Buford v. City of Tampa* (see chapter 1) describing the overflowed lands in the Hillsborough River as having

no value for purposes of commerce or navigation, and that the filling in of the lands as contemplated by the contract by dredging will, in reality, improve the navigability of Hillsborough Bay, and will add to the wealth of the city by re-moving the mud flats. . . .

It is also averred that the area embraced in the contract in its present condi-tion is *valueless for any purpose,* and the improvement as contemplated will ulti-mately add to the taxable value of property in the city of Tampa by several mil-lions of dollars, and that the contract is in the public interest of Tampa and the state of Florida.[78]

For over a century, Florida policymakers had imbibed the view that marshes, wetlands, swamps, mudflats, and tidelands were natural obstacles to human progress—"valueless for any purpose." Now, a handful of scientists were standing before the governor and cabinet declaring that "marshes are among the most productive systems of the world," that their value was inestimable to the support of life.[79] This at a time when ecology was a fledgling program in most universities—if it was present at all—at a time when the scientists themselves admitted that knowledge of the processes involved was still fairly unsophisticated. The successful channelization of the Kissimmee River had just been completed the year before. What were the state's policymakers to do?

In 1976 the Florida legislature passed the Kissimmee River Restoration Act, creating the Kissimmee River Coordinating Council (KRCC) to oversee the restoration of the Kissimmee-Okeechobee Basin. In 1978, the Florida congressional delegation asked Congress to direct the Corps of Engineers to reexamine the Kissimmee River Flood Control Project. Congress responded, requesting the corps to review the project "with a view to determining whether any modification . . . is advisable . . . with respect to questions of the quality of water . . . flood control, recreation, navigation, loss of fish and wildlife resources, other current and foreseeable environmental problems, and the loss of environmental amenities." In 1983 the corps' restoration feasibility study concluded that several options existed that could improve environmental conditions, and the KRCC eventually settled on a restoration plan designed to force flow back into the abandoned portions of the river's historic channel and floodplain.[80] This course of action necessitated one of the largest land acquisition initiatives in the state's history, and the South Florida Water Management District established a budget of some $81 million just to acquire the lands to be reflooded.

Now the question became: which lands lying along C-38 were private lands that the state must purchase and which were sovereignty lands already belonging to the state? The river's natural course had been obliterated, and the procedure for determining the OHWL in such a case was unprecedented.

*That land is a community is the basic
concept of ecology, but that land is to be
loved and respected is an extension of
ethics. That land yields a cultural harvest
is a fact long known, but latterly often
forgotten.*

ALDO LEOPOLD, *Sand County Almanac*

3   Custom, Criteria, and Community:
Clarifying the OHWL Concept

BY THE TIME the channelization of the Kissimmee River
was complete, controversy over the boundaries of Florida's freshwater
lakes and streams had been building for over a decade. During the 1960s,
the trustees' sovereignty lands policy on freshwater bodies evolved from
one that took little note of these lakes and streams to one of active protection of the public interest in these waters. With the passage of the Bulkhead Laws in 1957, familiarity with the terms *ordinary high water line*
(OHWL) and *mean high water line* (MHWL) had become increasingly
widespread because land lying between the MHWL and the bulkhead line
had to be purchased from the trustees and permitted if it was to be filled.
(The term *mean high water line* is used to designate on tidal waters what
ordinary high water line indicates on nontidal waters. The two terms were

used somewhat interchangeably until the Florida legislature, in 1974, prescribed a mathematical formulation for the establishment of tidal water boundaries. This mathematical average was designated as the "mean high water line" and applied only to tidal waters, while the term "ordinary high water line" remained in use for all nontidal waters.) [1]

Where bulkhead lines were concerned, local engineering and surveying firms frequently handled the job of determining where the MHWL was located, using such markers as the upland edge of the mangrove swamps and the debris or wash line—that line left by the reach of the ordinary high tide.[2] But the bulkhead laws were primarily intended to control bay fills on coastal water bodies. They did not contemplate the protection or acquisition of floodplains along freshwater streams and lakes. In fact, most state-lands policy until this time had remained focused on coastal problems, since coastal areas had developed so quickly. By the mid-1960s, however, development along Florida's many inland lakes and rivers was booming, thanks in large part to the flood control measures that had drained thousands of acres of floodplain and permanently lowered the levels of many lakes. In some instances, riparian landowners along lowered lakes began fencing lake basin areas and filling exposed lands adjacent to their properties.[3] Clearly a comprehensive policy was needed.

Freshwaters

In an effort to address the situation, Florida Attorney General Earl Faircloth proposed, in January 1967, a moratorium on the sale of reclaimed lake bottoms in order to give the legislature an opportunity to establish "sound, clear, consistent and comprehensive policies" concerning such lands.[4] The trustees approved a forty-five-day moratorium, which was later extended sixty days to the end of the legislative session, but the legislature failed to produce policy on the subject. In 1968 the trustees adopted as policy that "the mean high water line be the point of reference from which all bulkhead lines be established henceforth."[5] Bulkhead lines set farther offshore from the MHWL would have to be "fully justified as being in the public interest."[6] That same year the legislature passed a bill affirming the sovereignty character of freshwater lakes, rivers, and streams that had been navigable at the time of statehood: "For purposes of fixing bulkhead lines, restrictions on filling land and dredging beyond bulkhead lines, and permits required for filling and dredging, the board [of trustees] shall exercise the same authority over [sovereignty] submerged lands . . . in navigable fresh water lakes, rivers, and streams as it does over submerged lands otherwise defined in this subsection."[7] Meanwhile the trustees created the Interagency Advisory Committee on Submerged Land Management for the purpose of "reviewing existing bulkhead lines in coastal counties in the state and submitting recommendations concerning submerged land management policies."[8] Although the Interagency Advisory Committee did not address freshwater issues, it made a fundamental change in the bulkhead line approach to sovereignty lands problems: it recommended that the bulkhead line be located *at* the mean high water line. The trustees responded by announcing that their policy would henceforth be to refuse permits in areas where the bulkhead line had not been relocated to the MHWL as per the prescription of the Interagency Committee.[9] These actions, in effect, established the bulkhead line of navigable lakes, rivers, and streams at their OHWL, tying the sale of submerged lands and the permitting on those lands to the natural (OHWL) boundary, rather than to an artificial bulkhead line. In 1975 the legislature passed 75-22 requiring that the bulkhead line be the OHWL in navigable fresh waters.[10]

But much of natural Florida had by now been altered. With the massive flood control projects of the twentieth century—not to mention Hamilton Disston's drainage operations in the late 1800s—many of Florida's inland water bodies had been lowered from their natural levels. This condition sometimes resulted in impaired navigability and frequently left the new level of the lake or stream permanently below what its OHWL would otherwise have been. In 1927 the Florida Supreme Court had dealt with the problem of exposed sovereignty lands when Lake Okeechobee was lowered as part of the attempt to control devastating floods. In *Martin v. Busch,* "the Court determined that the lowering of the lake by government drainage projects did not change the public ownership of the exposed lands because the act of artificially lowering the lake could not be equated with the slow, imperceptible process of reliction." "Reliction" refers to an increase of the land by the natural, gradual, and imperceptible lowering of any body of water. Changes due to reliction result in changes in the boundary between the water body and the adjoining uplands. A later Florida Supreme Court decision explicitly equated the artificial lowering of a water body with avulsion.[11] "Avulsion" means the sudden or perceptible loss of or addition to land by the action of water, or a sudden change in the bed of a lake or the course of a stream. Avulsive changes do not operate to alter the boundary.[12] The problem with exposed sovereignty lands, then, was that most deeds to the riparian uplands surrounding these lowered water bodies would entitle their holders only to the OHWL of the water body in its natural state—a line which no longer adjoined the water.

In essence, deeds to what had once been waterfront property no longer reached the waterfront. One solution, of course, was for the trustees to sell the lands between the original OHWL and the new, lower OHWL, and this the trustees had been doing since 1919.[13] From that time thousands of acres of exposed lake bottom had been "randomly sold."[14]

By the end of the 1960s, however, the tide had turned on the sale of such sovereignty lands. Attorney General Earl Faircloth expressed this turn in 1967 when, proposing his moratorium on the further sales of submerged lands and reclaimed lake bottoms, he commented, "We seem anxious to sell public land when it should be just the opposite." In 1969, the trustees set about establishing a policy to deal with such reclaimed lake bottoms by putting forward a management plan for these lands. The plan defined reclaimed lake bottoms as "those lands which result from the permanent artificial lowering of a lake level by a legally constituted authority and which lie between *the line of the original (March 3, 1845) ordinary high water level* and the lowered ordinary high water level of the lake. Lands exposed by natural lowering of lake levels shall not be considered to be reclaimed under any circumstances."[15] Although, under this plan the trustees would be empowered to sell reclaimed lake bottoms if the sale was not contrary to public interest, no application for purchase of reclaimed lake bottom lands would be considered until "a specific contour or other acceptable boundary line representing the new, permanently lowered ordinary high water level [had] been determined and approved by the Trustees."[16] The very notion of an *original* OHWL—that being the OHWL of the water body at the time of statehood—seems to have had its beginnings in this effort to deal with reclaimed lake bottoms, and no one seems to have been especially concerned with whether this was the appropriate line of comparison with the new, lowered line. The plan did call for a technical advisory committee appointed by the trustees to advise and assist the trustees' staff in locating this original OHWL. The advisory group would consist of—at a minimum—an attorney, a registered land surveyor, a geologist, and a biologist.[17] But the determination of the "original" OHWL and the new "acceptable boundary line" was to be accomplished by the trustees' staff.

The proposed plan for dealing with reclaimed lake bottoms must have seemed adequate. Yet, the plan describes a task of potentially enormous proportions. Given the limited personnel and budget of the trustees' staff, the expectation must have been that few questions would arise concerning the OHWL of the state's many water bodies. Certainly there was little notion of—and no funding for—pursuing a statewide inventory of exposed sovereignty lands, in spite of a reference in the plan to the need for doing so. But more consequential perhaps than any of these difficulties was that the situation of exposed lake bottoms—which led the trustees to focus on the original OHWL—would further garble an already tenuous understanding of the ordinary high water line concept.

On January 20, 1970, the trustees adopted a revised version of the plan and passed the following resolution:

> the Governor and Cabinet, as the State of Florida Board of Trustees of the Internal Improvement Trust Fund, herewith declare it to be the policy of the Board that the Board will not approve any proposed bulkhead lines nor grant any dredge and fill permits waterward of the ordinary (historic) high water line in fresh water lakes except where other location of lines can be justified fully as being in the public interest.[18]

What the new policy meant to the average citizen was that the trustees had adopted a more conservative approach to disposing of exposed lake bottom and protecting the public trust in sovereignty freshwaters. To property owners on waters lowered by the Central and Southern Florida Flood Control District (or some other legally constituted authority), the new policy meant they could apply to purchase the strip of land lying between the OHWL of the water body at the time of statehood and the new, lowered OHWL—as soon as the trustees' staff could establish both of these lines. For property owners on waters lowered by Disston and others not considered "legally constituted authority," the new policy meant that their waterfront access remained in limbo—waiting for a state inventory. For all concerned, it was becoming increasingly clear that this boundary line— this OHWL—was crucial to the conception of waterfront property. Unfortunately, under the trustees' policy, the OHWL remained an amorphous concept, still lacking the countless practical applications that would clarify its use. And many people—including surveyors, landowners, and judges—held various befuddled notions of the OHWL. Not surprisingly, people came by these confusions honestly, imbibing the misconceptions and inconsistencies of the past.

Meandering Instructions

During the first hundred years of Florida's statehood, there was little awareness of sovereignty lands or the special situation of their ownership. The state of Florida owned the lands under its navigable water bodies by reason of its sovereignty, and title deeds were never created for

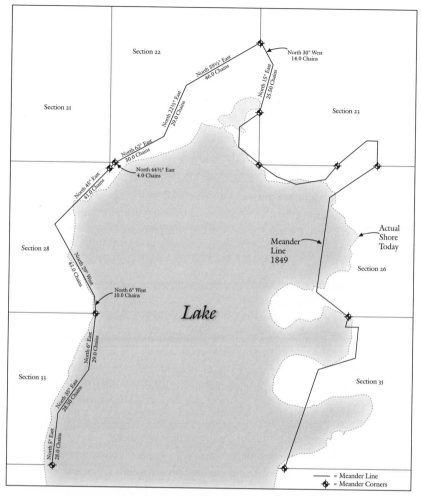

A portion of a lake showing the meander line placement when surveyed in 1849. Meander lines were used to approximate the sinuosities of a water body so that acreage of upland parcels could be estimated. They were not intended to function as boundaries. Meander corners were placed wherever the meander line intersected with a section line. Note the discrepancies between the 1849 meander line and the actual shore today. Many factors contribute to such discrepancies: actual changes to the shoreline from water control projects or other man-made or natural events; unclear and/or varying instructions provided to surveyors during the nineteenth and early twentieth centuries; changing water levels; and the harsh, impracticable conditions faced by surveyors. (A chain measures 66 feet.)

the state. Approximate boundaries of lands under navigable water bodies were to have been outlined during public land surveys by the surveying process called meandering. In this process, surveyors measure a series of straight lines along the curving shore of a water body and, with a transit, measure the angles between each consecutive set of line segments.[19] With these measurements the surveyor can represent the sinuosities of a river or shoreline of a lake. The process is time-consuming and painstaking. One surveying manual, originally published in 1928 and in its fifth edition during the 1960s, describes the process:

> **Meandering.** In the process of surveying the public lands, all navigable bodies of water and other important rivers and lakes below the line of mean high water are segregated from the lands which are open to private ownership. In the process of subdivision, the regular section lines are run to an intersection with the mean high-water mark of such a body of water, at which intersection corners called *meander corners* are established. The traverse which is run between meander corners, approximately following the margin of a permanent body of water, is called a *meander line*. . . .
>
> In running a meander line, the surveyor begins at a meander corner and follows the bank or shore line, as closely as convenience permits, to the next meander corner, the traverse being a succession of straight lines. The true length and bearing of each of the courses of the meander line are observed with precision, but for convenience in plotting and computing areas the intermediate courses are laid off to the exact quarter degree and each intermediate transit station is placed a whole number of chains, or at least a multiple of 10 links, from the preceding station. . . . When a meander line is "closed" on a second meander corner, the latitudes and departures of the courses bounding the fractional lot are computed and the error of closure is determined. If this exceeds the allowable value, the line is rerun until an error in bearing or distance is discovered which will bring the closure within the specified limits (maximum error in either latitude or departure 1/640).[20]

This straightforward description of meandering presents two points around which much confusion persists to this day. One is the question of navigability, and the other is the location of meander corners at the ordinary (or mean) high water mark.

The text remarks that in public land surveys all navigable water bodies as well as other "important" lakes and rivers will be meandered. The purpose of meandering a water body was to set it apart from lands that might be offered for sale and to provide a means of estimating the acreage of the upland tracts. This act in essence demonstrated that the watercourse was not part of the land being sold, that it was instead sovereignty land. Because public land surveys were to indicate navigable waters by meandering them, however, people came to think of meandering as the equivalent of a determination of navigability.[21] Conversely, in this logic, water bodies not meandered by the early surveys were—and still are—often considered to be non-navigable. The problem with this last assumption is perhaps best illustrated by the fact that *none* of the rivers supporting steamship lines during the 1800s were meandered in Florida's early public surveys.[22] This fact alone indicates that meandering is not a sufficient indication of a water body's navigability. In fact, only about 260 of Florida's thousands of lakes were finally meandered. Of the estimated 6,000 miles of navigable streams in Florida, some 1,250 miles are all that were meandered in the public land surveys.[23] These discrepancies between what is navigable in fact and what was meandered, however, are still not widely known, and countering pervasive assumptions about meandering comprises an important part of the state's efforts in sovereignty lands cases.[24]

The inconsistencies in meandering navigable water bodies resulted from several factors. Probably the most blameworthy of these, however, is that public land surveyors received their instructions from the General Land Office in Washington, and these instructions changed frequently and varied greatly. The first instructions used by Florida surveyors were issued in 1819 and made no direct mention of meandering.[25] Although the directives called for surveyors to record in their field books the "elevation of waters during their inundation and their greatest depression at low water," the instructions gave no directions for surveying the course of the water.[26] In 1825, the General Land Office instructions called for meandering the coastline of Florida as part of the first surveys of the range lines. The October 26, 1830, instructions included the following order to represent the surveyed area of an island at "ordinary low tide":

> If the island shall have a bluff coast the survey will be simple and easy. If however parts of it should more or less be affected by the tides, the survey is to be ordered as to exhibit the area at ordinary low tide, and it is further desired that you will Report as nearly as can be estimated the difference between the area of the island at ordinary low and ordinary high tide and indicate the same by some particular color on the plat of Survey.[27]

In this set of instructions we also find an early contemplation of the OHWL in the reference to the ordinary high tide.

In the General Instructions of 1831, surveyors were required to indicate the "general course" of non-navigable streams and to "truly" delineate navigable streams by meandering them. Inasmuch as the courts continue even today to sort out what constitutes a navigable stream in Florida, one can imagine that the early surveyors would have had similar difficulties: for example, depending on the time of year a stream was surveyed it might be completely dry, when in fact it served as a navigable stream at other times of the year. This type of seasonality has been compared with rivers in the north that ice over, in that, although this condition prevents their being navigable year-round, it does not render them non-navigable. Not until 1889, however, did the Supreme Court of Florida clarify this question. In *Bucki v. Cone* the court held that a stream need not run all year to qualify as navigable:

> A stream of sufficient capacity and volume of water to float to market the products of the country, of whatever kind or however floated, will answer the latter conditions of navigability, and it is not essential that the stream should be continuously in a state suited to the flotage.[28]

The 1831 instructions also required the "width of all water courses, rivers, creeks, etc." to be "represented in figures on the plat," although the instructions did not detail whether the width was to be determined at high water marks or low water marks or some place in between.[29] Section 4 directed that lakes and ponds of "*sufficient magnitude* to justify such expense are to be meandered and platted," while ponds and lakes not meandered were to be measured and exhibited on the plat "as accurately as practicable from careful occular [*sic*] observation to be made by the Deputy and noted in his field book." As survey historian Joe Knetsch has observed, there was no clear criterion for what constituted "sufficient magnitude":

> There is no definition of "sufficient magnitude" given in these directions (or special instructions in the files) to the deputy surveyors. This, like many other points, was discretionary for the surveyors in the field. The fact that the meander must justify the expense is also very discretionary for the individual surveyor who has a contract to run "x" number of miles in a given length of time. If the water course is of such a nature as to be surrounded or bordered by significant swamp lands and other difficulties that would detract from the sale of the land, was the surveyor *required* to meander the water course?[30]

Given the wide-ranging discretion surveyors had in such matters, any assumptions about meandered watercourses in the early surveys must be carefully examined. The 1845 instructions ordered surveyors to "meander all navigable streams, all lakes, and deep ponds, exceeding half a section

[320 acres] in area." In addition, swamps along the edges of such water-courses were not to be meandered but left as "unfinished" surveys.[31]

Then, in 1850, the passage of the Swamp and Overflowed Lands Act "changed everything," as Knetsch says. With these lands now added to the roster of saleable lands, surveying the swamps became much more important. Not surprisingly, however, instructions concerning this new situation left much to the discretion of the surveyors:

> Where the swamp or overflowed lands are on the borders of a stream or lake, the stream or lake could be meandered and ordinates surveyed at suitable intervals from the borders of the stream or lake to the margin of the swamp and over-flowed lands, and by connecting the ends of those ordinates, next to that margin by straight lines, the boundaries of the swamp or overflowed lands can be ascertained with sufficient accuracy.[32]

The instructions here suggest that where the situation is such that swamp borders a watercourse (navigable? non-navigable?) the stream or lake *could be meandered* (depending on what?) in the described way. Of course, such ambiguous phrases as "suitable intervals" and "sufficient accuracy" beg interpretation—which individual surveyors surely provided in individual ways. Then, somewhat perversely, the instructions go on to say that in "no case . . . should any such boundaries or ordinates be marked in the field, as they may produce difficulty in determining the lines and corners of the public surveys hereafter and thus lead to litigation."[33]

The "meander corners" of modern-day surveying texts made their first appearance in the 1855 revised instructions, although there is no direction concerning what elevation on the banks is to be used in establishing the corners (high water, low water?). Also, under this set of instructions, lakes and deep ponds of 25 acres or more were to be meandered, although ponds likely to dry up were not to be meandered. The change to meandering 25-acre ponds from the earlier instruction to meander lakes of 320 acres gives some indication of why Florida's meandered water bodies might appear to have been selected without rhyme or reason.

The 1881 instructions included several new directives regarding meandering. Meander lines were now to be established at the ordinary low water mark of rivers or lakes on which swamp or overflowed lands bordered. Rivers "not embraced in the class denominated 'navigable' under the statute, but which are well-defined natural arteries of internal communication," were to be meandered on one bank only. All lakes, bayous, and deep ponds that might "serve as public highways of commerce" were also to be meandered; shallow lakes or ponds "readily to be drained or likely to dry up" were not to be meandered.[34] Lakes, bayous, and ponds lying entirely within a section were, likewise, not to be meandered.

Several points of confusion emerged from these instructions. How was a surveyor to determine the ordinary low water mark of a watercourse if he happened to be surveying when the water was higher than the low water mark? As to the one-bank meanders, it is difficult to decide how exactly a "well-defined artery of internal communication" might differ from a navigable river. Here, some reference to the statutory definition of "navigable" might have been useful, if anyone had been clear as to what statute was intended. Practically speaking, though, this instruction probably indicated to surveyors that they need not restrict meandering to watercourses that would have met such federal guidelines for navigability as to be capable of interstate commerce, for example. Instead, they were to meander waters that were used more locally for communications and travel—that is, that were in fact navigable. Of course, the new instruction not to meander lakes and ponds lying entirely within a section (640 acres) tended to confuse the practice of the 1855 instructions to meander lakes and ponds as small as 25 acres. These two instructions taken together, however, seem to illustrate the possibility that in the surveys of the public lands meandering was not intended to provide a complete inventory of the state's water bodies.

More confusing still was the possible implication of the instruction to meander lakes and deep ponds if they served as public highways of commerce. Was the surveyor to infer that he should *not meander* lakes and ponds *not serving as public highways of commerce?* Many areas of Florida were, at the time of the public surveys, relatively unsettled, making it difficult to declare watercourses in those areas as public highways of commerce, even if those waters were in fact *capable of navigation.* Nineteenth-century surveyors often had to decide such questions for themselves. And any surveyor wondering exactly what was meant by "public highways of commerce" might continue to ponder this question until clarification came from the Florida Supreme Court in 1909. In *Broward v. Mabry,* the court established that if a water body "is permanent in character, and in its ordinary natural state is in fact navigable for useful purposes, and is of sufficient size and is so situated and conditioned that it may be used for purposes common to the public in the locality where it is located, such water may be regarded as being of public character."[35] Any water body meeting this test, the court said, could "be made useful for any considerable navigation or commercial intercourse between the people of a large area."[36] But pity the poor surveyor prior to these epiphanies.

In 1894, the 1881 instructions to meander at the ordinary low water mark were changed. The 1894 manual directed that "navigable rivers, as well as all rivers not embraced in the class denominated 'navigable,' the right-angle width of which is three chains and upward, will be meandered on both banks, at the *ordinary mean high water mark*."[37] Since the manual includes no rationale for the change from low water mark to high water mark, we can only guess at the surveyor general's thinking. Perhaps the weight of the accumulating case law concerning water boundaries motivated the change of instructions. In 1876, the U.S. Supreme Court had held, in *Barney v. Keokuk*, that the "bed of the Mississippi River and its banks to high-water mark belong to the State, and that the title of the riparian proprietor extends only to that line."[38] Whatever prompted the change, the 1894 manual gives the first indication that someone in the surveyor general's office was thinking long and hard about water boundaries. By 1902, the General Land Office had closed the gap between its instructions and established case law.

In the 1902 *Manual of Survey Instructions*, two new sections on meandering cite the defining case law. Section 154 begins with an instruction to meander water bodies at the mean high water mark and marks the General Land Office's first attempt to explain how to determine the mean high water mark:

> Lands bounded by waters are to be meandered at mean high water mark. This term has been defined in a State decision (47 Iowa, 370) in substance as follows: High water mark in the Mississippi River is to be determined from the river bed; and that only is river bed which the river occupies long enough to wrest it from vegetation.
>
> In another case (14 Penn. St. 59) a bank is defined as the continuous margin where vegetation ceases, and the shore is the sandy space between it and low-water mark.[39]

Such an "explanation" may seem rudimentary in light of all the considerations that go into determining an OHWL today.[40] Yet the importance of including the case law definitions and rationale lies in the possibility that the instructions may now be defended as something other than arbitrary. Even more remarkable is the final part of section 154:

> Numerous decisions in State and U.S. Supreme Courts, assert the principle that meander lines are not boundaries defining the area of ownership of tracts

adjacent to waters. The general rule is well set forth (10 Iowa, 549) by saying that in a navigable stream, as the Des Moines River in Iowa, high-water mark is the boundary line. When by action of the water the river bed changes, high-water mark changes and ownership of adjoining land changes with it. The location of meander lines does not affect the question.[41]

With these few lines the 1902 manual describes the relationship of meander lines and high water marks to ownership that will cause such consternation over the next century. Meander lines are not boundary lines. The mean high water mark is the boundary line. Section 155 expands on these points:

> Inasmuch as it is not practicable in public-land surveys to meander in such a way as to follow and reproduce all the minute windings of the high-water line, the U.S. Supreme Court has given the principles governing the use and purpose of meandering shores, in its decision in a noted case (R.R. Co *v*. Schurmeier, 7 Wallace, 286–7) as follows:
>
>> Meander lines are run in surveying fractional portions of the public lands bordering on navigable rivers, not as boundaries of the tract, but for the purpose of defining the sinuosities of the banks of the stream, and as the means of ascertaining the quantity of land in the fraction subject to sale, which is to be paid for by the purchaser. In preparing the official plat from the field notes, the meander line is represented as the border line of the stream, and shows to a demonstration that the watercourse, and not the meander line as actually run on the land, is the boundary.
>>
>> In cases where the deputy finds it impossible to carry his meander line along mean high-water mark, his notes should state the distance therefrom, and the obstacles which justify the deviation.[42]

But an even more remarkable point goes almost unnoticed at the end of section 154. "When by action of the water the river bed changes, high-water mark changes and ownership of adjoining land changes with it." This comment refers to the phenomenon of water bodies changing shape over extended periods of time due to natural processes such as accretion and erosion. But it also marks an important aspect of the emerging conception of the ordinary high water line: The OHWL is an *ambulatory* line that shifts in response to gradual, natural changes in the shoreline and water levels of a water body. The realization of this fact by the courts and the surveyor general at the turn of the century apparently did not guarantee that it would become common knowledge; more than sixty years later, it was this fact upon which the trustees would flounder in their efforts to protect sovereignty lands using an "original" OHWL.

The attempts of the 1902 manual to specify the mean high water mark more explicitly than had been done previously turned out to be inadequate—particularly for areas such as Florida where flat-banked streams and lakes are common. By 1930 the manual included an even more detailed attempt to describe mean high water. It contained a frustrating number of inaccuracies mixed with tantalizing insights into the problems of establishing an OHWL:

> Practically all inland bodies of water pass through an annual cycle of changes from mean low water to flood stages, between the extremes of which will be found mean high water. In regions of broken topography, especially where bodies of water are bounded by sharply sloping lands, the horizontal distance between the margins of the various water elevations is comparatively slight, and the engineer will not experience much difficulty in determining the horizontal position of mean high-water level with approximate accuracy; but in level regions, or *in any locality where the meanderable bodies of water are bordered by relatively flat lands,* the horizontal distance between the successive levels is relatively great. *The engineer will find the most reliable indication of mean high-water elevation* in the evidence made by the water's action at its various stages, which will generally be found *well marked in the soil,* and in timbered localities a very certain indication of the locus of the various important water levels will be found in the belting of the native forest species.[43]

In this paragraph we see the influence of the 1927 *Tilden* court, which described the criteria for locating the OHWL on both flat-banked and steep-banked water bodies. But, in spite of the manual's detailed description of the problems of flat-banked meandering (of which the surveyor was probably sufficiently aware already), the proffered solution—to find the marks of the various stages in the "well marked" soil—entirely contradicts *Tilden*. The *Tilden* court found that in places "where the banks are low and flat, the *water does not impress on the soil any well-defined line* of demarcation between the bed and the banks."[44] Instead, the court said the "ordinary agricultural crop" test should be the "principal test in determining the location of the high-water mark as a line between the riparian owner and the public."[45] That test establishes the "point up to which the presence and action of the water is so continuous as to destroy the value of the land for agricultural purposes by preventing the growth of vegetation, constituting what may be termed an ordinary agricultural crop."[46]

The 1930 manual then went on to even more torturous confusions, laudably suggesting the use of native forest trees to identify the various areas and durations of inundation, but completely botching the description of mean high water elevation. The manual states: "Mean high-water elevation will be found at the margin of the area occupied by the water for the greater portion of each average year." In fact, the area occupied by the water for the greater portion of each year describes the *low-water* elevation. That is, the percent of time water will occupy the low stage may well approach 100 percent ("the greater portion of each . . . year"); generally speaking, water may occupy the average stage something like 50 percent of the time, the high stage something less than 25 percent of the time, and flood stage only a small percent of the time. Therefore, the "margin of the area occupied by the water for the greater portion of each year" would lie *below* the average stage of water; it cannot possibly contain the mean *high water* elevation.

Obviously the changes and errors in surveying instructions perpetuated misconceptions about navigability and about the ordinary high water mark. When reading the transcripts of public hearings and trials, I see versions of these misunderstandings that persist today in the comments of landowners, surveyors, judges, and other interested citizens—among them the idea that the meander line *is* the OHWL and that only meandered water bodies are navigable. But looking at the history of surveying instructions—particularly when laid side by side with the history of case law on the OHWL—one can see that the confusions surrounding the OHWL arise in the very attempt to understand and use the concept.[47]

The boundary is a relatively simple idea—the place where the water ends and the land begins—that must be applied to a complex world. What happens when we begin to apply the concept is that we discover nature—actually meet the natural world in the way that one meets another face-to-face. Determining the OHWL is not something we can do to nature the way we dam a river. It requires that we listen and look and see. *There is a line there.* That is the premise of the concept and the evidence of what we have learned about the natural world. But, in Florida, it is not always what we thought it was before we actually looked for it—a well-marked line in the sand "needing no scientific exploration to find." Looking back over the course of the century and a half that Florida has been clarifying the concept of the OHWL, what one sees is a picture of people with certain ideas in mind learning to see what is in front of them. And we are still having to learn to say what we think that is.

"Original" Flounderings

Meandering instructions were not the only confusions the OHWL suffered. As early as 1952 a phrase began to appear in the trustees' correspondence on reclaimed lake bottoms that marked a mistake in the state's OHWL and sovereignty lands policy. In a report to the trustees, Chief Drainage Engineer F. C. Elliot wrote:

> Reclaimed Lake Bottoms of Meandered Lakes—Sale of: "The meander line is not the boundary line. The lakeward boundary of land bordering upon the lake is the *original, natural, ordinary high water mark*. Artificial changing of the lake level, either upward or downward, or raising the level of the land by filling, or lowering the same by excavation, does not change the ordinary, natural, high watermark or the location of the same as the lakeside boundary."[48]

This phrase—"the *original,* natural, ordinary high water mark"—seems to have arisen in the context of artificially altered lake levels as a way of contrasting the OHWL of manipulated water bodies with those of lakes in their natural state. Other documents—for example, the trustees' 1969 proposed plan to manage reclaimed lake bottoms—reveal that the word "original" referred to the time of statehood. Recall that in that plan, reclaimed lake bottoms were defined as:

> those lands which result from the permanent artificial lowering of a lake level by a legally constituted authority and which lie between the line of the *original (March 3, 1845) ordinary high water level* and the lowered ordinary high water level of the lake.[49]

In another document, a letter of July 18, 1957, Attorney General Richard Ervin wrote to the acting secretary of the trustees concerning Lake Gibson. Here, Erwin asserts that the *original high water mark* constitutes the boundary between sovereignty lands and private uplands:

> You point out that the application makes no reference to the *original high water mark—that is, the lakeward limit of private ownership.* Neither does the applicant offer any proof that the land applied for has been permanently reclaimed. The facts before us do not indicate that Lake Gibson is a permanently lowered lake and that the lands lying between the present water line of the lake and the original high water mark are subject to reclamation. *Navigable lake bottoms lying lakeward of the original high water mark are sovereignty lands* and the Legislature has not, in so far as I know, ever vested the Trustees of the Internal Improvement Fund with authority to sell such lands to private parties until the lands have been reclaimed and reclaimed lands may only be sold landward of the newly established ordinary high water mark.[50]

The mistake in Erwin's statement is in his assertion that the boundary of navigable waters is tied to the time of statehood (the *original* high water mark). Under the law, the boundary shifts as the dynamics of the water body shape and reshape the shore.

There is a tie between sovereignty lands and the time of statehood. The historic test for sovereignty lands is whether the water body was *navigable* at the time of statehood. The navigability has to be proved first. Only after the water body is identified as sovereignty land—that is, navigable at the time of statehood—does the OHWL become meaningful as the water body's boundary. But the boundary itself is not fixed at the time of statehood. The boundary is wherever the natural OHWL occurs.

In their attempts to deal with reclaimed lands, the trustees began by focusing on how the original OHWL (March 3, 1845) of water bodies differed from the artificially lowered OHWL. This approach was intended to sort out what was sovereignty land. The thinking went something like this: Lakes and streams that were *navigable at the time of statehood* are sovereignty lands. We have to determine *where the OHWL of these lakes and streams was at the time of statehood*. Then we can determine what is sovereignty land. However, this apparent logic concealed a key error: it blurred the criteria for sovereignty lands with the criteria for the OHWL. Sovereignty lands are determined by what water bodies were navigable at the time of statehood (because the state's sovereign rights and responsibilities pertaining to its navigable waters arise with its statehood). Therefore, navigability at statehood determines *which* water bodies the trustees are concerned with. The OHWL, however, is by definition a natural marker resulting from the complex hydrologic cycles affecting a given water body. The natural dynamics of submergence, reliction, erosion, and accretion (see glossary) can cause a slow migration of the shore over time. Such gradual changes in the shoreline and water level may alter the OHWL, shifting the boundary line between sovereignty lands and riparian uplands. Because this boundary is ambulatory, the horizontal location and/or elevation of the OHWL might be the same after 150 years, but it could be quite different.

However, when a water body is artificially lowered, the ambulatory movement of the natural OHWL is stopped and the water body's new physical boundary is determined by the water regime established for that water body. Unless this kind of manipulation is present, though, the *current* OHWL is always the legal boundary. When the trustees began pursuing a policy treating the *original* (at the time of statehood) OHWL as the "lakeward limit of private ownership," they mistook the original OHWL for the *natural* OHWL. But this misconception would not be clarified for many years.

In dealing with reclaimed lake bottoms, the trustees wanted a way to measure the change in the boundary—what the difference would be between a water body's new, lowered, fixed line and the boundary prior to the artificial manipulation of its hydrologic cycles. The idea here was that this quantification would allow the upland owner to apply to purchase that land necessary to restore waterfront status to the property. So, what the trustees really needed to know about reclaimed lake bottoms was how lowering a water body had affected its natural OHWL—not its *original* OHWL—or, more exactly, what the OHWL had been prior to man-made changes. In most instances, however, OHWL determinations of these water bodies had not been conducted prior to their being lowered. Often, the public surveys were considered to be the best (or only) indication of the OHWL prior to manipulation. Since this use of the original OHWL was the best available information for certain situations involving altered water bodies, it was easy to fall into thinking that the original OHWL determined water boundaries generally. With *lowered* water bodies, the thinking went, you needed to find the original OHWL and the "new, altered" OHWL; but within a very short time people began (mistakenly) to think of the original OHWL as simply the boundary—even when the water body hadn't been altered.

Compounding the confusion of an "original OHWL" was the generally held view that meander lines could substitute for the original OHWL in making boundary determinations. In 1960, the trustees prepared materials for a seminar on lake matters sought by Water Resources Commission and State Game and Fresh Water Fish Commission, which contained the following statements:

> Technically, private ownerships of upland extend to the original mean high water line as of the year 1845 when Florida became a State and was vested with the title to the bottom lands under navigable waters. *Determination of the 1845 mean high water line is generally impracticable,* expensive and hardly satisfactory to the present owners of abutting uplands. Unless there is evidence that the meanders in the official U.S. Surveys are erroneous or fraudulent *it is generally practicable and fair to present-day interests for the meander to be accepted as approximating the original normal high water line,* as basis for defining the lakeward boundary of private upland ownership.[51]

Of course, meander lines can provide the "best available evidence" in some cases for understanding what the situation was at the time of statehood. Given the inconsistencies and ambiguities of the public surveyors' instructions, however, the interpretation of meander-line evidence becomes a complicated procedure. In this light, the notion that erroneous or fraudulent meanders would somehow be evident—or that error or fraud would constitute the problem with meanders to begin with—seems refreshingly simple. In any case, resorting to meander lines for evidence of the OHWL probably contributed to thinking of the OHWL as something that was fixed in the past.

As the 1960s drew to a close, the trustees' focus on the state's freshwater lakes and streams intensified. On February 3, 1970, Governor Claude Kirk issued an executive order that must have struck terror into the heart of any person with a development plan and a lakefront property. The order, entitled "Emergency Immediate Action: Resolution for the People of the State of Florida for Their Survival," declared that, inasmuch as Florida's citizens needed drinking water to survive, the "257 state-owned lakes . . . at this time and any others as they become state owned" would be set aside to be "preserved in their natural condition." (The implication of the "257 state-owned lakes . . . at this time" language is that the count was made based on whether the lake was meandered in the original government surveys.) The doctrine guaranteed

> that from this date, . . . no further damage or risk to the present water quality of these lakes will occur and that no further degradation to the water quality or lakes will be permitted and that these lakes will not fall prey to further encroachment and there will be no further selling of these lakes which belong to all the people or new permits granted or old permits validated or rights of ways or easements granted as affects these 257 lakes, that in the public interest precedence be in this instance, the water of these lakes remain for drinking for survival of our people.

The order also gave one of the first directives on locating the OHWL of these lakes:

> That the bulkhead lines be determined as the mean high water line according to E.W. Bishop's recommendations as stated in the 1967 edition exclusively of Florida Lakes Part 1 & 2, all parties concerned are satisfied with these techniques established on said date for the best protection of these lakes and accepted and recommended by Game & Fresh Water Fish Commission, plus other valid biological and hydrographic information.[52]

E. W. Bishop, a geologist on the staff of Florida Board of Conservation, had endeavored to devise a field method for determining the high water line of water bodies that could be used when long-term hydrologic records of the water body were not available. His approach was to examine thirty

Florida lakes for which stage records did exist, correlating the lakes' shoreline features with their stage records. In his discussion of the study, Bishop explained what produced the high water line and how it correlated with the stage duration records:

When water occupies a depression in the earth surface long enough, it affects changes by its presence and by the action of the waves on its surface. Its presence will destroy any vegetation not adapted to spending at least part of its life cycle submerged or partially submerged in water and will promote the spread of those plants that are water tolerant. Its presence, in some instances, will cause the preservation of organic debris which can form a blanket over the original land surface and may in time fill up the lake. The waves act to erode the banks and supply the necessary energy to transport the eroded material into the lake bottom thereby enlarging the surface area and decreasing the depth of the lake. The highest extent of these changes is the high water line.[53]

The "landward termination of lake deposits," Bishop felt, was the feature "most likely to occur at or very near the same elevation at all points along the shore of any lake."[54] These terminal deposits would likely occur as stratified beach deposits at the base of beach scarps, or deposits of peat or sandy peat along sheltered parts of the shore. On average, Bishop found, the deposits indicated a 10 percent stage duration—that is, the water in the lake would be found at a higher stage than the deposits only 10 percent of the time. In contrast to the shoreline deposits, Bishop felt that plants provided indications of the OHWL with varying reliability:

It has been found that, in many instances, there is not a distinct break between the upland and lake bottom, if the lakeward or landward terminations of plant species are used to determine the high water line. . . . Because plant species have different degrees of tolerance to water standing above their roots, and these differences apparently are not consistent from lake to lake, they can be used only as a guide to the location of the high water line.[55]

Although, over the years, Bishop's approach to the OHWL has been refined (to rely on indicators of the *ordinary* high as indicated in case law), his studies provided some of the earliest fieldwork on Florida's lakes. It is also significant that actual fieldwork on Florida lakes suggested that the vegetative indicator was not wholly reliable on its own.

On June 16, 1970, the newly formed Technical Advisory Committee on Reclaimed Lake Bottom Lands[56] asked the trustees to authorize an expansion of the committee's investigation to include not only reclaimed lake bottom lands but also similar matters affecting all freshwater lakes, meandered or not. The trustees' policy that had been adopted on January 20 had been aimed only at lakes that had been permanently lowered. The committee felt, however, that it was "appropriate to determine methods for locating high water lines of all lakes," and not only those that had been permanently lowered.[57] The trustees responded by adopting a motion authorizing the committee to investigate "all fresh water lakes, meandered or not." In addition, the committee requested clarification as to whether the trustees' policy on the sale of reclaimed lake bottoms should be reinterpreted in light of the recently passed (June 2) policy that sales of sovereignty lands now meet the more stringent test of being "in the public interest." The trustees directed that the June 2 policy requiring sales to be in the public interest be applied also to reclaimed lake bottom lands.[58]

In their next meeting, the Technical Advisory Committee on Reclaimed Lake Bottom Lands—now renamed the Technical Advisory Committee on Fresh Water Lakes Management—heard testimony about various methods of locating the OHWL by determining vegetation patterns. As a follow-up, the committee scheduled a field trip to observe firsthand the vegetation methodology. The committee also agreed to recommend to the trustees' staff and board methods for the establishment of ordinary high water lines in all navigable Florida lakes.

Meanwhile, however, the legislature was charting a course of its own. On June 14, 1970, it passed an act amending and adding to chapter 253 of the *Florida Statutes,* which deals with sovereignty lands. The act provided that "submerged lands located under navigable meandered fresh water lakes shall be considered as a separate class of sovereignty lands."[59] Exactly what this separation was to accomplish the act did not make clear. In a new section, 253.151 Navigable meandered fresh water lakes, the act declared, "Such separate class of sovereignty lands shall not be construed to be of the same character as tidal lands, streams, watercourses, rivers, or as lakes attached to tidal waters by means of navigable watercourses, but rather, shall be administered in accordance with the provisions of this section."[60] Once again, this language seemed to allude to some obvious difference between freshwater lakes and all other water bodies, without specifying what constituted the difference. That freshwater lakes differ in character from other water bodies is a declaration that may indicate either a profound insight into Florida's various ecologies or a most inspired piece of political maneuvering. The new section described the boundary line of navigable meandered freshwater lakes to be that "line which separates the sovereignty lands of the state from those of a riparian upland owner," and stated that such line would be described in "terms of elevation above mean sea level." In section 3, dealing with establishing the boundary line, the act provided that evidence of where the water's edge was at the time of statehood would constitute the boundary.

> Where physical evidence exists indicating the actual water's edge of any navigable meandered fresh water lake as of the date such body came under the jurisdiction of the state, regardless of where the water's edge exists on the date of the determination of the boundary line, the water's edge as evidenced on the former date shall be deemed the boundary line.

With this statement, the legislature created its own version of the original OHWL, which the trustees had been trying to make workable. In their version, though, it was not even necessary to discover the original OHWL. Any indication of the water's edge at the time of statehood would now be sufficient to serve as a boundary. Of course, given the fact that many of the early surveys of the state's water bodies were conducted during the low-water season, placing the boundaries of these lakes at the water's edge—without reference to the OHWL—in effect relocated the boundary from the high-water to the low-water line.

The idea that the boundary of lakes could simply be "fixed" was an understandably appealing one, given the complications that had been encountered. In the long process of clarifying the concept of the OHWL, however, it is difficult to see how this legislative endeavor could stand as a contribution. Section 3 went on to say that in the absence of physical evidence of the original levels, long-time residents' affidavits attesting to the "average levels of such lakes" could be used instead. The act failed to specify whether these "average levels" were to constitute the boundary line elevation or be used as an indication of the OHWL. More puzzling still—given the anecdotal nature of this type of evidence—is the legislators' treatment of data that could actually specify the OHWL. Gauge-station data, the act said, if available for a period of no less than ten consecutive years, could also be used to determine lake boundaries. But this meant, in practice, that the actual hydrologic record of a water body might count for less than several affidavits of the average levels of the lake if the record did not comprise ten consecutive years. In the final instruction of the section, however, the legislature seemed ready to cast a grudging eye to existing case law on the matter, suggesting that physical evidence such as vegetation and watermarks might be useful:

> Actual on-site examination of the terrain (landward and lakeward of the existing waterline) and of plant life including upland and aquatic by qualified personnel,

and the other physical indications of present and past waterlines, which shall be deemed reasonable, may be used in determining the boundary line. This investigation may include public hearings, as well as examination of existing docks, structures, and other physical evidence which may properly be construed as germane to the location of the boundary line.

In this hodge-podge of "procedures" for establishing a boundary line, not only was it difficult to determine what counted as the best evidence of a boundary, it was all too easy to overlook the fact that the concept of the OHWL as the boundary between public and private lands had been completely jettisoned. Nowhere in the act is the ordinary high water line referred to as the legal boundary. Perhaps this is what the legislators had in mind when they declared that navigable meandered freshwater lakes were not of the "same character" as other navigable water courses: a way to get rid of the troublesome OHWL as the boundary between public and private lands. As it turned out, this was only the first of several attempts to establish a different boundary between public and private lands on navigable water bodies.

Swimming in a Mud Hole

On February 23, 1971, the trustees asked the Central and Southern Florida Flood Control District (CSFFCD) to hold public hearings "for the purpose of gathering evidence that would provide a means of establishing boundary lines"[61] for the upper Kissimmee Basin's "chain of lakes."[62] Citing the new law, *Florida Statutes,* section 253.151, the trustees noted that "one method of establishing lake boundaries includes holding public hearings at which time evidence is submitted that can be utilized by the Board of Trustees."[63] So, just as the ditching of the Kissimmee River was completed, public hearings began on the issue of where the boundary would be established for the lakes that formed the river's headwaters. On June 22, 1971, the hearings opened in Kissimmee, Florida, with hearing officer Don Morgan acknowledging the existing confusion. Morgan told the group that the trustees were asking for information from the public that would help in establishing the mean high water line. In spite of the fact that the newly passed law pertaining to lake boundaries did not call for the boundary to be set at the OHWL, Morgan and many others continued to refer to the boundary as the ordinary or mean high water line. Morgan emphasized that the meeting had nothing to do with regulating water levels of the lakes. "It is trying to establish the high water mark which divides private and public property," he said.[64] He then opened the floor for comments.

The first question raised the issue of what evidence the trustees were offering of the location of the boundary. Several participants at the hearing assumed the trustees would "come out with a proposal and ask for criticism." Morgan reiterated that the hearing was to gather information the public might have. Discussion then turned to the ordinary high water line. Understandably, there was confusion about what counted as the boundary. One attorney in the group stated that the boundary would be set at the level of the lake in 1845 (when Florida became a state). Jim Lane from the Engineering Division of the CSFFCD responded:

> It isn't the stage of the lake at the time that Florida went into the Union. It is the mean high water at that point. In other words, this could have been a period of drought when the lake was down to forty or something like that. The surveyors who went out at that time were supposed to look for evidence of mean high water such as tree lines and such, do their meander on that line rather than on the water line.[65]

Lane's "correction" seems based on the notion of the original OHWL that the trustees had been trying to make workable before the legislature passed 253.151. According to the new statute, however, evidence of the "water's edge" would determine the boundary, regardless of whether the lake was at high stage or low. Furthermore, Lane's comment contradicts the fact that surveyors prior to 1894 were not instructed to meander watercourses at the mean high water line.

The attorney then presented a copy of the original government survey of Lake Tohopekaliga (Lake Toho) and the Coast and Geodetic surveys of the lake, which were done in 1953. These surveys, he said, showed that the shorelines were almost identical on both maps. The 1953 survey had put the lake level at fifty-three feet. By comparing the two surveys, he said, one could conclude that the "best evidence of the mean high water level that is available historically is that original survey with respect to Lake Tohopekaliga; and we think it reflects a level of approximately 53 feet."[66] He went on to argue that the similarity of the shoreline in the two maps showed that Disston's drainage projects had not lowered the lake. He said he had examined the swamp and overflowed lands patent by which lands along the lake had been transferred from the federal government to the state. The evidence again seemed to point to a fifty-three-foot elevation. He had also spoken to surveyors who were locating section corners that coincided with the lake's meander line. He hoped that this information would provide a way to correlate lake levels with the shoreline at those corners. These remarks provided exactly the type of evidence the trustees' staff would want to review. For better or worse, however, the remaining speakers provided more questions about the state's intentions than evidence concerning the lakes.

The next person to speak was another attorney representing a large landholder in central Florida. He reiterated the concern that people had not had adequate time to prepare for the hearing "particularly in view of the fact that we are not advised as to the position the Trustees are going to take. We are trying to learn to swim in a mud hole," he said, "because we don't know what they're doing to us. It is a bad situation from the public standpoint and from a legal standpoint."[67] Clearly, the communications between the public and the trustees were not what they should have been to make the hearings their most productive. That the trustees' attempt to get public input concerning the line could evoke such suspicion, when it might have engendered trust and cooperation, boded poorly for the future of boundary determinations under the new statute.

Adding to the confusion, the speaker then made a garbled challenge of Jim Lane's remarks (above) concerning the mean high water line: "Apparently," he remarked, "you are taking the position in your capacity that the meander line doesn't mean anything, that the meander line is not significant in arriving at the mean ordinary mean high water mark [sic]."[68] Lane responded, "I say meander line was supposedly taken at the mean high water." Unheeding, the speaker continued: "Are you going to ignore it in connection with these? You indicate to us you will not pay any attention to the lines engineers put on there. You will look at what God put up there in the way of seashells, is that a correct statement? We don't know what the ground rules are."[69] And he went on to say again that without knowing the position of the trustees the landowners had nothing tangible to talk about. In spite of his non sequitur, it is interesting to note this speaker's concern that God's evidence (that is, natural indicators) will be considered more authoritative than the engineers' line. This opposition of human authority to the authority of the natural world, or God's evidence, would become a common theme over the ensuing years.

There followed a series of speakers who were concerned that setting the OHWL at the 1845 level would cut off their riparian access to the water. These cases raised one of the key questions facing the trustees' staff in the upper Kissimmee Basin. The chain of lakes forming the upper basin was now regulated as part of the flood control project that had ditched the river. With the lakes now lowered and held at consistent levels, the 1845

OHWL would surely be higher than the regulated water levels—a situation that would leave these landowners without riparian access to the lake. Furthermore, with the lakes now regulated, the idea of trying to determine a present-day OHWL as a boundary seemed unworkable. There was no longer a natural cycle to the lake's rising and falling levels—no longer an ordinary high water stage. Some of the speakers were clearly wondering what in the world the OHWL had to do with these lakes. And this bewilderment opened the door to some bleak speculation.

The next speaker was a former member and chairman of the Governing Board of the Flood Control District. He began by voicing frustration over the inadequacy of the notice for the hearing. "We have no idea what they [the state] are trying to accomplish," he said.[70] He then outlined his concerns regarding the state's motives for the water management policies they seemed intent on pursuing. He pointed out that the growing propensity of the state to acquire lands for the benefit of the public was costing taxpayers a great deal. At the same time it removed those lands from the tax rolls, placing a continuous upward pressure on the ad valorem tax rolls paid by private citizens. Therefore, he said, he opposed establishing the OHWL at "some tremendously high level for the benefit of the Trustees."[71]

This testimony raised another issue that was central to the problems of boundary establishment: the suspicion of the state's motivation for doing so. In contradiction to the trustees' stated purpose (establishing the legal boundary between public and private property), this speaker expressed the not-uncommon idea that the state had begun to "acquire private lands" for the "alleged" purpose of water management. Inherent in this concern, of course, is the idea that, in establishing the lake boundaries, the state is acquiring private lands as opposed to claiming public lands. The speaker suggests that the trustees—in order to gain control of waterfront property without having to pay for it—might set the boundary lines at a "tremendously high level." This argument details what would soon be dubbed the "state land-grab effort."

The concerns voiced in this hearing provide insight into an important moment in the history of the OHWL. The legislature, in its effort to make the establishment of waterfront boundaries workable, had "watered down" the OHWL as *the* boundary of sovereignty freshwaters. But this hosing may have increased the public's suspicions concerning the state's policy. As we have seen, the concept of the OHWL has evolved from some of the oldest laws still in use today, and the effort to simply drop this common-law doctrine as a matter of convenience might seem to fling to the high seas all that had been a source of stability. Remarkably, no one said so. As far as I can tell, no one commented on the legislature's omission of the OHWL from its description of the legal boundary of sovereignty freshwaters. In part, the failure to comment reflects the lack of clarity about the OHWL— one has to know what it means to know what it would mean to lose it. But the failure was even more complete: no one seemed even to notice the omission. In fact, agents of the state proceeded as if under the assumption that the "original OHWL" had been affirmed as the legal boundary. Reading the testimony of the public hearing, however, I can't help wondering how much of the frustration, suspicion, and confusion resulted from the legislature's muddled law and the trustees' failure to clarify the concept at the center of the chaos. When I first read the testimony suggesting that the trustees might be about to establish the boundary lines at "some tremendously high level," I penciled this question in the margin: What does he think determines the line? My assumption at the time was that he simply didn't understand what the ordinary high water line *means*—how it might protect his interests as well as serving those of the public. But after reading *Florida Statutes,* section 253.151, I realized his fears were well founded. According to the law, the procedures for establishing the boundary were so unclear as to allow for almost anything.

This is not to say that there was any great clarity of vision among those testifying at the hearing. Instead, a wealth of personal motivations interspersed with projections of what the state might "do to them" comprised the bulk of the later testimony. One witness, a realtor, testified that if the "state now attempts to use the original high water mark as a boundary of this area, it would in effect condemn thousands of acres of [privately owned] land." He advised that "the post-Disston high water mark is the original boundary rather than the ill defined and sometimes difficult-to-establish 1845 water mark."[72] Another attorney, representing property owners on several of the lakes, gave detailed testimony about the Disston system of canals. He asserted that Disston lowered the water table in the area as much as nine feet, allowing cultivation of thousands of acres of land that was previously overflowed lands. He feared that the state, in trying to establish the original OHWL of 1845 would "try to take some of the land from these people who have gotten these deeds in good faith believing they own the fee title down to today's ordinary high water mark, not 1845." He stated emphatically that he wanted on behalf of his clients "to definitely oppose any intention on the part of the Trustees or any other agency to adopt the ordinary high water mark at the time that Florida was admitted to the Union in 1845."[73] Clearly one of the most unfortunate omissions from the hearing was a representative who might have explained that the trustees' interest in the original high water mark was to enable some resolution to the problem of lands in this situation. This same speaker, however, went on to say that his clients' lands had never belonged to Florida, but had been patented to the individuals directly from the U.S. government (an unusual situation, but not unheard of).

Other residents seemed to confuse the "ordinary high water mark" with flood marks and were concerned that the boundary would be placed accordingly. The confusion here stems from the common misconception that the high water mark that is used as the legal boundary was derived from the highest watermark—that is, the flood mark. In this instance, the contribution of the word *ordinary* to the concept of the OHWL goes unrecognized.

Another speaker testified that he "owned from Ox Pond here half a mile up Boggy Creek." He went on to explain that in a previous meeting with District personnel he had asked who owns East Lake Toho and was told that the state did. "That kind of upset me," he said. "I had my land surveyed. I have been paying taxes on about a mile or two of East Lake out there for forty years. Looks to me like that I have been selling hunting and fishing rights on my land out there and I think maybe the State owed me something."[74] In this complaint the authority of surveying and the payment of taxes seem to amount to incontrovertible evidence of ownership. In fact, many deeds deriving from swamp and overflowed patents to the state include navigable waters in the deed description. That those lands under navigable waters are excepted from private ownership is not widely understood.

Some riparian owners wanted the regulated water levels of the lakes raised; some thought the lakes were already being held at flood levels. Hearing officer Morgan explained again that the regulation levels had nothing to do with the boundary separating private and public lands. One speaker complained that having "to buy from the old high water mark down to the present high water mark" was "grossly unfair," saying that people owning waterfront had thought all along that they owned to the water.[75] Another speaker remarked, "We are getting so much government we hardly know what to expect from them. We can't live with it."[76]

At this point, W. Turner Wallis spoke, offering a positive suggestion. "I am a professional engineer and registered land surveyor," he explained. "I am a former employee of both the Trustees and of the Flood Control District. My residence in Florida dates back to 1920." Wallis went on to say that he was in agreement with the purpose of the hearing and to urge that the boundary establishment be expanded to include the "entire chain of

lakes in the watershed for both the Kissimmee and the St. Johns Rivers."
In addition, he argued that the boundary determination should be approached within the discussion of the lakes' regulation since the problems of each were "inseparable."[77] Then he argued for an expanded research program not only for purposes of boundary determination but out of concern for water conservation. This call for additional (scientific) study of the lakes and Wallis's suggestion that the boundary determination be considered with the necessity of conserving groundwater met with mixed responses.

An attorney from St. Cloud noted that although he was not satisfied with the meander line as an indication of "where this fictitious mean high water line was back in the 1885's," what Wallis was suggesting was no better. "There is a good deal of guess work and speculation on [the surveyors'] part in these old government surveys so, as to the meander line of the old government surveys, they are subject to question as to accuracy," he noted. "On the other hand," he went on to say, "if we are going to use a so-called scientific test as to the fossils, so-called, to determine the mean high water level, you have a problem that is equally speculative. I might say they're still trying to find out where Noah's Ark came to rest." He concluded: "In reading the memorandum here, my question is: Are the Trustees committed to determining that boundary line, this ownership line? Are they committed that it will be the 1845 line as it is subsequently determined to be or are the Trustees open to having the ownership line or this boundary line established by other criteria based upon logic and reason?"[78]

This response exemplifies a dilemma the trustees' staff would encounter repeatedly in the following years. People unversed in the history of surveying lacked any capacity to determine what was useful about the original government surveys and what was less than reliable. The realization that surveys might require interpretation rendered them useless in the minds of many laypersons. A similar difficulty existed with regard to scientific evidence. People unfamiliar with the practice of science or unaccustomed to interpreting its data tended to approach scientific findings with suspicion, if not outright dismissal. The idea that the trustees would base the lake boundaries on further scientific study (of the lakes' hydrologic cycles) was, therefore, not reassuring to many. And yet, there is the appeal to logic and reason. *Can't the boundary be determined by other criteria based on logic and reason?* I have to admit that when I first encountered this question, it frustrated and bewildered me. What do people think scientific study is based on if not logic and reason? Has it been possible for people to live in this century, in this country, and not realize that they depend on the logic and reason of science? (Do they wash their hands before preparing a meal? Do they use plastic gate handles on their electric fences? Do they use sunscreen? Vaccinate their children, pets, livestock?) Can people really form sentences with the words *criteria, logic,* and *reason,* while equating a geological survey to "so-called fossils" and a failure to find Noah's Ark? Self-interest certainly plays a role in what we come to know, and an even larger role in what we (will or won't) acknowledge. Understandably, the people who would benefit from the evidence of the old surveys saw no problem with surveys. Those who enjoyed favorable scientific findings on their properties embraced scientific determinations. But there is something more than self-interest in this appeal for criteria based on logic and reason.

Stanley Cavell says that establishing criteria makes the process of judging "more open, less private or arbitrary."[79] His idea suggests that the call to establish criteria doesn't arise from petty self-interest. Establishing criteria does, however, indicate something important about the community:

> [E]stablishing criteria allows us to *settle* judgments publicly—not exactly by making them certain, but by declaring what the points are at issue in various judgments, and then making them *final* (on a given occasion). That is a practice worth having; human decisions cannot wait upon certainty. But it is therefore one which can be abused. In assuming the burden of finality in the absence of certainty, an authority stakes the virtue of its community: if its judgments are not accepted as scrupulously fair, in its criteria and in its application of criteria, the community is shown to that extent not to provide a secure human habitation for its members; it fails to take up the slack between the uncertainty of judgment and the finality of decision. A virtue of sports is their celebration of the community's ability to take up its own slack—to provide an arena in which finality of judgment about actions is backed up by certainty, and in which certainty is essentially a matter of seeing.[80]

In light of Cavell's remarks, the speaker's appeal to establish criteria can be seen as a question of community. In essence, the speaker rejects what he perceives to be the trustees' criteria for establishing the boundary: the old government surveys and scientific evidence. This rejection implies that the state has failed the test of community. In this case, I think the charge is that it has failed utterly—it is an outsider. What this speaker and several other participants seem to want is to do things the way they have done them in the past, the way they have worked it out over years of day-in and day-out—the way they have been done customarily. Theirs is an appeal to the outsider to acknowledge local logic. *People have thought all along that they owned to the water line. I've paid taxes on that property for thirty years. My deed says I own it.* These statements say again and again essentially the same thing: we have had an orderly way of living here.

The early 1970s, however, was a dangerous time to stake one's argument on the customary. The communities of central Florida, which had in the early part of the century been dominated by ranching, were now populated by people with more diverse interests. In particular, environmental thinkers had increasingly begun to challenge the customary ways of rural communities. Somewhat surprisingly, however, such challenges frequently came not from newcomers to the community but from long-time residents. The next testimony given in the public hearings was from just such a person. She had lived in Kissimmee since 1937. She had flown over much of the surrounding area frequently over the years and observed that the fluctuation in lake levels had been "exceedingly great." At one time, she stated, "I flew over the southern end of Lake Tohopekaliga when all the surrounding prairie was flooded so that the outline of Lake Cypress, for instance, could be made out only from the tops of the cypress trees sticking out above the water. From Kissimmee south to Lake Kissimmee, including Lakes Cypress and Hatchineha, there was only one big lake." Thus, she said, it seemed "obvious that all of this area should be considered part of the flood plain of these lakes and I should like to see legislation passed forbidding development of this area except for grazing, agriculture, recreation, or such uses." She went on, "In setting the boundaries or shorelines of these lakes, it should be remembered that in some years there is a phenomenal rise in water levels, and provision should be left for this."[81]

This perspective identifies the speaker not only as a more environmental thinker, but as an early proponent of a biocentric view of nature. Her idea is that we should take natural ways into account in determining how we should live—that a right relationship with our environment means we live within the limits imposed by the natural world. Today, the biocentric approach to environmental protection forms the basis of Florida's ecosystem management. According to Pam McVety, executive coordinator of Ecosystem Management for Florida's Department of Environmental Protection during the late 1990s, "The role of science and technology in this view is to help us understand our environmental constraints, to develop strategies for living in harmony with nature, and to identify and mitigate damage caused by past mistakes."[82] This view contrasts sharply with an anthropocentric view of nature, which stems from the belief that the "environment is here solely for exploitation to meet human needs. The role of science and technology in this view," McVety says, is to "allow us to fully understand and manipulate ecosystems in order to extract ever greater quantities of resources to meet the needs of a growing human population."[83]

Of particular interest in the public hearing is this last speaker's perception of the state. Her reference to protective legislation implies that the state forms a working part of her community at large. There is no hint of suspicion toward the state's authority and no attempt to define it as an outsider. This stance may well be typical of those who have long held minority views in traditional communities. They look to a broader community to discover like-minded people and appeal to nonlocal authority for their representation. Her trust of state authority is evident in her idea that the state should own the floodplains surrounding the lakes. She finds it reasonable to assume that the state would uphold traditional uses of the lands (grazing, agriculture, and recreation) while protecting the property from development. These attitudes contrast strongly with the riparian landowners' nervousness about the state's proprietary role, a nervousness that —at least in part—is tied to the issue of development. Property rights advocates resist any limitations on what uses they may make of their property, and, no doubt, many riparian landowners had already glimpsed the tremendous profits to be made from waterfront development. Although some landowners favored state ownership of the floodplains primarily in order to protect traditional agricultural uses, others wanted no interference from the state regardless of what they chose to do with the land.

Although there was an array of other positions as well, the issue of development probably did more to reconfigure traditional alliances than any issue had to that point. Ranchers and farmers had typically shared similar interests, and usually acted in unison to protect those interests from urbanization pressures. With the influx of new residents, however, landowners with large holdings on lakes and riverfronts could be tempted by the enormous profits residential development offered. This concern tended to ally those landowners with realtors, development contractors, and financiers—those interested in development. But it would also put them in league with other groups opposing government protection of water bodies, such as phosphate mining companies. This type of "defection" from traditional ranching concerns often coincided with the land passing to a new generation. A ranch was more susceptible to being developed when a son or daughter who had no interest in ranching inherited the property.

Next to speak in the hearing was Martin Northrup, assistant director of the Florida Audubon Society. He summarized the trustees' actions concerning the OHWL on freshwater lakes, reading into the record the governor and cabinet's February 3, 1970, resolution protecting the lakes from development. He discussed E. W. Bishop's studies to develop criteria for determining the OHWL in the absence of sufficient stage records. He then read a letter from the Department of Natural Resources (DNR) responding to the trustees' proposal to survey the OHWL on Florida's sovereignty freshwater lakes. The letter, dated March 10, 1970, noted that, although the DNR agreed with the intent and purpose of the trustees' resolution to protect the meandered lakes of the state, it did not have the personnel or funds to establish mean high water lines for the lakes.

Although this information slips by without comment in the hearings, this situation was to become one of the most insidious barriers to protecting sovereignty lands. The trustees not only lacked the resources to survey and inventory sovereignty lands, they also possessed little or no enforcement staff to deal with sovereignty lands encroachment. This shortage of personnel would, by the end of the 1970s, contribute to the loss of thousands of acres of public lands.

Northrup then discussed the possible participation of other agencies in the boundary surveys, suggesting that a joint effort might make their completion possible. He submitted correspondence from the District Chief for the U.S. Department of the Interior, Geological Survey (GS), who offered the assistance of the GS in Florida's OHWL surveys. The letter supported Northrup's idea that aerial photography could be used to delineate the upland areas along water bodies. "We are presently using aerial photography and other remote sensing techniques . . . as an aid in the evaluation of certain hydrologic, geologic and biologic features with encouraging success," the GS chief wrote.[84] Northrup concluded by saying, "It looks like we do need surveys involving many fields of interest."[85] But Northrup's testimony focused on the commitment of federal agencies to assist in the state project, and there were no further objections to the repeated hints that an OHWL determination was no longer simply a surveying activity. The proposition that hydrology, geology, biology, and aerial photography form an integral part of the OHWL determination may have seemed to garner acceptance that day. This silence, however, was merely the calm before the storm.

Back to Square One

Soon after the upper Kissimmee Basin public hearing was conducted, a sovereignty lands dispute arose when a riparian landowner in Highlands County, Florida, began to develop lands along the shore of Lake Istokpoga for resale as a residential community. The trustees maintained that, pursuant to section 253.151, *Florida Statutes*, the boundary line between private uplands and sovereignty lands should be located at a contour 41.6 feet above mean sea level. This boundary, based primarily upon the evidence of a fifty-year-old government survey, was unacceptable to the upland owner, since at this location the boundary would claim approximately half the property he had slated for development. The upland owner maintained that the boundary was the actual ordinary high water line, which he placed at 38.5 feet above mean sea level. In addition, he argued that a controversial lowering of the lake by riparian owners constituted reliction since it was to provide relief from a flood caused by a hurricane. The case was brought as *State of Florida and Board of Trustees of the Internal Improvement Trust Fund v. Florida National Properties, Inc.* Following a two-day trial in Highlands County, the circuit court ruled that the "boundary line between [the upland property] and the sovereignty lands was the present ordinary high water mark of Lake Istokpoga." [86] In addition, the court found that the trustees' claim to the 41.6-feet contour had been based on section 253.151, *Florida Statutes,* which the court adjudged to be unconstitutional:

> Other than Section 253.151, the Court can find no authority whatsoever for *fixing* the boundary line at a particular elevation as urged by the Trustees [*sic*]. . . . In *Hughes* [*v. Washington*] the Supreme Court stated:
>
> > A long and unbroken line of decisions of this Court establishes that the grantee of land bounded by a body of navigable water acquires a right to any natural and gradual accretion formed along the shore. . . . Any other rule would leave riparian owners continually in danger of losing the access to water which is often the most valuable feature of their property, and continually vulnerable to harassing litigation challenging the location of the original water lines. . . .
>
> Fla. Statute Section 253.151 which purports to fix the public/private boundary line as of the date of Statehood, suffers from the same infirmities as the constitutional provision under consideration in *Hughes;* and it is likewise unconstitutional. . . . By requiring the establishment of a fixed boundary line between sovereignty bottom lands and Plaintiff's riparian lands, Fla. Stat. Section 253.151 as applied by the Trustees in the instant case, constitutes a taking of Plaintiff's property, including its riparian rights to future alluvion or accretion, without compensation in violation of the Fourteenth Amendment of the United States Constitution and the due process clause of Art. I, Sec. 9, of the Florida Constitution.[87]

The trustees appealed, and the Supreme Court of Florida, on July 14, 1976, heard the case. Agreeing with the lower court that section 253.151 of the statute was unconstitutional, the court noted that the state's right to exercise control over sovereignty lands is so inherent in the state that no specific statutory authority was needed. The court then confirmed the ordinary high water mark as the indicator of the boundary:

> while the Appellee is entitled to the land down to the present ordinary high water line, as held by the lower court, it is not because of the doctrine of reliction but because of the location of the actual, present high water mark. . . . It is our opinion . . . that the property line separating sovereignty and riparian property rights is the ordinary high-water mark in meandered fresh water lakes. In doing so we recognize that such line is subject to change from natural causes or with joint consent of the State and private riparian owners. . . . An inflexible meander demarcation line would not comply with the spirit or letter of our Federal or State Constitutions nor meet present requirements of society. . . . Accordingly, the judgment of the trial court is affirmed.[88]

With the court's ruling, the OHWL was upheld as the boundary between private uplands and sovereignty lands, and the boundary's ambulatory nature was confirmed in law. Furthermore, the court's recognition that the OHWL is the sovereignty/riparian boundary line and that it is subject to "change from natural causes" established the legal status of the natural indicators of the line. Once again, the focus turned to questions of how to determine the OHWL of the state's many water bodies in their varying natural conditions.

By the Distinctive Appearances They Present

In a 1972 review of OHWL cases, entitled "Legal Standards for Determining the Ordinary High Water Mark," Richard Warner Winesett pointed out that throughout the development of American case law the courts had consistently held that the ordinary high water mark "is a question of fact to be found by the trier of fact under proper legal standards. It is to be determined from visual examination of the bank by witnesses or the finder of fact."[89] In addition, no one type of evidence could of itself be sufficient to prove an OHWL if it appeared contrary to evidence of other types. In one case the court ruled that a record of lake levels extending almost a century was not, of itself, sufficient to establish the OHWL. Citing *Tilden v. Smith,* the court reiterated that the proper test must consider the action of the water upon the soil and the corresponding destruction of the value of the land for agricultural purposes.[90] In a 1965 case, *Borough of Ford City v. United States,* the trial court adopted the findings of Ford City's witness, who used the vegetation test exclusively, choosing to ignore three well-qualified government witnesses who considered shelving, erosion, and litter as well as vegetation in determining the OHWL. The appellate court held that the findings were in error because the Ford City witness had not considered at what point the soil could not be used for agricultural purposes. According to the court, the riverbed of a navigational stream is "the land upon which the waters have visibly asserted their dominion, the value of which for agricultural purposes has been destroyed. The value for agricultural purposes is destroyed where *terrestrial* plants *not all plant life* ceases to grow."[91] In other words, the vegetation test alone was not sufficient to locate the OHWL. Winesett outlined the types of evidence upon which various cases attempted to establish ordinary high water marks: vegetation, hydrologic records, the averaging of water levels, agricultural tests, the physical characteristics of the shore, and so forth. Again and again, the courts indicated that "it was necessary to take into consideration all the circumstances and natural conditions . . . in finding the mark."[92]

Interestingly, when one goes back through the keystone cases for OHWL a subtle but persistent theme emerges in the language of the courts' holdings: because water bodies are natural entities, they are each distinct in their characteristics, and they, therefore—to a certain extent— refuse categorical definition. As early as 1851, in *Howard v. Ingersoll*, Justice Curtis wrote: "But in all cases the bed of a river is a natural object; and is to be sought for, not merely by the application of any abstract rules, but as other natural objects are sought for and found, by the distinctive appearances they present."[93] As the effort to establish a methodology for determining the OHWL intensified during the 1980s, the "distinctive appearances" of natural water bodies became an increasingly difficult obstacle. Not only did the characteristic natural indicators of individual water bodies have to be taken into account in determining their OHWLs, but the understanding of natural indicators had become vastly more complex than was the case a century previous.

In 1976, the Boundary Determination Section of the Department of Natural Resources issued a report determining the OHWL of four lakes in the upper Kissimmee River Basin: Lake Tohopekaliga, Lake Hatchineha, Lake Kissimmee, and East Lake Tohopekaliga. The situation of these headwater lakes was that regulation had since the mid-1960s "greatly restricted the range of lake level fluctuations and prevented the occurrence of the high lake levels previously recorded."[94] Because of this change in the water regime, formerly submerged lake bottomlands were now exposed. Florida courts had held that such reclaimed lake bottom resulting from drainage operations was classified as artificial reliction, thus title of these exposed lands remained in the state.[95] The Boundary Determination Section, under the direction of Douglas Schneider, set out to determine the present-day or postregulation OHWL of the lakes. One of the questions hinging on the outcome of the study was what, if any, disposition of the reclaimed lake bottoms would be considered. Upland owners, separated from the waterfront they formerly adjoined, were anxious to regain title down to the new, postregulation OHWL.

Schneider's team conducted fieldwork at each of the lakes to gather biological and geological data and establish elevations of prominent topographical features. After a preliminary examination of soil types was made with a small auger three-quarters of an inch in diameter, holes were dug along a transect, elevations of the different soil layers measured, and samples of the layers recovered for further analysis. These samples were processed to determine the percentage of organics contained in the soil. This information was pertinent because changes in soil types—from soils formed by wave action or continual submergence to soils characteristic of more upland environments—provide evidence for the action of the water on the lake margin. Fieldwork also included measuring the elevations of tree bases. This data helped indicate inundation history, since some species of trees are more water tolerant than others. Live oak, for example, is an upland tree, killed or injured by water standing over the roots for extensive periods of time, while cypress is well adapted to inundation.

Schneider's team also analyzed hydrologic records for each of the lakes. These records allowed the team to determine both extreme highs and lows prior to regulation and to establish ordinary high water levels. Historic data of human activities affecting the water bodies' levels was also reviewed. Reclamation projects, canals, dikes, and so forth were considered for their effects on the lakes. Schneider's report concluded that, since "in three of the lakes the current ordinary high water elevation is below the maximum regulation level and since the state may desire to raise the regulation level in the future, it is recommended that the state ensure that it retains title to the reclaimed lake bottom above the current ordinary high water line."[96] Although, no doubt, a farsighted and sound recommendation for managing public lands, Schneider's advice was certainly not what riparian landowners wanted to hear.

Later that year, Schneider teamed up with Ernest Bishop in the Bureau of Geology to determine ordinary high water elevations "such as existed prior to the onset of regulation in 1964, at selected sites on the Kissimmee

River."[97] Their report, based on two days of fieldwork, was intended only as a preliminary investigation of the river's elevations, and both authors stressed in their conclusion the need for further investigation to resolve discrepancies their work uncovered. Still, their report provides a thumbnail sketch of the efforts in the mid-1970s to follow the courts' direction concerning OHWL methodology. Schneider and Bishop noted in the introduction to their report that because of the trustees' contract with Hamilton Disston to reclaim lands adjoining the Kissimmee River, the "boundary abutting the Kissimmee River in the state conveyances made in the late nineteenth and early twentieth century was intended to be the post-drainage ordinary high water line." In addition, they said, because the OHWL is an ambulatory line, the OHWL might have moved from the OHWL at the time immediately following Disston's drainage operations. "Therefore," Schneider and Bishop wrote, the OHWL "as it existed [just] before the onset of regulation (1964) is the one of interest in determining the extent of state ownership prior to the channelization of the river."[98]

To study the three sites they had chosen, Schneider and Bishop established temporary benchmarks, which could be used to determine river levels, elevations of selected tree bases, and elevations of soil layers. They then examined geological and biological evidence. At all three sites, they reported, the basic lithology was the same:

> fine grained quartz sand deposited off shore on a shallow bottom during high stands of Pleistocene seas. The sand is highly uniform in its fineness and contains a very low percentage of accessory minerals. . . . The principal post depositional changes have been the cutting and filling of the Kissimmee River Valley and the deposition of organic material in the interstices (hardpan) and on top (peat) of the flood plain deposits of fine sand. The term "flood plain" is probably a misnomer as hydrologically the pre-regulation Kissimmee River exhibited more characteristics of a lake than a river. As the term implies, flood plains are inundated only during the flooding of streams whereas the flood plain deposits of the Kissimmee were under water most of the time.
>
> Carbonaceous hardpan in the banks of the river valley is a reliable indicator of the normal range of fluctuations of the river stage and the immediately adjacent ground water table. The upper surface of this material is the pre-regulation high water mark at any given point along the river bank. Peat deposits, where they are still preserved, are also good indicators provided that elevations of these deposits are determined where they wedge out against the uplands.[99]

The biological evidence was similar at the three sites as well:

trees, mainly live oaks . . . grew at elevations considerably above current river levels and somewhat higher than the investigated soil changes indicative of standing water. Live oaks are upland trees that are killed or injured by water standing over the roots for extended periods. The lowest live oak found at the site south of Structure S-65 was a 1.05-foot diameter tree growing at an elevation of 53.74 feet. At Fort Kissimmee, the lowest live oak was a 1.3-foot diameter tree situated at an elevation of 47.27 feet. A lower upland tree was encountered at this site: a persimmon . . . with a diameter of 0.25 foot was growing at 46.24 feet. The small size of this tree means that it probably became established during the post-regulation period or during the three dry years preceding the onset of regulation.[100]

Two general points of interest emerge from the report: First, there is a clear effort to follow the courts' guidance concerning the evidence of the OHWL. The authors outline a methodology defining the natural indicators of the OHWL prior to regulation and present detailed evidence of those indicators. Second, it is apparent that the type of training required to produce and interpret evidence of an OHWL has clearly moved beyond what a layperson—perhaps even a surveyor—could be expected to have. It seems that as the trustees and their staff moved to bring their understanding of the OHWL into compliance with the ruling case law, their methodology would necessarily move beyond what would be immediately apparent to an ordinary person.

In October 1978, Attorney General Robert Shevin called a meeting with key personnel from the state's Departments of Natural Resources, Environmental Regulation, and Administration to formulate a plan for the protection of sovereignty lands. As part of the strategy developed during the meeting, Shevin wrote, "The DNR and the Attorney General's Office will work to produce a modern practical definition of 'navigable waters,' 'ordinary high water,' and 'mean high water' to be used by the state and adopted by rule or statute, as appropriate."[101] After all that had happened, it seemed impossible that the OHWL was still without statutory certification or common understanding. Perhaps it could be counted as progress, however, that, like the students of Socrates, Florida's sovereignty land managers were finally being called upon to define what had so long been spoken of without clarity.

The Bureau of Coastal and Land Boundaries, under the guidance of Chief George M. Cole, responded to the attorney general's request with a draft of proposed water boundary legislation. The draft proposed a definition of navigable water bodies, declaring those to be owned by the state;

defined standards to be used in determining the boundaries of navigable, nontidal waters; and provided for a procedure for approval of the location of such water boundaries by the trustees. Cole's definition of navigable waters followed closely the prescription of case law: "All natural waters are deemed navigable and under the public trust so long as they are in fact navigable to the extent that said waters are used, or susceptible of being used, in their ordinary condition as highways for commerce over which trade and travel are, or may be, conducted in the customary modes of travel on water."[102] Cole then expanded on the phrase "customary modes of travel," interpreting the court's words thus: "Commercial navigation, as used here, shall be construed to mean easily navigated, at average or ordinary high water, by vessels such as commercial fishing vessels such as mullet boats."[103] Cole's attempt to prescribe the customary modes of travel over Florida's inland streams and rivers would become controversial in the coming decades, especially as the courts began to hear testimony from historians concerning the actual types of vessels customarily used in trade during the mid-1800s.[104]

The bureau's proposal also included "Standards for Establishment of Boundaries of Non-Tidal Water Bodies." This section described the means of determining the OHWL, saying it would be located "at the intersection of the rising bank and the water body at the stage which is exceeded only 25 percent of the time." Daily water stage records made over the ten-year period immediately preceding the determination were to be used for the stage determination. In the absence of adequate stage records, the OHWL was to be located "as indicated by physical characteristics such as a natural line impressed on the bank; shelving; changes in the character of the soil; destruction of terrestrial vegetation; the presence of litter and debris; or other appropriate means that consider the characteristics of the surrounding areas."[105] The proposal further stipulated that locating and mapping an OHWL was to be performed "by or under the direction of qualified personnel licensed by the Florida State Board of Professional Engineers and Land Surveyors or, when accepted by the staff of the Division [of State Lands], by representatives of the United States Government."[106] Notice to the DNR and approval by the board of trustees was required for any boundary of any natural, nontidal water body, and the department was charged with coordinating the efforts of all public and private agencies making OHWL determinations. In light of the division's limited investigatory capabilities, it was hoped that the provisions for notice and trustee approval would help the state detect adverse claims on sovereignty lands before illegal encroachments became securely established. But the legislature failed to act on the bureau's proposal, and no law was forthcoming concerning the location of the OHWL.

The Urgent Need for Sovereignty Lands Protection

By the middle of the twentieth century, the buying and selling of land in this country had become mired in the difficulty of obtaining a marketable title record. Exhaustive title searches going back to the root of title were required under the then-current laws, and the time and expense of such searches severely hindered the transfer of property. In Florida, finding the root of title usually meant searching back to the time of statehood or further into the past, to the Spanish or British period. "In answer to the problem," explained one report to the Florida Department of Natural Resources, "state legislatures created laws enabling titles more easily to possess a marketable record. This usually was done stipulating a fair period of time after which liens and claims against property were extinguished. A title search, therefore, was confined to a much shorter recent period, and titles became more marketable by reason of having no old, hidden claims upon them."[107]

In 1963, Florida passed its Marketable Record Title Act (MRTA), which facilitated land transactions by extinguishing any claim more than thirty years old against the property being transacted. The law worked very well for its intended purposes. Unfortunately, because the legislature failed to specifically exempt sovereignty lands from the effect of MRTA—also called the Title Act—riparian landowners soon discovered that the law worked equally well for an unintended purpose: the transfer of thousands of acres of sovereignty lands into private hands. The first hint that sovereign lands could be in trouble came a decade after the Title Act was passed. A report to the DNR described how the crisis began:

> A case involving only 4 acres along the intracoastal waterway in Palm Beach County was won when the defendant claimed that, under MRTA and his 30-year chain of title, the state's sovereignty claim was extinguished. Four years later, the Deltona Corporation used MRTA to win title to several lakes in central Florida ranging from 140 acres to less than 50. . . . These cases started a landslide of similar legal actions when landowners adjacent to sovereign lands began to realize that, under the 30-year provision of MRTA, the state was unable to maintain its ownership.[108]

Although many of these lakes were too small to be considered by the state as sovereignty lands, the use of MRTA to affirm their private ownership opened the door to much more substantial claims on large, navigable water bodies that did contain sovereignty lands. In 1978, alarmed by the loss of sovereignty lands under the Title Act's operation, the legislature enacted an amendment clarifying that MRTA did not apply to sovereign lands. However, because the measure failed to stipulate that it was retroactive to 1963, when MRTA became law, the courts ruled that the sovereign lands exception applied only from 1978 onward.[109] As a result, the state continued losing sovereignty lands in the cases already filed. In one case alone involving Lake Poinsett (on the St. Johns River) five entire sections and parts of three more sections of sovereignty lands were converted to private ownership.[110] By 1985, some 55,000 acres of sovereignty lands had been converted to private property, and it was clear that with the Title Act's unrestrained operation, Florida's sovereignty lands were in danger of evaporating altogether. But when bills to repeal MRTA were introduced in the senate that year, strong opposition arose from the phosphate industry, cattlemen, developers, ranchers, agribusiness, foresters, the Farm Bureau, and others, arguing that the state was trying to take their property.[111]

"The row got so loud," the report noted, "that the legislature enacted a one-year temporary moratorium on the use of MRTA as a legal vehicle to divest the state of its sovereign lands, and created a Marketable Record Title Act Study Commission to study the effects of MRTA on state lands." In February 1986, the commission recommended that "the legislature enact a statute clarifying that Chapter 63-133 did not and was never intended to be utilized to deprive the State of ownership of sovereignty lands." In addition, the commission stated: "We also believe a methodology must be adopted for administrative resolution of boundaries between sovereignty and non-sovereignty lands."[112]

In the meantime, the DNR, as staff to the trustees, had issued a contract for the determination of the OHWL of Lake Kissimmee in the upper Kissimmee River Valley. Following case law, the department had developed a methodology it hoped would be defensible in the almost inevitable court challenges that would result from establishing the line. But the challengers were not about to wait for the line to be set.

Looking out over the cove I felt a strong
sense of the interchangeability of land and
sea in this marginal world of the shore,
and of the links between the life of the two.
RACHEL CARSON, *The Edge of the Sea*

4 Drawing the Line: The Changing Status of the Natural World

THE LEGISLATURE'S DECISION in 1976 to restore the Kissimmee River Basin signaled the blossoming of ecological policymaking in Florida. In the late 1940s, the Water Control District had recognized the need for a coordinated approach to central and south Florida's water problems; but with the focus on controlling the waters, an understanding of the ecological relationships in the basin was hardly pursued.[1] To a large degree, it was the unprecedented success of the Army Corps in containing the Kissimmee in the 1960s that galvanized environmental research, for the very reason that the project's accomplishment produced such widespread environmental damage.[2] By the late 1970s, biologists, botanists, geologists, hydrologists, and ecologists had amassed a substantial body of scientific data that made possible a more complex understanding of the Kissimmee River Basin—and of the natural world in general.

The ditching of the river also had a far-reaching effect in that it provided a highly visible example of the power of technology to overrun the ways of the natural world—an example understandable not only to scientists, but to people in all walks of life. Lifetime area resident Scott Boland describes his experience:

> We were all for it [the channelization of the Kissimmee] because they sold it to us in a way that they were just going to run a canal right down the middle of the river and all of the oxbows and riverbends would be places to hunt and fish. The water would be regulated with a series of dams, and in front of every dam would be virtually a large lake that we visualized would be more area to hunt and fish— and for recreation. When I came down here [to the river] and they were doing [the dredging], I had a lot of second thoughts. It looked like they were digging the Panama Canal. They had giant dredges pumping the spoil out into the woods—into what was the marsh. The dead rivers or oxbows, a lot of them were filled up with the spoil. Spoil banks went all the way to the hammocks.[3]

The enormous scale of the project and such immediate, obvious effects as the decimation of the fish and wading bird populations distressed people who had known the natural river. (Scientists reported an "immediate 90% reduction in waterfowl" when the river was ditched.)[4] As a result, the destruction of the Kissimmee Valley's ecosystem gave wide currency to important fundamentals of ecology, which, in turn, changed the way people thought about the river.

The River Lost, the River Found

If the voice of the river had long been drowned out by the din of building the Florida empire, the ideas that now began emerging from the ongoing environmental studies made the river central to a very different story. Observers of the river now began focusing on the elegance of nature's design and how the impact of human engineering had destroyed much of the river's capacity to sustain life. William Barada pointed out that prior to human interference the basin's natural ecosystem had kept its shallow lakes and rivers healthy and productive through a complex combination of interactions. Seasonal fluctuations in the water levels resulted from prevailing rainfall and weather conditions. When water levels dropped during dry periods, shorelines were exposed, organic muck and detritus dried and oxidized, and seeds germinated to produce prolific marsh-type vegetation. This plant growth, in turn, allowed a host of organisms and wildlife to thrive. During times of heavy rainfall, runoff from upland areas made its way through the marshes and floodplains. Here the nutrient-rich storm water was filtered by the marsh vegetation, which converted dissolved minerals and chemicals into additional food for fish and other organisms. As storm waters made their way downstream to Lake Okeechobee and on into the Everglades, the Kissimmee's vast floodplains cleaned and slowed the waters, ensuring high water quality and conserving fresh water in the basin where it would be needed in times of drought.[5] "It was an abundance of wildlife," Scott Boland recalls. "Any kind of wildlife that Florida might grow was in this river valley."

Prior to the channelization, this abundance was taken for granted; it seemed a given. "No one here realized the awesome destruction that would occur to the aquatic system or to the terrestrial systems," says longtime river observer Roy Coffee, "in other words that through the destruction of habitat the wildlife would be just decimated."[6] By the late 1970s, however, it had become well known that destroying a river's marshes and floodplains also destroyed its capacity for self-cleansing and its ability to retain water. As a result, the river's value as a life-supporting habitat for fish and wildlife were decimated. Osceola County Commissioner Chuck Dunnick, asked in an interview what people had learned from the Kissimmee's story, commented, "Number one—the environment and how fragile it is in this state. . . . Anytime you start fooling with the natural way that things have been—which is the reason why everything's so pristine and pretty— once you change that, there are going to be some things happen that you might not know about 'til fifteen or twenty years down the line."[7]

Restoring the river, however, was expected to cost some $343 million and involve years of work. To sustain such an investment would require a broad-based political will rooted in the new ecological awareness. Restoring the river would also depend on the acceptance of the science that had developed as the means to this new understanding—not only for the technical know-how needed to recover the Kissimmee, but to make plain why the recovery was essential. For in the opinion of some people, the idea of spending millions of taxpayer dollars to restore the river was simply unnecessary: nature would take care of the problems. "The environment has healed itself, the animals are all back at home," Dunnick commented. "Let's just leave it alone."[8] For other people—including most of the waterfront property owners from Kissimmee to the Everglades—the idea of taking back the very benefits the ditching had provided showed that the state agencies had been overrun with "tree huggers," who would take a person's private property or cut off his or her means of making a living in order to preserve a bird habitat. In an interview with WFTV, one rancher expressed his fears that a restored river would not provide the flood protection afforded by the channel. Although relatively few people would be affected by reflooding the old river, he said, "those people are being sacrificed. There are many things that could be done for half a billion dollars that would be more appreciated by the general public," the rancher noted. "I am opposed to spending it on the river."[9]

Perhaps most controversial of all, however, was the use of the "new" environmental sciences to establish the boundary lines between private and public lands along the river. Under the restoration proposal, some 75,000 acres of land were to be acquired for reflooding. This meant that the controversial ordinary high water line would once more come to the forefront in an already tense situation. For many of the people holding deeds to lands along the river, the use of botany, hydrology, and geology as a basis for setting boundary lines seemed a radical departure from time-honored means of determining property ownership and setting public land policy. The commitment to go forward with the restoration demonstrated a heightened consciousness among Floridians of how vulnerable natural ecosystems are to human tampering and how important they are to sustaining all life. But the practical problems faced by those responsible for the actual restoration were anything but solved.

The Authority of Marshmallows

In the early 1980s, trouble erupted at the river's headwaters in Lake Kissimmee. Part of the chain of lakes forming the upper Kissimmee Valley watershed, Lake Kissimmee in its natural state had flowed directly into the Kissimmee River. With the channelization of the river in the 1960s, ordinary high fluctuations in Lake Kissimmee's water levels were significantly reduced,[10] and the lake was regulated by a control structure (S-65) at its juncture with the river. When, in 1980, a drought caused the lake to recede still further,[11] developers around the lake began dredging large trenches along the shoreline. Department of Natural Resources staff stepped in, claiming the developers were encroaching on sovereignty lands. Preliminary investigations indicated that the OHWL would have to be determined in order to substantiate the state's claims, but obtaining funds for such a massive project would require cabinet involvement.

Bureau of Surveying and Mapping records contain notes prepared for presenting the case to the cabinet.[12] The talk, entitled "The Kissimmee Dilemma," began by outlining five points illustrating how the dilemma came about:

1. Prior to regulation Lake Kissimmee varied from a high of 56.6 msl [mean sea level] (in 1953) down to 44.2 msl (in 1962).
2. Various governmental agencies have since taken artificial control of the water levels of Lake Kissimmee.
3. Pre-regulation studies *were conducted* and determined the OHW level prior to regulation to be 53.75 msl. However, this level was *never submitted to or approved by the Board of Trustees* of the Internal Improvement Trust Fund. The top of the spillway gate at structure S-65 was, however, placed at elevation 53.4 msl and is representative of those studies.
4. Due to the shortfall of rain over the past 20 years and the lack of flexibility to compensate accordingly on the part of the regulating agencies the regulated high pool stage of 52.5 msl was reached only 3 times between 1970 and 1980. Naturally **the wetland vegetation, which is the basis of most environmental regulatory authority,** disappeared with the water.
5. In 1980 development-oriented interests began purchasing the historical flood prone pasture along the shore of Lake Kissimmee and immediately began dig and fill development operations.[13]

In summary, the talk stated, with no wetland vegetation and no cabinet-approved OHWL, there could be no control of these activities. Remarkable in point four is the unabashed statement that wetland vegetation forms the basis of regulatory authority. The assertion that the authority to regulate water levels is based not solely in statutes or judicial determinations, but in such things as buttonbushes and marshmallows, illustrates the degree to which state policymakers have incorporated the findings of the environmental sciences. It is an indication of the changing status of the natural world.

The second part of the Kissimmee Dilemma talk took up the issue of enforcement status in three points:

1. The Corps of Engineers and South Florida Water Management District *claim no jurisdiction whatever* over dig and fill [*sic*] activities located landward of the berm, even though they know the area will be under water at their own high pool control elevation. Reason—the State has never officially confirmed an OHW line on Lake Kissimmee.
2. The Department of Environmental Regulation served notice on 11/24/81 stating their jurisdiction up to elevation 53.74 msl. However, *no further ju-*

risdictional action will take place until the OHW line is officially confirmed by the Cabinet.

3. The DNR, which is the responsible agency for making this determination, now states there are *no funds available* to do the survey. ($96,000).[14]

A handwritten comment in the margins pleads: "20 months have now past [*sic*] since this issue was brought to the State's attention. Help!" In conclusion the talk detailed four points:

1. Until the DNR and Cabinet officially confirm the OHW Line of Lake Kissimmee, the public interest is solely at the mercy of the actual water level on any given day in question.

2. In essence, if the subject area is dry at the time of dig and fill, it is considered permissible and one must remember that this lake is scheduled to fluctuate 4 feet every year (48.5 to 52.5).

3. The public interest and the health of Lake Kissimmee is [*sic*] in jeopardy until the OHW Line is established by the Cabinet.

4. $96,000 is actually a meager sum to spend to protect the public interest when compared to the vast lake bottom acreage that will otherwise be lost to private development interests. (8500 acres as per the last page in this book.)[15]

As the Division of State Lands undertook measures to go forward with the OHWL, landowners around Lake Kissimmee began organizing to protect their interests. Generally, the landowners divided into two groups: those (landowners and others) who opposed the recent lake-bottom dredging by developers and looked to the state to protect the lake, and those who wanted no interference from the state in their use of (what they perceived to be their) private property.

Correspondence between the landowners and various members of the trustees' staff indicates that the prevailing understandings of exactly what constituted an OHWL determination still comprised a broad range. In a letter to Department of Natural Resources counsel Lee Rohe, the attorney for several small landowners on the lake wrote that he would be glad to meet with Rohe at the contested site. "I hope," he wrote, "it will be possible to also have your technical person on the site to point out his determination of the ordinary high water mark."[16] In light of the brouhaha about to unfold, the attorney's assumption that a "technical person" could simply show up and "point out his determination" of the OHWL appears as the last vestige of the era when it was believed that the mark needed "no scientific exploration to find."[17] Especially considering the near certainty that the Lake Kissimmee line would be challenged in court, an informal indication of the boundary would not be sufficient. But DNR's response is nearly as nostalgic. In a memo to Douglas Thompson, chief of the Bureau of Surveying and Mapping, Rohe wrote:

> Rather than leave it up to laymen or strictly to the discretion of a private surveyor, I think it important that you play a role in helping us find the "historic" ohw mark or approximation thereof. Then, perhaps we could enter into a boundary agreement with these two small lot owners without spending time or money on a formal determination.[18]

Set aside the fact that the "historic" OHWL Rohe alludes to has been ruled an improper boundary by the Supreme Court; Rohe's hope that such an approximation of the OHWL to settle the boundary with two small lot owners would avoid a formal determination on Lake Kissimmee dredges up the image of a boy with his finger in the dike. Of course, it's possible that what Rohe had in mind was having Thompson locate the prechannelization or postdrainage OHWL, but his use of the term "historic" nevertheless indicates the prevailing confusion.

At the other end of the scale, however, is correspondence indicating a remarkably comprehensive understanding of the OHWL and its current situation. In a letter to the State Lands Division director Henry Dean in late 1982, Bob Quinn, serving as Polk County Director of the Save Our Lakes organization, expressed the group's concern over the proposed methodology for establishing the OHWL. In doing so, Quinn gave early voice to a problem that would, by decade's end, escalate into a full-scale crisis for the surveying profession. Quinn opened his letter:

> I have several reservations concerning the wisdom of placing the *prime contract* to conduct the Kissimmee ordinary high water elevation determination in the hands of an ordinary surveyor.
>
> As I am sure you are aware, the *expertise* required to make such determination rests primarily in the academic and practical training of the Geologist, Botanist, Soil Scientist, Hydrologist and Dendro Chronologist, trained specifically in wetland boundary and ordinary high water determinations, wetlands distinction, the geology and botany of uplands and wetlands environments and transition areas. The chain puller, or surveyor, is normally the least technically trained member of the team, as shooting an elevation or laying a line is the same as any other ordinary survey, for all practical purposes.
>
> To place the *prime contract* in the hands of an ordinary surveyor and depend upon him to select and evaluate the quality of the academic and practical train-

ing expertise of the individual team members, borders on the absurd. It would be the same as giving the prime contract to construct a skyscraper to the painter and depending upon his knowledge to qualify and intelligently select the appropriate architect and general contractor. He couldn't.[19]

Quinn then went on to detail the reasons why State Lands could ill afford to make a mistake in establishing the OHWL:

The ordinary high water determination of Lake Kissimmee is *most critical* to the public interest for several reasons.

Lake bottom development encroachment has been going on for the past 20 months and continues in process.

No state, federal or local agency can, or will, take effective enforcement action until the D.N.R. has established this line.

Lake Kissimmee is only the first in a chain of several lakes that will eventually experience this problem and the decisions made on Kissimmee will set the precedent for the others.

Whatever the ordinary high water decision turns out to be it will surely be contested in court and it is just too damned important to let this project be botched by a bunch of amateurs and trainees.[20]

Quinn then outlined qualifying requirements of the OHWL team and prime contractor that he felt should "go out with the invitations to bid":

(1) All team members must have had academic and practical training and experience (in their respective fields) in wetlands boundary and ordinary high water line determinations, wetlands distinction and the geology and botany of wetlands and uplands environments and transition areas.

(2) The team must include a geologist, botanist, soil scientist, hydrologist and dendro chronologist, each with previous experience in southern ecosystems in riparian and littoral situations, specifically here in Florida, in the determination of ordinary high water lines for legal/scientific purposes.

(3) Each team member must also have a working knowledge of the applicable law relative to ordinary high water line determination.

(4) Each team member must have a working knowledge of case law history pertaining to ordinary high water line determination and what it means.

(5) In addition to all of the above the surveyor that is to act as the *prime contractor* must also have had *extensive* ordinary high water line determination experience including the evaluation, selection, assembly and successful leadership of such a team. Any surveyor that does not meet these requirements should not be allowed to bid on this job.

In spite of Quinn's obvious distrust of surveyors acting as the prime contractors for OHWL determinations, his letter leaves little doubt of the sophistication of at least some Floridians with regard to the intricacies of the OHWL. His comments also suggest, however, the view that such professionals as he described—having extensive experience and academic training in ordinary high water line determinations—were actually plentiful, or at least existent. In actuality, professionals were only beginning to wrestle with the controversies of OHWL determinations.

Drawing the Line

In January 1983, Florida's governor and cabinet authorized the Department of Natural Resources to determine Lake Kissimmee's OHWL, and on June 17 the department contracted E. R. Brownell and Associates—a surveying group—to determine, with the aid of scientists, what the OHWL of the lake was prior to the channelization of the Kissimmee River.[21] The *Daily Highlander,* a local newspaper, reported in July that a "state Cabinet-authorized survey team seeking to legally define the ordinary high-water level of Lake Kissimmee today is operating out of Camp Lester east of Lake Wales."[22] The report detailed two reasons why the survey was of critical interest to those in the region:

> First, [the survey] should determine where state land, or the lake and its edges, ends and where private property begins. That question has long thrown a hitch into plans by private owners to develop properties around the lake.
>
> Second, and more importantly, the survey's findings could have far-reaching effects on the lake itself and its levels, on plans to return the Kissimmee River to a more natural state, and on recurrent man-caused flooding of the Florida Everglades.
>
> Environmentalists believe the whole water problem begins with Lake Kissimmee and its river. Many feel the lake, and the river if put into a more natural state, could hold a lot more water than they do now.
>
> They say that by storing more water upstream, the controlling South Florida Water Management District wouldn't have to release tons of water from Lake Okeechobee into the Everglades during wet weather.
>
> Private property owners around Lake Kissimmee, the river, Lake Okeechobee and the Everglades view the entire idea with a jaundiced eye. Many are afraid higher water levels upstream would cause them to lose land recovered from swamp when the river was channelized by the U.S. Corps of Engineers.[23]

The *Highlander* article went on to describe the methodology being used to determine the OHWL. A botanist on the surveying team told the *Highlander* the survey was to be "highly scientific in methodology. Using surveying instruments, we're laying out transects from the present water edge and shooting to high points." [24] By analyzing plant samples from each transect, scientists could determine the elevations where shifts from more aquatic to more upland plants occurred. Likewise, soil samples would indicate the lake's movement and where the upland soils began.

Early in 1984 notice of public meetings and articles discussing the OHWL determination began appearing in local newspapers. An article in the *Orlando Sentinel* pointed out that the state wasn't the only group hosting public meetings on the controversial topic. "The state Department of Natural Resources and a landowners group—the two competing interests fighting over Lake Kissimmee's legal boundary—will hold separate public meetings this month to explain where they think the line ought to be drawn." The landowners organized as the Chain of Lakes Property Owners, "a group composed mostly of ranchers," the *Sentinel* said, and their meeting was "simply to air the association's side of the dispute." The DNR meeting, to be held at the Osceola County Courthouse, would provide the last opportunity for public input before the agency made its final recommendation on the boundary to the trustees. [25]

Consultants hired by the ranchers' group estimated that the OHWL would fall at about 50 feet above mean sea level. The DNR proposal put the line at 53.1 feet above mean sea level. At stake in the discrepancy between the two figures were thousands of acres of prime cattle pasture. "The property owners association sees that [OHWL elevation] as a state-supported grab for land that the ranchers have used for three or four generations," the *Sentinel* reported. On the other hand, "DNR officials say they are trying to establish what legally belongs to the state. If the boundary is set at 53.1 feet, the state automatically would assume ownership of several thousands of acres of land," estimated between 2,000 and 10,000 acres. "State officials think the lower number [of acres] is correct; the ranchers say the higher figure is more accurate."

According to Allen Whitson, director of the ranchers' group, "What we are trying to get across to the public is that this is not a large-landowner issue and it's not an environmental issue, but it's a property owner issue." The *Sentinel* went on to explain that the "argument over the boundary goes back to the 1981 drought. In that year, four Polk County developers started dredging large trenches along the lake's shoreline. State officials claimed the developers were digging up state-owned lake bottom, but they couldn't prove it. The wetland vegetation that by law must be present to prove it was lake bottom had been killed by the drought."[26]

On February 15, 1984, the ranchers' group held its public meeting in Kissimmee, Florida, to discuss the state's boundary determination along the shorelines of the various waterbodies in the Kissimmee Chain of Lakes. (The lakes comprising this chain include Lake Kissimmee, Lake Cypress, Lake Rosalie, Lake Hatchineha, and Lake Tohopekaliga. These lakes lie upstream of the Kissimmee River and constitute a major source of the river's water.) Among those present at the meeting were Whitson and some forty-two property owners; the group's attorney, Alan Cummings of the Holland and Knight firm; and Douglas Thompson of DNR's Bureau of Surveying and Mapping.

Thompson's report describes Whitson opening the meeting with several comments, among them that the ranchers' group had already paid over $61,000 in legal and engineering fees for preliminary OHWL strategies and that they "haven't even started yet."[27] Whitson bemoaned their "unfortunate position fighting an opponent who uses taxpayer dollars to oppose us." There followed a presentation on early statehood history concerning the state's early efforts to establish a healthy tax base and outlining the state's flood control efforts.[28] Next, their lawyer addressed the group. He discussed a current lawsuit Holland and Knight was handling on Lake Cypress concerning the OHWL and asserted that, "because Lake Cypress is a non-meandered lake, private ownership extends to the lake's center." (Lake Cypress—like all navigable freshwaters, meandered or not—is considered by the state to be sovereignty lands.) "Today," Cummings noted, "we filed a lawsuit on Lake Kissimmee," which he characterized as a meandered lake requiring the establishment of OHW elevation. Following a discussion by Cummings of OHWL definitions and how to establish OHWL, the meeting was opened to public questions. In his report, Thompson paraphrased several of the questions along with Cummings's answers:

Q. (Whitson) Would the State "take" a man's house and land if below OHW?
A. (Cummings) What you think you own, you may not own under the theory of OHW.
Q. Does the State have a bureau that assures all OHW surveys are consistent?
A. (Cummings) The State does not have a State Land Inventory. However, no bureau really polices all state-owned land boundary problems.

Q. Does the State use the same laws (interpretation) in residential areas as in agricultural lands?

A. (Cummings) In the Peace River case the State made a claim against the phosphate industry which is different from Lake Kissimmee v. Ranchers—it seems inconsistent to me.[29]

The questions at this meeting address much the same concerns as the 1971 public hearings on the Kissimmee Lakes boundary lines. People are concerned about losing their property and about the fairness and consistency of the state's proceedings. And, once again, there are inaccuracies in the information being distributed.

Perhaps the most startling aspect of the ranchers' meeting, however, addressed the issue of scientific data and its use in establishing the OHWL. In the earlier (1971) public hearings some objection to the state's use of scientific evidence had surfaced. But at the conclusion of the meeting, a new strategy marked a step-up in organized resistance to the state's reliance on scientific evidence. Whitson asked all attendees to sign a petition stating:

> We, the undersigned, petition the State of Florida, more specifically the Trustees of the Internal Improvement Fund, to oppose the establishment of private property ownership through the application of scientific methodologies. We further petition that establishment of private property ownership should, as it has been in the past, be established by but not limited to original conveyances, warranty deeds, federal land patents, property tax payments and legisled law currently in existence.[30]

Although the petitioners here object to the use of science to establish private property boundaries and to make title determinations, I don't think we read this as an objection to science per se. I don't imagine, for example, that these same petitioners would object to scientifically tested methods their surgeons might require to perform bypass surgery or Monsanto engineers might need to provide new pesticides. Nor does their objection seem aimed at a surveyor's use of triangulation, for example, in establishing a boundary line (even though triangulation would seem to qualify as an application of science to private property determinations).

To understand what's at stake in the objection, it's helpful to note that the petitioners also object to what they perceive as a departure from established ways of determining property title—that is, the science they object to is not part of *the way things have been done in the past*. They cite what they see as traditional practices of establishing ownership in contrast to the use of scientific methodologies—original conveyances, warranty deeds, federal land patents, property tax payments. This objection—that the trustees have changed the rules pertaining to sovereignty lands boundaries—remains a key complaint in current OHWL conflicts. In one such instance a riparian owner complained that:

> The State's OHWL determinations in the past were made in the context of a federal and state goal to facilitate the improvement of the millions of acres of swamp and overflowed lands that were patented to the State. However, the methodology used by the Division of State Lands has changed in recent years due primarily to the advent of state interest in environmental protection.[31]

In this charge, which is meant to demonstrate that the state has been unjust, the plaintiff relies on a basic argument that policy has changed. But it is quite normal for policy to change over the course of a century and a half, and this does not of itself prove the state's injustice. The state's responsibilities in the context of a nineteenth-century frontier requiring internal improvements and settlement would reasonably differ from those the state would face in the context of a modern technological society, already highly populated and rapidly developing. As to the specific complaint that the OHWL methodology has changed, the methodology for determining the OHWL has been developing in response to case law since the time of Justinian (circa 534 C.E.), through British law to the thirteen American colonies, through statehood of the colonies in 1776 to each new state joining the Union on an equal footing with the original thirteen. In reality this methodology existed in an embryonic stage 1,500 years ago, evolving sporadically over the centuries until the problems of the modern state compelled its clarification.

But this particular grievance reveals much in its last eight words: "the advent of state interest in environmental protection." I think this plaintiff's grievance, and that of the rancher petitioners, has to do not with science and not with the fact that state policy changes; it has to do with the changing status of the natural world in the American consciousness and courts.[32] This is a different phenomenon than the objection to science as untrustworthy. For the rancher plaintiffs, the authority of science is a given, and that is why its findings are so troubling. The plaintiffs are well aware of the weight scientific findings will have in any reasoned decision. Their opposition to the "application of scientific methodologies" objects not to science, but to the authority science gives to the evidence of the natural world—evidence that the plaintiffs see as adverse to their interests. In effect, the involvement of science in locating the ordinary high water line gives the natural world a legal standing it did not have in the past, and such plaintiffs see this change as one more infringement on their already shrinking rights.

Scientific Evidence

Whether the ranchers' petition ever found its way to the trustees is not a matter of record, but what might have served as a decisive answer to their appeal was not long in coming. The state opened its public hearing on February 28, 1984, with a detailed and comprehensive presentation by the team of scientists and surveyors who had been working for six months to determine the ordinary high water line of Lake Kissimmee. DNR Executive Director Elton Gissendanner opened the hearing by reviewing the situation of Lake Kissimmee, pointing out that the drought two years previous had exposed a lot of land and resulted in encroachment on the lake bottom. "The Department was asked to protect state lands," Gissendanner said. "There was no intent to take land, but simply to find out what is owned by the public. . . . Let the consultants tell you what they've done. Ask questions. By July we'll have a more complete database; we'll put some monuments on the ground and have some maps you can look at."[33]

Gissendanner introduced E. R. Brownell, project manager and surveyor in charge of coordinating the team's efforts. Brownell began the presentation by citing the Florida statutes guiding the effort and then stated the goal: "The object of our efforts was to identify the ordinary high water line of Lake Kissimmee as it existed prior to the construction of the water control structure at the south end of the lake in 1964." (It was important to clarify this purpose because many of those attending had brought concerns about how Lake Kissimmee was being regulated, and the state hoped to keep clear the point that this hearing was over the sovereignty lands boundary—not the lake level regulation schedule.) Brownell explained that in order to prepare a survey in accordance with the legal definition of the OHWL, a multidisciplinary team of scientists and professionals[34] followed the "physical fact" method indicated by such court decisions as *Tilden v. Smith* and *Howard v. Ingersoll*. He then outlined the procedure that the OHWL team had followed in order to decide where the line would have been on Lake Kissimmee prior to its control. The characteristics of the vegetation, the soils, and the geomorphology; the information from the literature, maps, and documents; the items of historical significance; and the compilation of the hydrological data, Brownell explained, were examined by the surveyors in order to make a physical comparison of evidence. "Each of these items must correlate," he said, "or we must know the reason why they do not."[35]

Brownell then described how the transects were laid out. "Transects," he explained, "are lines that are cut at a 90 degree angle to the lake shore through an area that we want to investigate. The line is made long enough to cover all the pertinent data—up to an elevation high enough that no water level could possibly go any higher. Then a stake is placed every 20 feet along the transect." Once the transects were laid out, he said, the botanist identified the vegetation along the length of each transect and, at locations where the vegetation noticeably changed, additional stakes were placed and samples were taken. "The botanist, the dendrochronologist (who determines the age of the trees and studies the vegetation), the geologist, and surveyor all worked together," Brownell pointed out. "The botanist identified and measured the abundance and density of the plant species at each sampling station. The dendrochronologist took core samples from the dominant trees to determine age (and we found the trees that were older than 20 years—those that had been there since before the dam went in—were growing above the 53′ elevation; those that were below 53′ were young trees)," he added. The surveyor took the elevation at the base of each tree that the dendrochronologist sampled and marked the tree with a numbered aluminum tag. The geologist identified the relevant sites in the land surface and the lakeshore geological features. The surveyor took the elevation where each sampling was made and each feature was found. "The features were analyzed for continuity," Brownell said, "for uniformity of elevation—in other words, if you have a certain thing happening at one elevation we found it happening at that same elevation at a different spot. The surveyor plotted each elevation and prepared profile drawings so that a comparison of these locations could be made. Then a comparison of the things that were happening at each location on the transect was made."[36]

The geologist collected core or trench samples at each sampling station where noticeable changes in the vegetation occurred. Soil sediment samples were taken with a hand auger or by trenching, and organic compounds, the grain size, and sorting characteristics were determined for each sample. "All the vertical data pertaining to the transect study lines were related to the National Geodetic Vertical Datum (NGVD) of 1929," Brownell explained, "and the surveyor provided an overall plan-view showing the horizontal location of all the study transects." The surveying was carried out using calibrated electronic distance measuring equipment and precision leveling equipment to second-order standards. "Pertinent precipitation and lake level data was obtained by the hydrologist," Brownell went on, "and the levels that he found also correlated with and confirmed the studies made before him. He made a detailed hydrologic analysis based on the records collected after 50 years. The surveyor assisted in gathering wind factor data to determine if the wind blowing across the lake makes a difference as to elevation." [37]

"One other thing we did was to go into the history of [the area]," Brownell pointed out. By comparing aerial photos of the same scale dating back to 1937, the team was able to see the advancement of the trees toward the lake after the dam was put in. "We were also able to see some changes in the configurations of the berms in the lake," Brownell said. "This was very useful." The team found that post-1960 was a drier cycle than any other in the period of record. Whereas the average annual rainfall for the entire period of record (back to 1929) was approximately fifty inches, rainfall for 1980 was only thirty inches, and for 1981 and 1982 only forty-five inches. Brownell also interviewed long-time residents in the area. They provided information about changes going back to the 1930s and in one case back to 1925. "They said there used to be less coot grass," Brownell noted. "Wider lake level fluctuations back then kept the grass from growing as well. They also said the shore was sandy, the fishing was better, and the water higher. They said the big differences were pollution, the numbers of people, and people's signs—they're unhappy with the things people throw overboard and the bottles they leave around when they camp nearby." [38]

Detailed presentations by a geologist, a botanist, and a hydrologist followed. The geologist, Dr. Thomas Patten, explained that the physical fact criteria indicating the OHWL formed the basis of his work. His job was to determine the features of the lake that revealed its geomorphic history, which would indicate where the OHWL was or had been at some point in the past. "We look at soils and sediments, soils beneath the surface, features eroded by waves at the edge of the lake. We do a reconnaissance of the lake, looking for geologic features such as scarps, terraces, former beaches," he said. "We set up transects based on undisturbed natural features. Then any feature that is distinctive, we measure to note the location on our transect." The surveyor measures the horizontal distance of the feature from the shoreline and marks its elevation. Then a geologic profile is created. Soil samples are taken and examined for the sorting and winnowing of sediments, sand grain sizes, and the amount of clay and organic material in each sample. "These aspects are indicative of water levels and the degree of submergence in that area over a period of time," he said.[39]

After the data is gathered, the elevations of distinctive features are plotted. "What we are looking for is whether the geomorphic features we think are indicating the level of the OHW submergence correlate at the same elevation. Does the scarp we think represents the former OHWL occur at a consistent elevation around the lake?" the geologist asked. "These features correlate and occur at the same elevation within a few tenths of a foot with amazing regularity." On Lake Kissimmee several sets of scarps were found indicating shifts in the lake levels. "There were very high historic elevations from thousands of years in the past to very low levels below even the present controlled levels," he observed. "We had to find where the last real impression of the lake was before control." Three sets of scarps fell into that hydrological range: one set at about 52 feet, one set at approximately 53–53.5 feet, and one set at a little above 54 feet. "At the lower part of the range (52 feet) the extent of geological working indicated the water levels were at that elevation too long for a high water level. The submergence was too frequent, indicating something more like an average," he explained. "At the other extreme (54+ feet) the soils and sediments were alluviated [distributed, disturbed]. The clay and organic material deposited had been emergent for so long that they were moving down through the profile and had not been replenished by submergence." The set of scarps occurring higher than fifty-three feet mean sea level presented the profile most closely fitting the OHWL criteria. "Here, organic material was undisturbed—unalluviated—indicating that emergence was not prolonged," he said. "And we always encountered organic muck at this elevation, showing that this area had been underwater for a significant period of time." The average elevation of these scarps over all the transects was 53.1 feet.[40]

The botanical component of the OHWL study was then detailed in a report from the team botanist.[41] Because plant communities along lakes and streams respond very closely to changes in water regimes and elevational gradients along the beds and banks of the water bodies, he explained, they produce a physical fact representation of the OHWL. Due to their ability to withstand flooding, many plant species along water bodies exist in community associations dependent upon the specific species' abilities to tolerate the many factors involved in their growth and reproduction, such as available light, moisture, flooding, and nutrient relationship. The typical community response to increased or reduced inundation is that of a community successional change, which responds to higher or lower water levels and durations. In the case of Lake Kissimmee today, he noted, water levels are artificially maintained at particular elevations for fairly long periods of time, and woody vegetative communities are completely removed in the inundated areas—with the exception of strongly tolerant species such as cypress. With rising water levels, he pointed out, a somewhat disjunct plant community of younger, more water tolerant species becomes established up to a higher level where very old, less hydric vegetation is met. Conversely, during very low water conditions or receding water level conditions, the successional trend of the drier-type species occupying higher elevations could be expected to move down and position themselves closer to water levels of the lake. "An abrupt change will generally leave large and older trees positioned at higher elevations with a very rapid invasion by younger species of a fairly even age class at the lower elevations," the botanist said in his report. "More gradual reductions in water levels around a water body could be expected to produce a very graduated or mixed age class distribution of plants from higher elevations down to lower levels." This type of gradation would generally show plant species ranging from seedling to sapling to larger size classes in a progression from near water's edge to higher elevations. These kinds of signatures in the plant communities indicate water levels and durations that allow us to determine the OHWL.[42]

"The primary species indicating ordinary high water conditions on Lake Kissimmee in the past are live oak and slash pine," he noted. "These communities can tolerate water conditions for several days out of the year but cannot withstand prolonged durations of very high water conditions or general lake stillstands which would occur below the OHWL." Conditions prior to the channelization of the Kissimmee River and stabilization of lake levels, he said, very likely allowed a forest community typical of elevations 53.5 feet and higher to occur around the lake. The present successional trend generally is seen occurring below 54-foot elevation down to approximately 52 feet. "This significant change in age class distribution," he said, "provides strong weight to a physical fact OHWL of approximately 53.1 feet, the general point at which the age class of invading oaks and pines show a clear successional trend or change which took place approximately 20 years ago." Only two cases were found in which older live oaks were growing at elevations below 53 feet, he noted, and these were in areas where the erosion of material from the berm created the effect of higher ground. "Older oaks around the 53.3-foot line and the successional trend of the live oaks generally less than 20–25 years old below this level provide a clear physical fact criterion for determination of the OHWL of Lake Kissimmee," he concluded.

The team hydrologist, Dr. Raul McQuivey, then presented the hydrological aspects of the study and explained that the data gathered at Lake Kissimmee was correlated with the hydrological record as one aspect of interpreting the physical evidence. "The hydrological record of Lake Kissimmee goes back to August of 1929," he said, "so that gives us a great deal of data." The hydrologic record reports a daily average, which is based on measurements of the lake level taken every fifteen minutes each day. "Two time frames were of interest to us: the period from 1929 (when the record began) to 1964—just before the control structure was placed at the south end of the lake; and 1965 to the present." Plots were created demonstrating the percent of time elevations were equaled or exceeded by the lake's water levels. "Analysis of 12,705 days of record (the pre-regulation period) would suggest that the OHWL is at an elevation of at least 53 feet NGVD," he said. "This corresponds to a 15 percent time that the Kissimmee Lake elevation has been equaled or exceeded for the uncontrolled/unregulated period of record (1929–1964)."[43]

Gissendanner then opened the floor to comments and questions from audience members. "This is a very complicated piece of business," the first respondent observed. "About 90 percent of the time they were talking over my head, but I was able to follow them sufficiently to realize that the Department has approached this in a very precise and scientific manner." Following this comment, several other hearing participants expressed their appreciation for all the work the team had done to protect public lands, the fisheries, and the future health of the Kissimmee River Valley. Many specifically supported the 53.1-foot OHWL finding the team was recommending as the sovereignty lands boundary line. Yet, problems remained. One homeowner raised the issue of homes that had been built with all the required permits, but which now were found to be on state land. This man had used a USGS quad map to determine where to build his house. "Your experts come here saying 53 feet," he said, "but the USGS map I have says Lake Kissimmee is at 49 feet." In response, state counsel Lee Rohe explained, "You have a quad map based on a photograph taken on a particular day when the lake was at 49 feet elevation. That has nothing to do with the OHWL."[44]

At that point, a local county commissioner rose to speak. He noted that the county was charged with issuing building permits, but that "we did not foresee development as it is occurring." Polk County, he noted, exempts grazing and agricultural activities from permitting. "You can do that anywhere regardless of zoning," he explained. "But you can't build houses, dig canals, dredge and fill regardless of zoning and without permits." The problem for the county and the homeowners, he said, came from the state not setting the OHWL. "We need the state to determine the boundary," he said. "We haven't the funds or the expertise, but we need to know if we're permitting activities on state land." The county had had to establish a moratorium on building on the eastern border of Lake Kissimmee, he noted, until the line was authorized by the governor and cabinet.[45]

A homeowner on Lake Ruby rose to speak. "The public land belongs to the people," she began, "and the state is the guardian. You've just completed the best survey that money and expertise can provide to determine what is public and what is private. Now go the next step. The large landowners are going to challenge the survey in court and they have many thousands of dollars and expert legal help," she said. "Don't be stingy in your defense of your trust."[46]

Another Polk County resident then addressed the survey team. "I've heard the accusation that this survey was told at the outset to establish a certain level. Could the surveyor tell us what his criteria was and just exactly how much influence the state brought to bear on the surveyor to establish the OHWL at a certain level?" To which Brownell responded, "We were asked to determine the OHWL of Lake Kissimmee. We would be subject to license revocation if we did anything else. We were never told or even given a hint of anything else." Gissendanner followed with a further comment. "There was a lot of discussion about whether Dr. Patton (the team geologist) was going to be the prime contractor on this job or whether the licensed surveyor was going to be the prime contractor. As you can tell by what you've heard tonight," he noted, "most of the work has been done by those folks who were not the prime contractor. We made a decision up front that we would have a licensed surveyor be the prime contractor so we could hold that person—like we do a member of the bar—to their professional standards, ethics, and regulations, so that nobody could accuse us of playing any games here. His livelihood is at stake," Gissendanner said. "I can tell you now without any equivocation, he wasn't told anything to do except go out and find the OHWL."[47]

Several participants then rose to support the state protection of the marshes, the restoration of the Kissimmee River, and the raising of Lake Kissimmee's water levels to the 53.1-foot elevation. Gissendanner reminded the group that "we're not trying to supply water to Miami by doing this—we're trying to find the OHWL for this lake." He also cautioned that determining the OHWL would not directly affect the control levels of Lake Kissimmee. One man pointed out that the conflict seemed to be between the ranchers and the city folks. He complained that the state was telling him that "deeds didn't mean anything and if we've been paying taxes on land we didn't own it was just our own tough luck." Another man wanted to know if the meander line was considered the wrong boundary "just because the fellows that did it lived a hundred years ago." Then, one person pointed out that if the trustees set the OHWL at 53.1 feet, "700 acres of what we thought was ours now will be the state's. We don't want to develop it," the man said. "We've had it for hundreds of years. We want our daughters to inherit it. We'd like the state to stop the pollution coming in from Orlando," he concluded. Another man rose to say that it seemed the state was trying to gain control of the land in an unfair manner. "There are plenty of zoning laws to safe keep the land—the controls are there—but the state is overstepping its margins. We've owned this land for hundreds of years," he echoed the previous speaker. "I want to hand this land down to my children, not hand down junk. We're having to defend something that belongs to us—it's an emotional case as well as a technical case. I think the line needs to be set, and if we can keep the emotional side down, we can do that. But I feel like the state is illegally trying to control the land and we have enough controls." He went on to say that "the emotional aspect is being put in the eyes of some of the people wrongly by the [claim that] 'we've got to have these marshes to save our lakes and our livelihoods and our lives.' Well you may have to have the marshes," he said, "but they may belong to someone else." [48]

Gissendanner responded, "The State did not enter into this to get anybody's land. Let me tell you there's more ways to take your property than by saying your deed's no good. I've got 125 acres that's got my life savings tied up in it and it's wet. So I can't use it—no question the deed is good—but I can't use it. There's a lot of ways to get your land besides what you fear this exercise will do. We are really not trying to get more land. We've got more land than we can find now. So we're not looking for extra land. What we're looking for is what is legitimately owned by the private owners and what is legitimately owned by the public—part of which you and I are." At the end of the hearing Save Our Lakes chairman Bob Quinn urged people to "Support the DER [sic] and let's get on to the courts. The Lightseys [a large landowner family on Lake Kissimmee] have filed suit claiming ownership out into the lake down to elevation 50 feet," he said, "lands which are currently two and a half feet under water three months out of each year." [49] At last it seemed a determination was at hand.

Restoration Woes

Meanwhile, plans for restoring the Kissimmee River were going forward, but the need to acquire lands for the project soon created conflicts not only between landowners and state agencies but between the agencies themselves. In August 1983, the Coordinating Council on the Restoration of the Kissimmee River Valley had issued a Public Hearing Discussion Paper outlining various issues the hearing participants might want to discuss during upcoming public hearings on the project. Noting that the DNR's OHWL determination—which would establish state/private ownership boundaries on Lake Kissimmee—was presently under way, the council outlined the issue of land acquisition:

> There has been continuing debate about the need to reacquire lands which may be flooded by restoration. For the Partial Backfill plan, several legal analyses have suggested that since the plan simply re-establishes the natural hydroperiods of the Kissimmee River Valley, there is no obligation to acquire title or flowage easements for land which may flood. Others argue that basin landowners improved their property in good faith, depending on the government to maintain the canal.[50]

By March 1984, regional water managers were proposing to "buy the entire floodplain of the channelized Kissimmee River—a one-mile wide, 50-mile-long corridor through Central Florida—to stop development and protect South Florida's water supplies."[51] The *Miami Herald* described the plan, put forward by the South Florida Water Management District staff, as placing some "62 square miles in five counties under public ownership, including extensive pastures and several residential subdivisions, at a cost of $40 million to $60 million." Such a purchase, the *Herald* noted, "would be among Florida's most sweeping attempts to halt growth in sensitive ecological areas and would mark a dramatic new chapter in the 20-year-old fight over the formerly twisting Kissimmee, which giant dredges converted to a wide, straight, deep canal in the 1960s."[52] A Water Management District deputy director, John R. Wodraska, said that the purchase proposal was needed to stop further development between Lake Kissimmee and the backup water supply for more than 3 million south Floridians, Lake Okeechobee. He pointed out that, under the plan, land presently used for grazing cattle would probably be leased back to ranchers. Artificial drainage or other improvements on the land, however, would be prohibited. "If the Kissimmee is restored and its marshes reflooded, cattle still could graze there when water receded in winter and spring," he noted. Current residents of subdivisions affected by the proposal would "be allowed to remain indefinitely, but the district would buy their land and houses." He went on to say, however, that as restoration proceeded affected residents would have to move.[53]

Opponents of the river's restoration, in the meantime, filed a request for a formal administrative hearing in order to delay a $1.4 million restoration experiment the district had planned. The experiment called for installation of three steel walls in the canal to force water back into the river's old channels. In response to the delay, district administrators said they would continue working to move the floodplain purchase forward regardless of whether the Kissimmee was ever restored.[54]

On April 2, 1984, the ranchers' attorney, Cummings, wrote to Gissendanner asking why the state was pursuing an inconsistent policy that favored property owners along the Kissimmee River over owners on Lake Kissimmee. Cummings asserted that property owners along the river were being paid for land lying below the OHWL, while owners on Lake Kissimmee were receiving no compensation for exposed lands below the boundary line. "The position of the Lake Kissimmee property owners is essentially the same as the Kissimmee River property owners," Cummings wrote. "If the State needs the land to protect water supplies and to prevent development then it should buy the land."[55] Gissendanner replied on May 23 saying the state had consistently taken the position that "lands below the OWH of the Kissimmee River remain sovereign unless previously alienated. . . . I quite agree with your letter and see no reason why Lake Kissimmee should be treated differently than the Kissimmee River since both waterbodies are under regulation." Gissendanner outlined the state's position in several cases in order to demonstrate its consistency. He then concluded, "By copy of this letter, I am going to alert the South Florida Water Management District that the question of ownership ought to be carefully addressed before any land acquisition begins. Thank you for calling this matter to my attention."[56]

On June 4, 1984, Robert Grafton, South Florida Water Management District Coordinator of the Kissimmee River land acquisition project, wrote to Gissendanner. Citing Gissendanner's letter to Cummings, Grafton noted, "it appears reference is being made to distinction between publicly and privately owned lands along the Kissimmee River south of State Road 60. You refer to state ownership of 'lands below the OHW of the Kissimmee River.'" Grafton asked for copies of the relevant correspondence and citations of the lawsuits Gissendanner had cited in his letter. "The District is greatly interested in any determination you may have made as to the OHW line of the Kissimmee River immediately prior to regulation under the Central and Southern Florida Flood Control Project," Grafton said. By way of reply, DNR counsel provided the requested information and referred Grafton to State Lands administrator Jim McFarland for further information concerning the OHWL of the Kissimmee River.[57]

On October 8, 1984, Kirby B. Green, Bureau of Surveying and Mapping Chief, wrote to Grafton. Green noted that the preregulatory OHWL of the Kissimmee River had not yet been established, but offered to make available some preliminary work that evaluated high waters along the Kissimmee Basin from a geological and botanical viewpoint.[58] Two weeks later, McFarland also wrote to Grafton to say that he had noticed in the newspapers that the Water Management District was about to buy 7,700 acres in Polk County from the GAC Realty Trust. "It sounds like an outstanding purchase," McFarland said, "that will go a long way in the state's efforts to preserve the Kissimmee River Floodplain. . . . However, I would like to take this opportunity to make you aware of a potential survey issue concerning the determination of the OHWL when purchasing lake or river properties within the State." McFarland went on to warn Grafton that "the determination of the OHW is both a costly and complex process that involves not only technical considerations, but legal considerations as well." He suggested that Grafton call Kirby Green to discuss OHWL issues "to see if they would be applicable to your proposed purchase in the Kissimmee River chain."[59] Grafton noted on November 2 at the bottom of Green's letter that he had talked to Green on the phone. "He cannot advise OHWL—needs extensive physical survey—he estimates cost at $300,000—this seems low to me."[60]

Grafton then composed a memorandum to the Water Management District Governing Board members, attaching copies of McFarland's letter. "What the letter does not explicitly say, but which is implicit therein," Grafton wrote, "is that the [DNR] *may* claim ownership of the GAC lands below the OHWL." Grafton further noted that Green had "verified the State would claim the Kissimmee River flood plain, if, after a survey complete with review of vegetative indications, the Department felt a claim of state ownership could be made." Grafton explained that a survey would cost approximately $300,000 and take six months to a year to complete. Furthermore, he said, if the survey indicated that a state claim could be made to the GAC land, he would anticipate a fight between the present landowners and the state.

Grafton outlined another situation that he felt was comparable to the Kissimmee situation. "There is ongoing litigation concerning lands along the Peace River. The State has claimed a large flood plain area of that river, which landowners have claimed, used and paid taxes on for many years." Grafton noted that the case had been in litigation for over six years and was still not decided. "In view of the action taken by the State with regard to the Peace River," he said, "there may be a State claim along the Kissimmee River." Such a claim would "arouse instant united opposition from the landowners," causing a delay in the acquisition program of from five to ten years. Such a delay would jeopardize the district's plans to restore the river to more natural conditions, since without the land rights the restoration could not proceed. In view of all these considerations, Grafton said, "I believe we should go ahead with our purchase from GAC." On November 9, the Water Management District governing board unanimously agreed.[61]

Soon thereafter, Cummings complained again to Gissendanner that the South Florida Water Management District governing board was considering purchasing thousands of acres of land lying below the 50-foot contour. Inasmuch as the trustees had officially recognized the 53.1 foot elevation as the official OHWL of Lake Kissimmee, Cummings argued, "lands bordering the Kissimmee River immediately south of Lake Kissimmee and lying below the fifty foot contour are assuredly below the OHWL of the Kissimmee River. . . . Again, why does the State of Florida persist in what appears to be a blatantly inconsistent approach to the lands lying along the Kissimmee River and to the lands surrounding Lake Kissimmee and the other lakes in that chain?" Cummings asked. "It is a matter of great concern and frustration to those who own property on the Lakes that the State of Florida would take their land under the guise of a revamped theory of ordinary high water line while at the same time purchasing at fair market value identically situated lands along the River."[62] In a February 19, 1985, response, Gissendanner told Cummings, "We have advised the SFWMD [the Water Management District] of our position, but our correspondence may not have reached Mr. Grafton before the September 14 meeting of the SFWMD." Then, in a handwritten note at the bottom of the letter, he added, "Alan, SFWMD is not operating under the law and rules of DNR and Trustees. I tried to get that in the Save Our River law, but failed. Please call me if you wish to discuss further."[63]

Gissendanner's candid note provides insight into the DNR's perspective: the Water Management District's practice of paying for lands below the OHWL runs afoul of the rules and threatens much needed cooperation from landowners. In view of Grafton's analysis of the situation, however, one can understand the temptation to the strategy he outlines. This dispute—between the trustees, who were responsible for protecting public lands, and the Water Management District, which was charged with the restoration of the Kissimmee River—would threaten the state's accord with the restoration proceedings for nearly a decade before it was resolved.

The correspondence concerning the Kissimmee River land acquisition deal reveals many interesting points, perhaps most remarkably how little communication seemed to exist between the Department of Natural Resources and the Water Management District during the time Lake Kissimmee was being surveyed. In late 1984, it seems the only citizens who tended to know anything about sovereignty lands issues were the landowners contesting state claims to properties waterward of the OHWL. But that was all about to change.

MRTA and the Growing Public Uproar

As the OHWL conflicts on Lake Kissimmee and the Kissimmee River escalated into eviction surveys, lawsuits, and clashes among the trustees' staff, landowners, water management district personnel, and the concerned public, other interested groups began forming alliances with these embattled parties. Associations of farmers, realtors, foresters, miners, and landowners, seeing what was taking place in the heart of the state, began gathering more information and moving to protect their interests. At the same time, these alliances were furthered, and the oppositions intensified, by a related issue—that of the Marketable Record Title Act (MRTA), also called the Title Act. Under the operation of this new law, the ordinary high water line—and its value in delineating public lands from private—very nearly became completely inconsequential.

In 1963, the Florida legislature had created MRTA in order to simplify property title searches. The act provides that any person whose chain of title extends from a title transaction recorded thirty years or longer and free and clear of all claims during that time has a marketable record title, with some exceptions set out in the statute.[64] The act undoubtedly relieved a situation in which buying and selling properties required title searches all the way back to the time of Florida's statehood in 1845. But in the 1970s owners of private lands began using MRTA as a tool to gain title to sovereignty lands adjacent to their properties. It worked like this: During the rush to develop Florida in the later nineteenth century, the state conveyed some two-thirds of its total surface—or 22 million of its 35 million acres—into private hands under the Swamp and Overflowed Lands Act. Because many of these transactions involved huge tracts of land, the state tended to use broad legal descriptions. For example, a single land patent might include all or most of the sections of several townships and ranges. The navigable rivers, lakes, and streams lying within these vast tracts were sometimes described and meandered by the surveyors and, thus, reserved by the state as sovereignty lands. But often these waters were not specifically described—even when they were obviously navigable. This failure to designate sovereignty lands within the swamp and overflowed land patents did not change the fact that the state had neither the authority nor the intent to convey title to sovereignty lands in disposing of swamp and overflowed lands. Instead, as Florida law pertaining to sovereignty lands developed during the nineteenth century, the notion that private lands ended at the shore of navigable waters became the law of the land. Buyers were to take title to swamp and overflowed lands "with notice" that navigable waterways were excluded. Or so it seemed until 1976 when the Florida Supreme Court ruled that under the new law of MRTA a landowner who holds an unchallenged deed owns all the land within the legal description of the deed—including beds of navigable waters. Private landowners with deed descriptions including navigable waters began filing quiet title actions against the Board of Trustees, and, in many cases, winning large tracts of sovereignty lands on summary judgment motions.

Blindsided by the 1976 ruling, the state began the frantic scramble to stem the loss of sovereignty lands. Governor Reubin Askew called a special session of the Florida legislature to exempt sovereign lands from the Title Act. The amendment passed in 1978, but the courts subsequently ruled that the amendment was not retroactive.[65] This decision meant not only that the lost sovereignty lands could not be recovered, but that those cases still in the courts on appeal would continue to be considered under the operation of MRTA. In the 1982 appeal of such a case, *Board of Trustees v. Paradise Fruit Company, Inc.,* involving some two thousand acres of Lake Poinsett, Justice Cowart held that, although the trustees were arguing for the amendment to be applied retroactively, any such construction would be unconstitutional inasmuch as the Title Act had operated to perfect appellee's title in 1963. He further complained that, although the trustees had made an impassioned plea for the court to save and preserve sovereignty lands for the benefit of all the people of the state,

> it was the state legislature that omitted an exception in favor of sovereignty lands from the original enactment in 1963 of the Marketable Record title Act, thereby perfecting appellee's title. Under our constitutional separation of powers doctrine, the state judiciary has no alternative but to read the plain language of MRTA as it existed prior to the 1978 amendment.[66]

In 1985, Senator Tom McPherson, a Democrat from Fort Lauderdale, backed by Governor Bob Graham and the DNR, introduced a bill that would have made the 1978 amendment retroactive. The proposed legislation drew so much opposition from special interest groups that legislators agreed to create a MRTA study commission and place a one-year freeze on MRTA-based court actions.[67] The study commission held fact-finding sessions and hearings, and, over the course of 1985, associations of farmers, realtors, miners, foresters, and other concerned groups held meetings and workshops as well. Unfortunately, as time went on, one outcome of the increased participation of interest groups was an overall decline in responsible discussion of sovereignty lands issues, and inflammatory rhetoric and reportage tended to dominate much of the ensuing discourse.

In February 1985 the Florida Forestry Association held a sovereignty lands workshop, which was presented by DNR staff and legal experts. Over 125 association members and guests met to learn about the issue. According to *Pines and Needles*, the association newsletter, "The issue affects landowners whose property contains or borders on a navigable lake, stream or river—or timber operators who work those lands." The article stated that the DNR had recently increased its efforts to claim state-owned land lying below these navigable waters. "The key to this issue is the location of the ordinary high-water line (OHWL) which serves as the dividing line between private property ownership and state ownership," the article explained. "Establishing this line is not easy." Locating the line, the article said, involved scientific exploration, interviews, and historical research, as well as surveying. Furthermore, a small difference in the placement of the OHWL could be very significant. "In many areas of Florida where the terrain is relatively flat, it can mean hundreds or even thousands of acres lost to the private landowner," the article pointed out. "This often includes land used for grazing or timber production."[68]

One association member pointed out to the DNR representatives that establishing the OHWL in a timely fashion was a critical concern. "If a timber supplier has a lease on timber which might be in the 'gray area' between private and state ownership," he said, "it is costly to hold that lease because we're paying interest on that money. The state expects the private owner to get the line established, but then goes to court if it doesn't agree with the line's location. We're in danger, then of having the lease expire." In addition, he noted, "It's almost a no-win situation for the landowner. Eventually, the cost of establishing the line and defending it in court outweighs the value derived from the timber or the pasture use." The article also pointed out that the "DNR has not only brought the landowner to court in disputes, but also forestry consultants and timber suppliers operating on property claimed by the state."[69]

The possibility of a "simpler and less costly" way of establishing the OHWL was discussed during the workshop. One presenter from State Lands Management, Ted Forsgren, spoke about the state's costs to protect sovereignty lands. "We have spent eight million dollars defending the state's rights to land in Central Florida," he said. Litigating cases, he said, was "a cost we feel we must endure. However, we have to be sensitive to the tremendous cost of litigating every contested boundary. We would be receptive," he concluded, "to the establishment of a committee which brings all interested parties together and develops a method we can send to the Legislature which quickly and reasonably sets the OHWL."[70]

The Forestry Association Executive vice president, Carroll Lamb, pledged to work with the DNR and the legislature to find solutions. "This is one of the most important issues we've faced in a while," he said. "Over the whole state, hundreds of thousands of acres are at issue. These acres cannot be managed properly if they are tied up in dispute over months and years. . . . There aren't many issues more emotional and basic than property rights. When you add boundary lines to the problem, you've really got a volatile situation."[71]

On July 4, 1985, the *Graceville News*—the rural newspaper of a north Florida farming community—reported that the Florida Farm Bureau Federation was taking legal action to find out whether the state's plan to assert sovereignty over existing river and lake bottoms would include millions of acres of land currently held by private citizens.[72] According to the report, the federation had served the DNR with a public records request seeking "all documents indicating the identity and locations of land over which the state intends to assert sovereignty." The article relied heavily on Farm Bureau Director of Public Affairs Al French for its explication of the issues. "Although it may have been submerged prior to the state's development," French was quoted as saying, "much of this land is high and dry today and has been in private ownership for almost 150 years. During this time the owners have improved and developed their land. They may have also paid taxes on the land for many years. The state conveyed title to much of this land on the condition that it be drained," French continued. "If the state is now going to claim that it never sold these lands, then property owners should have a right to know whether or not they are affected . . . whether their property is in jeopardy."[73]

French's comments provide an indication of the muddle into which sovereignty lands issues had now fallen. By allowing lands under navigable water bodies to be claimed as private property in the same manner as swamp and overflowed uplands, the Title Act had contributed to the confusion French expresses. Although it was never the state's intention to claim lands above the OHWL, French's remarks miss this all-important distinction, and the article contains no mention of the OHWL. Instead, French cites areas that were "submerged in the 1800's" including millions of acres and "large portions of cities such as Belle Glade, Kissimmee, Naples, most of Dade County, and perhaps even Walt Disney World," as if these lands were in danger of being claimed by the trustees.[74]

The *Graceville News* went on to say that the DNR told inquiring legislators that the extent of the state's claim was as yet "undetermined." This characterization of the state's claim as "undetermined" was, very likely, read by many as *unlimited*. Of course, from the DNR's perspective, providing an estimation of sovereignty lands must have seemed a formidable if not impossible task, given the complexity of each water body and the necessity of acquiring the physical fact evidence in order to determine its actual boundary line. The article, however, giving no account from the DNR, went on: "Nevertheless, the department's memorandum indicates the claim would affect 180,929 ownerships." French demanded, "If they can count them, why can't they tell us who they are?" This question could have been answered quite simply by an inquiry to the Bureau of State Lands Management. It is a straightforward matter of compiling information from tax records, deeds, or plats to know *how many* properties border on navigable water bodies. Anyone who owns property adjacent to or containing a navigable water body would potentially be affected by a sovereignty lands claim. That the state could not indicate the extent of the potential claim means that, without establishing the OHWL for every navigable water body in the state, it could not specify the affected acreage or map the boundary of its ownership.

However, these clarifications were not sought after by the Farm Bureau Director of Public Affairs. "The potential for damage to property owners is enormous," French warned, "whatever the current intentions of the state may be. . . . These people have had no indication that their titles were flawed."[75] This final word, once again, indicates the perceptual problems that followed the Title Act even after its amendment, which exempted sovereignty lands from the act's operation. French's comment indicates that deeds are somehow flawed if their holders cannot sustain a claim to lands described in the deeds lying below the OHWL of navigable waters. But the idea that this condition constituted a "flaw" only arose with the attempt to use MRTA to divest the state of sovereignty lands.

A week later the *Gainesville Sun* ran an article about MRTA entitled "Land Dispute Pits State against Private Interests." Once again, French detailed the landowners' position, but the *Sun*'s article included the comments of DNR general counsel Kevin Crowley, who provided the state's perspective. "Is it a land grab by the state or a steal by private property owners?" the opening line queried. In the article, French cautioned that state actions could result in "farmers and other property owners losing thousands of acres of land which they had improved, used and paid taxes on." From the state's point of view, the article stated, "without an amendment to MRTA the state (read public) could similarly lose its right to thousands of acres of navigable lakes, rivers and streams." According to Crowley, by 1985 the state had lost over 50,000 acres of sovereignty lands.[76]

French, however, challenged what "losing" the land really meant to the state. He argued that "nobody has lost their right to fish, swim or boat and there has been no effect on navigable waterways over the disputed land." In fact, much of the land the state was claiming it could lose, French said, had been converted to uplands since it was transferred and was no longer under navigable lakes and rivers. The problem, he contended, comes in determining what high water mark will be used in resolving disputed boundaries where "once-encouraged" dredge-and-fill operations have taken place. According to French, the state's authority to regulate navigable waterways was unrelated to its ownership of the submerged lands anyway. He suggested that the "state give up its claim where permanent improvements have made former swamps and overflows into uplands."[77]

The following day, the *Florida Times-Union* took up the issue in its article "Panel Dives into Submerged-Land Fray." "Despite court rulings to the contrary, the Legislature never intended to give away land under and beside Florida's navigable waters," Hyatt Brown said. Brown, a former speaker of the state House of Representatives, had just been named chairman of the seventeen-member commission appointed by Governor Bob Graham to study the MRTA problem. Brown called the court rulings "erroneous," but noted that it was going to be difficult to find a constitutional "cure" for the problem. Brown announced that the commission would hold five public hearings across the state. But, he said, citizens needed to be educated that "they have a stake in the lands that are in danger of being lost to private interests. The average guy on the street's reaction is 'That doesn't affect me—I don't own any state lands.'"[78]

On July 26, 1985, the *Orlando Sentinel* reported, "A Central Florida environmental group, sensing the state is losing a battle over public ownership of river and lake bottoms, said it plans to skip the legislative fight and head straight to federal court."[79] The group, Save Our Lakes, planned to raise $50,000 for legal fees to press the case against MRTA, according to the *Sentinel*. Bob Quinn, president of Save Our Lakes, said that developers had abused the MRTA law, gaining title to lands that were part of the river and lake bottoms. Construction so close to waters, he noted, is environmentally destructive.[80]

In September, the *News-Tribune* ran a series of articles continuing the MRTA discussion. The articles summarized the issues in the fray and detailed a few new points. The Florida Farm Bureau, they noted, was stating that local governments would lose millions of dollars a year in property taxes if the state prevailed in its claim to nearly 3 million acres around and beneath the state's waterways. On the other hand, unless the Title Act was revised, the state "could face more than 40,000 court cases from people fighting the state's effort to claim its land." One article noted that state representative Irlo "Bud" Bronson of St. Lucie County (in the northern Kissimmee Valley Basin) was fighting a state claim that could cost him half his 20,000-acre ranch around Lake Cypress and Lake Kissimmee. "The argument has to do with the definition of 'submerged,'" the article explained. "The general agreement is that anything below mean high water mark is 'submerged' even if it is land that is only submerged once in a while. The problem . . . is to locate the high water mark." St. Lucie County Commissioners would consider a request from the Farm Bureau the following Tuesday to help lobby against a revision of MRTA.[81]

At the commission meeting the St. Lucie County Farm Bureau president argued that private ownership of river and lake bottoms would not keep people from using the water. "The public trust doctrine gives everyone the right to use the water," he said. He urged the commissioners to oppose any changes in the Title Act, saying "Just try to sell or get loans on property without clear title." But an area resident advised the commissioners to seek more information before deciding. She argued, "MRTA was drawn up in a rather sloppy fashion." Rather than the state taking private property, she said, "there had been more of a problem with private landowners trying to grab the state's land." The commissioners decided to write to the governor's office for more information on the proposed changes before making a decision.[82]

On September 18, 1985, the *Daytona Beach Journal* reported that in a fact-finding session area interests "painted two pictures here Tuesday for a state commission studying the Marketable Record Title Act." More than a dozen speakers addressed the blue-ribbon commission, arguing on both sides of the state's efforts to change MRTA. A Daytona Beach attorney who wanted the law changed said the act was being used to clear titles of land ownership in instances where the person's deed itself was not sufficient. "It was not the intent of the 1963 legislature to divest the people of sovereignty lands," said the attorney, who was a senator's aide during the 1963 legislative session. "If a man's only claim to land is MRTA then he doesn't own it."[83]

The president of the Seminole County Farm Bureau attacked the plan to change the law. "He railed against the change," the article noted, "and said the law was 'not designed to be used by Governor Graham and his henchmen. The public is being misled by the governor and his gang.'" The speaker claimed there was "nothing wrong with MRTA. It's working and it's fair and equitable to all." The vice president of Consolidated Tomoka Land, which owned 46,000 acres in the Volusia County area, agreed. "Definitions within the law on mean high water boundaries and definitions of navigable waters . . . could mean vast differences in acreage."[84]

DNR general counsel Kevin Crowley told the commission that MRTA had helped simplify title transactions, but had "gone further and allowed Florida citizens to be dispossessed of public lands." On the Peace and Alafia Rivers alone, he said, 640 acres of land and twenty-one miles of river bottom had been lost to private ownership. Those opposing a change in MRTA, he observed, cite a "litany of mistakes" made by the Board of Trustees and others to justify transfer of public lands to the private sector. Crowley advised the commission to rely on the Florida Constitution, which states: "Sale of [sovereignty] lands may be authorized by law, but only when in the public interest. Private use of portions of such lands may be authorized by law, but only when not contrary to the public interest."[85]

That same week in rural north Florida, the *Jackson County Floridan* reported on a meeting of the Chipola Area Board of Realtors at the Beefmaster in Chipley, Florida. "These kinds of things happen in non-democratic countries," one participant cried, "not America." The unanimous anger of the group, according to the article, was aimed at Governor Bob Graham and the DNR, "who, if they have their way, [will reclaim] much of the land conveyed in the past by the state of Florida to private owners." The article went on to describe MRTA as an act that "actually gave the people the right to buy and sell land." Now state officials, it said, wanted to take back the land without paying the individual landowner "any compensation for the taxes that have been paid on the property and may even charge the landowner for punitive damages. Needless to say," the article stated, "realtors are in an uproar." The article then queried, "So what are deeds worth? If the state accomplishes its task, any landowner can be subject or victim to having their land reclaimed by the state of Florida and be left with nothing. As for realtors," the article concluded, "no title, no mortgage, no sales."[86]

On September 19, 1985, the *Lake Ledger* reported that a large crowd of some two hundred people packed the MRTA commission hearing in Orlando that week worried about the state's push to have MRTA changed. "As [DNR counsel] Crowley . . . pointed to a state map that showed what he said are 16 cases where 'state-owned' water bodies have been lost to private interests, a voice from the rear of the Orlando City Council chambers asked, 'Don't you mean privately owned lands the state has tried to claim?'" Many of the same issues heard in other forums were discussed in the hearing, and eventually Bob Elrod, president of the Florida Association of Realtors and member of the 1963 (MRTA) legislature, suggested that the commission simply wait until the Florida Supreme Court ruled on MRTA in the "Mobil case" before taking any action. The case Elrod was referring to was in fact *Coastal Petroleum Co. v. American Cyanamid Co.* in which Mobil Oil Corporation was a party.[87] Of all the litigation involving private landowners claiming ownership of submerged lands, the *Coastal* case was perhaps the most complex—and eventually the most significant.

Reining in MRTA

The *Coastal* case began when Coastal Petroleum Corporation, which held shares in the state's mineral resources, sued several companies (American Cyanamid and Mobil Oil) for phosphate mining operations they were conducting in the bed of Florida's Peace River. The phosphate companies asserted that the Peace River was not navigable, at which point the Board of Trustees of the Internal Improvement Fund became a party to the suit—counterclaiming that the river was in fact navigable and sovereign. When the state conducted a survey to establish the OHWL, it was determined that ownership of some twenty-one miles of the Peace River and five miles of the Alafia River was at stake and that the OHWL lay considerably farther landward than the phosphate companies placed it. Before the OHWL dispute could be tried, however, a court had to rule on whether the state had been divested of title to the bed of the river by swamp and overflowed lands patents, the Marketable Record Title Act, or the doctrine of estoppel by deed.[88] American Cyanamid and Mobil Oil entered summary judgment motions, and the trial court granted the motions. With the state's ownership of six thousand miles of streams and rivers and over six hundred lakes at stake in the legal issues,[89] the Board of Trustees (with Coastal Petroleum) appealed. The District Court of Appeals affirmed the summary judgments.[90] The trustees again appealed to the Florida Supreme Court to review the case.

Early in 1986 the court ruled, reversing the lower court and finding for the state on all three ownership issues. Writing for the court, Justice Shaw specified that:

> (1) swamp and overflowed lands deeds issued by Board of Trustees in 1883 did not include state sovereignty lands below ordinary high-water mark of navigable rivers; (2) the doctrine of legal estoppel or estoppel by deed did not apply to 1883 swamp and overflow deeds so as to bar Trustees' assertion of title to state sovereignty lands; and, (3) the Marketable Record Title Act did not operate to divest Trustees of title to state sovereignty lands below ordinary high-water mark of navigable rivers, despite conveyances to private interests encompassing sovereignty lands within swamp and overflowed lands being conveyed.[91]

In deciding the ownership questions that had so thoroughly divided Floridians—particularly regarding the MRTA, the court's ruling in *Coastal Petroleum v. American Cyanamid* became the modern-day cornerstone for the protection of sovereignty lands, providing the basis for the future development of Florida's state lands policies. Essentially, this ruling upheld the ancient Public Trust Doctrine on which the state relied for its protection of navigable waters, and, in doing so, brought a much-needed historical perspective to the controversy at hand. In 1987, in the wake of the *Coastal* decision, Florida Attorney General Bob Butterworth negotiated a settlement between the parties confirming state ownership of thousands of acres under and beside the Peace River. But the proponents of privately owned navigable waters were not about to accept the Supreme Court's ruling as final.

The Kissimmee River. In Florida's flat terrain, rivers often show a low- or flat-banked profile, making it difficult to tell where the water ends and the land begins. During the twentieth century, the courts began recognizing the complexities of these slow, low-energy systems and began providing guidance for establishing the ordinary high water line on water bodies exhibiting this low-banked characteristic. (Courtesy of the South Florida Water Management District.)

Kissimmee River, showing full channel and extensive floodplain, 1919.
John Kunkel Small photo. (Courtesy of the Florida State Archives.)

Steamboat landing and ferry, Kissimmee River, circa 1912.
(Courtesy of the Florida State Archives.)

The Kissimmee River, 1961, showing braided channel formation, prior to channelization. In flat terrain, water tends to spread out and form multiple, meandering channels with lower banks. This characteristic is in contrast with rivers of the high-bank variety, in which water, flowing more rapidly down a steeper grade, cuts a well-defined bank. (Courtesy of the South Florida Water Management District.)

Kissimmee train station, 1942 flood. (Courtesy of the South Florida Water Management District.)

Kissimmee River flooding in 1948 at Highway 70 in Okeechobee County. (Courtesy of the South Florida Water Management District.)

Hurricane winds, Lake Okeechobee, probably 1948. (Courtesy of the South Florida Water Management District.)

Everglades National Park, Lake Okeechobee, drought. (Courtesy of the South Florida Water Management District.)

Floodwaters at B&B Cash Grocery in Kissimmee, Florida, probably 1942 or 1948. (Courtesy of the South Florida Water Management District.)

Kissimmee River Basin flooding. (Courtesy of the South Florida Water Management District.)

Survey crew in thickly vegetated river, 1952. (Courtesy of the South Florida Water Management District.)

Dredge on the Kissimmee River, 1962. (Courtesy of the South Florida Water Management District.)

Rock cutter from dredge. (Courtesy of the South Florida Water Management District.)

Construction of S-65 locks, 1965. (Courtesy of the South Florida Water Management District.)

Spillway dam and lock S-65E, 1964. Note the extensive spoil deposits of white sand. (Courtesy of the Florida State Archives.)

A dredge channelizing the Kissimmee River, 1965. Note the massive spoil piles of light-colored sand. (Courtesy of the South Florida Water Management District.)

Left: C-38 at Lake Kissimmee. Note the disconnected oxbow of the former river. (Courtesy of the South Florida Water Management District.)

Below: C-38 Pool C, showing restored oxbow of the Kissimmee River. The weir across the canal helps push water back into the original, meandering river channel. (Courtesy of the South Florida Water Management District.)

Mouth of the Miami River, circa 1914. (Courtesy of the South Florida Water
Management District.)

Mouth of the Miami River, circa 1995. (Courtesy of the South Florida Water
Management District.)

Flooding from Tropical Storm Jerry, 1985. It's difficult to imagine when the water is at lower stages that it will ever get this high. Yet in Florida, tropical storms and deluging rains are regularly occurring, seasonal events and should be considered typical—not anomalous. (Courtesy of the South Florida Water Management District.)

Knowing something is ineluctably a matter
of aligning concepts with the world.
STANLEY CAVELL, *The Claim of Reason*

Lawyers, Landowners, Surveyors, and the State: The OHWL Language Wars

WITH the 1986 *Coastal* court finding for the public trust on each of the ownership questions at issue, proponents of privately owned navigable waters suffered a severe defeat.[1] They had contended that they held title to the beds of navigable waters flowing on lands described in their deeds. They had declared that their deeds—derived from deeds issued by the state—prevented the state from claiming ownership of the submerged lands. They had, in some cases, paid taxes on lands below the ordinary high water line, which they argued proved their ownership. With the use of the Marketable Record Title Act to convert sovereignty lands into private property, they'd felt their ownership of the beds of navigable waters described in their deeds was assured. Now the Florida Supreme Court had asserted that swamp-and-overflowed-lands deeds did not convey lands below the ordinary high water mark of navigable waters, that these deeds did not bar the trustees' assertion to title of sovereignty lands, and that MRTA did not operate to divest the trustees of title to state sovereignty lands below ordinary high water mark. "[B]ecause grantees of swamp and overflowed lands took with notice that such grants did not convey sovereignty lands," the court explained, "neither they nor their successors have any moral or legal claim to these lands."[2] Although an OHWL argument had originally been planned as part of their case, counsel for American Cyanamid and Mobil Oil Corporation now saw no way to proceed with it.[3] Instead they pulled back, settling the ten-year dispute and conceding that the land beneath the Peace River, up to the state-determined OHWL, was publicly owned. They were not about to accept the court's holdings as final, but one thing was now clear: if property rights proponents were going to make any headway against the state's sovereignty lands claim, they would have to find another avenue. They now turned their efforts to defining the criteria and methodology by which ordinary high water line determinations were made.

Dueling Rules and the Question of Authority

In June 1985, the Bureau of Surveying and Mapping acting as staff to the trustees had contracted with the University of Florida to answer questions about the methodology of OHWL determinations.[4] As part of the endeavor to establish the boundary line in the Peace River (*Coastal*) case and in response to more general concerns and questions that pertained to sovereignty lands, trustees' staff at DNR sought development of a procedures manual that surveyors could use when determining the OHWL. To this end, the bureau in 1986 obtained a STAR grant for the university's primary research and by July 1987 was ready to ask the legislature to fund the contract for development of the manual. The legislature appropriated the funds and the contract was let to the University of Florida team that had done the primary research. In November 1987, while considering a settlement agreement with Mobil Oil Corporation (one of the parties in *Coastal*), the trustees instructed their staff to "commence rule-making to define the methodology for the determination of ordinary high water lines."[5] Over the next year, the trustees' staff drafted proposed rules on navigability, OHWL determination, and safe upland line determination;[6] participated in a field test of the university procedures manual; and, in October 1988, held workshops on the proposed rules in four cities around the state.[7]

By mid-1988, however, it had become apparent that the Board of Professional Land Surveyors (BPLS), a five-member board charged with setting technical standards for surveyors, was acting to establish its own rules on navigability and the ordinary high water line.[8] DNR correspondence at the time acknowledges the BPLS activity, anticipates working together on the rule, and asks to be kept informed of meetings, given "the public's interest in submerged lands."[9] But the DNR was not asked to help draft the BPLS rule. Instead, the BPLS rule was drafted by the attorneys for the defeated mining companies in the *Coastal* case. In a workshop conducted May 11, 1988, the BPLS presented its draft rule before an audience of surveyors, title insurance underwriters, cattlemen, foresters, and other interested persons.[10]

Among the first to speak was Robert Feagin from the law firm of Holland and Knight, whose representation of phosphate mining companies had involved him directly in the *Coastal* case.[11] Feagin said he was attending the BPLS workshop on behalf of "landowners whom we have represented in litigation involving what is called the sovereignty lands issue. We've been involved in that litigation—principally involved in rivers in central Florida—for the past 11 years." Feagin briefly discussed the issue of navigability, which he felt could be resolved through legislation. "The most important issue, I think, however, and one that creates the greatest controversy between the state and private landowners is the question of the ordinary high water line," he said. "And *our interest*," he went on, "*is that this Board adopt a rule establishing standards for determining the ordinary high water line* as a real property boundary in accordance with existing law and *in accordance with* the long standing *practices* of surveyors *as we understand them and as we have studied them in connection with this litigation in which we've been involved.*" Feagin continued: "And so we're here today to support an effort by this Board to adopt such a rule. . . . *We participated with other attorneys and other interested parties in preparing that draft and providing it to the board for distribution* at the last meeting. . . . [A]s you discuss it and questions come up, I will be happy to participate by answering questions."[12]

Feagin then discussed two concerns his draft addressed that were to become enduring points of confusion over the next two decades: the role of the surveyor in determining the OHWL and the idea that the state's method of setting the OHWL confused it with a (much more landward) wetlands jurisdictional line (a line used in enforcing regulatory requirements—not a boundary line determining ownership). "[I]t has traditionally been the role of surveyors to establish the ordinary high water line as a real property boundary," Feagin said. "I want to distinguish that [boundary], distinguish it carefully and clearly from the regulatory line that marks the edge of wetlands that are subject to jurisdiction by various state, local and federal agencies. That regulatory line is an entirely different line. But because some of the concepts involved in establishing that regulatory line involve some of the same disciplines and expertise that are involved in establishing the ordinary high water, they have become, I'm afraid, confused."[13]

The "disciplines and expertise" Feagin mentions here, as he would later make clear, referred to the state's use of botanists, hydrologists, and geologists in establishing the OHWL on the Kissimmee lakes and river and on the Peace River. But exactly who is confusing the wetlands jurisdiction line for an OHWL is never specified. Feagin believed that the state was asserting absurdly high OHWL boundaries on the Kissimmee and Peace Rivers and maintained that the state's methodology places the boundary line too far landward, robbing upland owners of lands that are rightfully theirs. Presumably his statement that expert evidence has led to the confusion of the OHWL with a wetlands jurisdictional line is meant to explain how the state has—in his view—gone awry. But no evidence has ever been presented that the bureau confused the criteria of ordinary high water lines with wetlands jurisdictional lines. What one sees in bureau records of this period is ongoing research to determine what in fact are the best indicators of the "true ordinary high water line" (in accordance with case law), and painstaking efforts to gather and correlate all pertinent information in situations such as the Kissimmee Basin, where so much was at stake in the outcome.

Feagin then stressed "what we think is the compelling logic and efficiency of having the surveyors establish the line. It does not aid the cause of stability of real property . . . or efficient and sure resolution of property boundary disputes," he said, "to submit that issue to a panel of experts with the surveyor standing at the end of the line simply to implement what some committee of botanists and biologists and other scientists have jointly determined is the line. That," he added, "as I can testify from my own experience in this litigation which I've been involved, is a terribly, terribly expensive, terribly, terribly time consuming process and not one that I think can be reduced in its cost."

Somewhat ironically, Feagin then introduced two speakers he had invited to present information to the board—both of them scientists. First was Dr. Les Bromwell, an engineer whom Feagin characterized as having "worked very closely" with him as an expert witness in litigation on behalf of property owners. Bromwell began by explaining that he was a "consulting engineer . . . specializing in geotechnical, hydrological and environmental consulting work. For the past ten years, I've been involved in scientific studies in support of ordinary high water line surveys on various lakes and rivers." Bromwell characterized his purpose in conducting his "scientific studies" as determining "whether modern scientific disciplines would support the surveying practices and principle that has been used to locate water boundaries in Florida going back to the time of statehood." He went on to say that the "conclusion of all these studies has been that the surveyor's traditional placement of the mark on the bank or on the shore of a water body is supported by modern scientific evidence based on soils, vegetation and geology."[14] Bromwell's statement is especially interesting in light of assertions Feagin would make over the next thirteen years. Despite his own expert's view that scientific studies support the OHWL determinations made by surveyors, Feagin held and continued to espouse the view that the state was creating a "new methodology" based on "highly scientific studies" that placed the OHWL much higher than the "traditional method" on which "everyone had always agreed."[15]

Feagin's second speaker was Dr. Michael Dennis, a botanist with an environmental consulting firm. Dennis asserted that "as a botanist, I don't feel it's my charge to establish ordinary high water lines. It seems clear from all that I understand that that's the duty and responsibility of the surveyor." He discussed issues of jurisdictional (regulatory) lines and the problems that arise when those are confused with boundary lines. One of Dennis's remarks stands out in retrospect. He characterizes the botanist's role in OHWL determinations as one supporting a surveyor's determination in situations where litigation is involved.[16] (Because courts have sometimes been reluctant to allow testimony from surveyors concerning vegetation, hydrology, geology, and so forth, it has been necessary to engage experts to present such evidence.) In spite of this reality, Feagin would continue during the long battles ahead to characterize the state's similar use of experts as a "new methodology" designed to "take" private property.

In actuality, the state's use of scientific experts seems closely akin to what Feagin advocates. DNR's first studies in the late 1970s using scientific evidence of the OHWL were originated and directed by surveyors (in DNR's boundary determination section that would later become the Bureau of Surveying and Mapping).[17] The use of scientific evidence was motivated at that time by two factors: the need to determine predrainage boundary lines on lakes that had been permanently lowered—a situation calling for substantiation of traditional surveying methods,[18] and increasing signals from courts nationwide that the various indicators of the ordinary high water line would be considered evidence of the boundary.[19] In addition, the use of expert testimony in litigation, as Feagin well knew, was often necessitated because a surveyor's testimony regarding vegetation, soils, and hydrology might be challenged by opposing counsel as outside the surveyor's area of expertise. In fact, the Division of State Lands (DSL) and its Bureau of Surveying and Mapping—that part of the trustees' staff charged with issues concerning the OHWL—has always supported the role of the surveyor as *the* professional responsible for determining the OHWL. When public opposition to having a surveyor maintain the lead role arose in 1982 during the OHWL determination on Lake Kissimmee, DSL Director Henry Dean stood firm on the matter. And, since it is the Bureau of Surveying and Mapping that contracts work concerning the determination of an OHWL, the work done with scientists has always been under the direction of professional land surveyors. Given these actualities, Feagin's interpretation of the issues seems somewhat confounding. Often this kind of confusion in language signals a disagreement at a deeper level than the one being discussed—a disagreement, for instance, over authority or criteria. And, in the ensuing discussion at the BPLS workshop, this kind of conflict did emerge—again rather ironically, in response to the comments of a surveyor.

After several short statements from the floor supporting the Board's initiative, Dave Gibson, a surveying professor from the University of Florida and project director of the DNR-initiated research contract, rose to speak. Gibson began by explaining that he had come to give further information on the OHWL issue, "not taking a scientific position but just to let you know what's going on on this particular subject." He described the contract the university had from the DNR to study ordinary high water and explained that the end result was to be an OHWL manual that "would then be proposed to the survey community in Florida as a procedure that would be repeatable and legally and scientifically defensible." Gibson pointed out that a great deal of research was currently under way that would address the board's proposed rule on OHWL. "I think that the rule that I see a copy of here today of course is an end product of research and so forth," he said. "But I believe we're a certain time distance away from a resolution of that particular scientific problem and the rule making process that would follow that resolution." Gibson went on to say that surveyors take their direction from the courts. "We wait," he said, "until a court decides a particular issue and then that gives the surveyor a mechanism for resolving . . . boundary problems. And I believe this particular subject area is very active in the courts and . . . there has not been a very definite answer given to the surveyor community directly from the courts," he said. "So I believe there's a little more time required before the survey procedure rule making process should proceed."

At this point BPLS chairman, Bruce Durden, interrupted to ask: "Did you say you are—as a part of your study you are going to come up with a manual for surveyors?"

"Yes," Gibson answered. "In fact, that's the title of—"

"Who instructed you to develop a manual for surveyors?" Durden asked.

Gibson explained that he was project director of the research team under contract at the university, that he represented the "practicing community bringing the surveyor's history, the viewpoints and so forth into the process." He explained that the Peace River and Lake Kissimmee litigation that had raised questions over the past ten years had prompted the DNR to develop procedures that the surveying community could rely on as repeatable and scientifically valid.

Chairman Durden responded, "So this manual is being developed under contract to DNR?"

"That's right," Gibson answered.

"And it will so state that it's a DNR document?" Durden asked.

"No," Gibson explained, "it's going to be a University of Florida document."

"Prepared from funds furnished from DNR?" Durden asked.

"That's right," Gibson replied. "And we are very careful in the formulation of the project, that it was a university team that's putting it together and it was never intended as—in concept that it would automatically be turned around to be the DNR manual. It would be input to DNR as a result of our university study. And then they can do what they want with it," Gibson explained.

"I'm just concerned," Durden said, "of course, about how a manual of instruction on how to survey anything can come from someone without— in other words, just by coming from the University of Florida, it's going to have some implied authority to it. And if it's contrary to something that this Board believes, it could create some tremendous problems in the surveying community."

"Well that's the reason I came here today when I heard that this particular subject was on the Board agenda. So my presence here is just to relate to the Board what's going on because I could also see a conflict coming if that were the case," Gibson replied.

"Dave, if it's contrary to a rule that we might adopt, it could develop into a very serious problem, yes," Durden reiterated.

"Yes," Gibson agreed. "But since it's the university project, it will be a technique that we, as a team at the university, think would be scientifically defensible and repeatable by the surveying community. And so, of course, we have a broad range of solutions to this problem and this would be a solution. And it would stand on its own merits once it's published."

After several more exchanges, Gibson concluded, "So my reason for being here is because I know from our studies the last couple of years how complex this issue is. I felt that the Board needed to know what's going on in a different forum, what we're doing at the university and how it all ties in."[20]

After several comments from the floor, Patrick McCaffrey of the Florida Cattlemen's Association rose to speak. He prefaced his remarks by saying that he had "in another life" overseen "millions of hours of state research monies through the Department of Pollution Control . . . [which] went into research a good bit of which was performed by various elements from the state university system. But never," McCaffrey asserted, "in all those millions of dollars and never in forty some different projects that we funded did I have a researcher come before a regulatory body with an advocacy position to not take a course of action until I finish my particular piece of research. I can't think of an action that more thoroughly and completely jeopardizes the opportunity of the research team than to put itself in that kind of a posture," he said. "So as long as they can maintain their objectivity, whatever product they produce should be welcomed to take unto your bosom. But I submit to you that when they come in with an advocacy posture, that that immediately taints whatever product they might produce. And I would urge you to convey to the university research team that they ought to be very careful before putting themselves in that type of posture," McCaffrey concluded.

Two more speakers, both from title companies, then responded to Gibson's remarks. The first characterized Gibson's research project as "a subjective study" under the control of the DNR. "There cannot be a report given to you or to anybody else that is contrary to the individual that's paying the bill or paying the contract," he asserted. "They're [the University of Florida team] going to hire a lawyer from the University of Florida law school. That lawyer is going to work for the Department of Natural Resources, who is paying him a contractual sum. What we have here is a vague line between contractual parties . . . [that's] no more clear than the high water line that they're trying to solve," he said. "I think this body should keep in mind where that information is coming from and who is paying for it," he concluded.

The second speaker added: "I'm sorry. If the end product of the research is to develop a book which explains how to do a survey of ordinary high water line, then it should—that effort should have come from this group to begin with. It seems to me to be in recognition of the fact it's within the prerogative of this board regulating the surveyors to develop those standards," he said.

Part of what's remarkable about the reaction to Gibson's presentation is the conviction that his research, merely by being government supported, will be biased. Clearly, in the minds of some participants the mere fact of state funding provides sufficient motivation for tenured university professors to skew their findings and publish scientifically indefensible results, despite the sizeable risk that such incompetence would entail for their standing within professional organizations and scientific and legal communities. What this suspicion reveals is these participants' conception of the state as an *interested party*, as though civil service professionals and state agencies, like landowners and private developers, stood to profit from the OHWL's location. Chairman Durden's anxiety over the University of Florida's producing a surveying manual ignores the fact that university professors are expected, indeed *required*, as a contractual part of their job, to produce textbooks, train surveyors, obtain grants, and undertake (and publish) research, none of which professional regulatory boards are required to do. But even more remarkable is that, while distrusting guidelines reviewed by the University of Florida Law School and published by a University of Florida surveying professor, not one participant or any member of the board questioned the reliability of a draft rule written by lawyers representing explicitly interested parties—as Feagin himself had pointed out was the case with the BPLS rule at the outset of the meeting.

Board member Dan Gentry, however, did urge the board to give everyone "a chance to absorb [the rule] and to understand all the different aspects of it." Gentry argued that the BPLS should not just "adopt it the way it is," and cautioned that it might need "a long process." [21]

Durden, on the other hand, responded that he didn't "see any necessity for . . . the adoption of this rule being delayed. I think we need to move right on with the program myself," Durden argued.

Gentry pointed out several areas he felt needed clarification and "expansion," saying he wanted to see the board "come out with a document that ultimately will stand the test in the court system. I don't want us to create a document that's not going to represent what case law has told us in the past," Gentry cautioned.

But Durden persisted: "I think we need to go ahead and proceed with the adoption of the rule and I personally don't see any need to delay it and . . . I don't see any need for more public workshops on it. We've had a workshop with the opportunity for input, we've had input, it's all positive for the rule, and I think if we need to clean up some of the language, then let's do that within the next meeting and proceed with adoption."[22] With that Durden called for any final comments and brought the rule workshop to a close. The time elapsed from start to finish of the BPLS workshop on the OHWL rule was one hour and fifteen minutes.

It isn't clear what motivated Durden's desire to adopt the OHWL draft rule so quickly. Surely it was apparent to all that the OHWL issue was complex and controversial. One would think that the chair of the professional regulatory board overseeing the adoption of this rule would welcome due process. Adding to this puzzlement, Durden urged the hurried adoption of the draft rule with a fundamental issue of authority as yet unsettled. At the very beginning of the meeting, before presentations about the rule had even begun, Gentry had pointed out that at the previous meeting he had asked attorney Susan Proctor, liaison to the BPLS from the attorney general's office, to find out two things: whether or not the BPLS was legally authorized to promulgate these rules (on navigability and OHWL) and also whether or not the DNR was so authorized.

Proctor reported that the question had not yet been answered, although her office had recently received a request from the DNR for the attorney general's opinion of whether the DNR had the authority to promulgate these rules. Proctor pointed out that as a result of the *Coastal* settlement agreement in November 1987, the Board of Trustees had instructed DNR to write a rule on ordinary high water line. "Because of the situation," she said, "I do not feel I can tell you today who has the authority to write the rule. I would suggest if we discuss this rule today, that it be discussed in terms of the methodology, deferring for the moment the question of who is authorized to adopt the rule."[23]

Durden then proceeded to question Proctor: "DNR requested that you do something or DNR requested the Attorney General?"

Proctor responded: "DNR has requested the Attorney General issue his opinion as to their authority to adopt this rule." She went on to point out that several bills currently pending in the legislature might also affect the

OHWL issue and suggested again that the BPLS proceed with discussion keeping in mind the possible effects of these actions.[24]

But Feagin and associates had already been working on the question of who had authority to pass a rule on OHWL determinations. During the workshop he made available copies of a "Memorandum of Law," written for the BPLS in early 1988 by L. M. "Buddy" Blain and Douglas Manson—two attorneys representing private landowners. In their memorandum, Blain and Manson asserted that the BPLS was "the only agency with statutory authority to adopt rules governing the procedure for locating the ordinary high water line."[25] The memorandum went on to point out, however, that the "surveyor does *not* define the OHWL." Courts define the OHWL, Blain and Manson explained, and the surveyor locates it.[26] In conclusion, Blain and Manson claimed:

> The TIITF [trustees], the DNR and the DER all lack the necessary authority to promulgate rules to be used in determining the location of the ordinary high water line. None have the authority to regulate the practice of land surveying. Regulation of land surveyors is under the sole discretion of the Board of Professional Land Surveyors of the Department of Professional Regulation pursuant to Chapter 472 and *only licensed land surveyors can perform actual surveys*. . . . Therefore, the Board of Professional Land Surveyors is the only agency that possesses such authority.[27]

However, on June 1, 1988, Florida Attorney General Robert A. Butterworth, responding to the query from DNR Executive Director Tom Gardner, declared he was of the opinion that "The Board of Trustees possesses sufficient authority to establish a method by which the ordinary high water line shall be determined."[28] And so, new battle lines were drawn.

The BPLS Conception of OHWL

Over the next two months the BPLS did hold several public workshops (under a new chairman—Buell Harper) and undertook to define in its OHWL rule such critical terms as *navigable, riverbed, banks, erosion,* and *terrestrial vegetation*. These activities began to make clear the differences between the BPLS notion of the OHWL and the idea of the line that the DNR's Bureau of Surveying and Mapping had. As it turned out, these differences were not fundamentally disagreements about methodology—although Feagin and other supporters of the BPLS rule usually characterized them as such. Instead, the BPLS rule comprised a wholly different idea of where the boundary between sovereignty lands and private uplands should lie. Illogically, proponents of the BPLS rule continued to speak of their boundary as the OHWL even though it was increasingly apparent that the line they described bore no relation to the concept *ordinary high water line.*

As surveyors and lawyers at the DNR began analyzing the BPLS rule during the summer and early fall of 1988, they realized that the rule would be unacceptable to the trustees because its effect was to relocate the public/private boundary from a line marked by the ordinary high water stage to a line resulting from the low or average water stage. This change would, in effect, convert the shore—that area between the high and low water lines—from public to private ownership. In December 1988, the Senate Economic, Community, and Consumer Affairs Committee asked State Lands director Percy Mallison to estimate the number of acres that would be lost by the state if the BPLS rule were to be adopted. Mallison replied,

> It is the position of the Department of Natural Resources (DNR) that the BPLS rule attempts to amend State law by moving the OHWL [established in case law] from the ordinary high stage to the low water channel of rivers and the low water stage on lakes. It does this, in part, by identifying all trees, including cypress, as upland species and dictates that the OHWL is to be found below or waterward of trees. Next, it defines land suitable for normal agricultural purposes to include cattle grazing. Cattle will graze on aquatic vegetation when they are belly-deep in water.

The acreage difference between the two rules (the BPLS and the DNR rules), Mallison went on to explain, could not be precisely stated without surveying the lines described by the two rules on every state-owned water body.

But Mallison did provide calculations for three water bodies of the types typically found in Florida: an unregulated lake, an artificially regulated lake, and a river. The BPLS version of the OHWL on the unregulated lake, Mallison wrote, constituted a 41 percent decrease of state-owned acres; on a regulated lake, there was a 60 percent loss of sovereignty land. "Finally," Mallison said, "we made calculations for a ten-mile reach of the Peace River in Polk County. This is an area that was the subject of years of litigation," he wrote. "The State's survey results were contrasted with the line proposed by the State's opponents—in this case, two phosphate companies. The State claims 1,252 acres below the OHWL. The opponents' OHWL, which would be the same line defined by the BPLS's rule, shows 73 acres. The difference is 1,179 acres, or a 94% difference in land area."[29]

This wide gap between the BPLS proposed line and the Bureau of Surveying and Mapping's placement of the line begs the question of how the surveying community viewed this discrepancy. To a degree, however, the response of surveyors was overshadowed by the reaction of such interest groups as the Cattlemen's Association, title insurance companies, and other supporters of a low water boundary between public and private lands. In many instances, opinions of these groups that were published in newspaper reports, newsletters, and other documents conflated the surveying community with the BPLS, as if the five-member regulatory board spoke for Florida's professional land surveyors.

In one such example, Vice President and Regional Counsel of the American Title Insurance Company, Michael S. Davis, wrote to the BPLS: "Upon review of these two proposed rules we have determined that the recommendations of the Florida Board of Professional Land Surveyors is the only acceptable method for determining the OHWL. The DNR, in its zeal to accomplish a particular end, has proposed a means that is impractical and unworkable. We feel that *the surveyors' approach* is definitely more logical, efficient and consistent with existing Florida case law." [30] It's important to observe here that, although Davis's letter describes the BPLS rule as the *surveyors' approach,* the board-sponsored rule did not represent a consensus among surveyors on issues pertaining to the OHWL. In fact, as we have seen, the rule was drafted by attorneys for large riparian landowners. In actuality, many Florida surveyors were—in the words of one— "just waiting for the smoke to clear so they could figure out what they were supposed to do under the law." [31]

But interest groups supporting the BPLS rule continued to insist that the bureau location of the sovereign/upland boundary resulted from a radically new methodology—a departure from the way things were done in the past when "everyone agreed on the boundary." Davis, in his letter representing American Title Insurance, claimed that the case law had actually "evolved" as a result of the DNR's "efforts to claim for the state as much land as possible by radically changing how the 'ordinary high water line' is determined." (He didn't cite the cases, and it's not clear what cases would support this claim.) Bob O'Brien, Jr., on behalf of Carteret Savings Bank, also expressed this idea when he wrote to Governor Bob Martinez that some "activists" in the State Lands Division were "now trying to redefine OHWL to include present and former swamps and overflowed lands." [32] This idea, that the state was redefining the boundary's location, seemed to go hand-in-glove with the fear that under this new policy surveyors would no longer determine the OHWL but would be replaced by scientists. Ticor Title Insurance Senior Vice President and Title Counsel

John S. Thorton expressed this anxiety in a letter to BPLS director Allen Rex Smith, saying that Ticor "enthusiastically supports [the BPLS] Proposed Rule. . . . We wholeheartedly agree with the proposal that this important task be performed only by certified land surveyors based upon evidence that is readily observable by them and not by scientists based upon laboratory analyses that would not be observable by the average citizen."[33]

To a degree, the worry over a scientific method expressed the desire by all concerned that the boundary between public and private property be apparent, easy to locate, and uncontestable. The idea of a clearly observable line that needed "no scientific exploration" to discover appealed to surveyors as well as upland owners.[34] But, as Florida courts had long recognized, Florida's topography did not always oblige the cause of simplicity.[35] Perhaps what is best revealed in these writings is the notion that the location of the OHWL can be *chosen*—by any particular group, radical or not. What has seemed most difficult to grasp is that the OHWL is a line existing in the natural world, a line that must be found. Unlike a concept such as *the northeast quarter of section 6,* which has no meaning (that is, no corollary) in the natural world, the concept *ordinary high water line* describes a natural indicator—the concept follows from the natural phenomenon. The criteria establishing the legal concept of an ordinary high water line have for thousands of years reflected this fundamental connection. If the citizens of Florida now want to change the location of the boundary between public and private lands from what it has—by law—been, we should stop calling this new boundary the ordinary high water line. To persist in a way of speaking that ignores the limits of our concepts is to render our words meaningless, ourselves nonsensical. Unfortunately, this manner of speaking still persists today in much of the debate pertaining to the OHWL.

There are a few extant records of surveyors' reactions to the BPLS rule. In one such example, professional land surveyor Vince Martinez provided a nine-page (single-spaced), carefully prepared commentary to the BPLS critical of certain portions of its proposed rule during the late spring of 1988. He dealt with questions about meandered and nonmeandered water bodies, about who should determine navigability, and about whether the OHWL should be monumented given its ambulatory nature. He suggested that surveyors should be required to submit certified copies of OHWL determinations to the DNR since the state "lacked the resources to know where such surveys are being performed that directly affects the State's lands." He pointed out that if there were a disagreement about the boundary, "the State would rely on the PLS [Professional Land Surveyor], whether a State employee or a private consultant" to resolve the dispute.

He then raised a question at the heart of the discrepancy between the BPLS location of the sovereignty/uplands boundary and the bureau's location of the OHWL: "Can [the BPLS] Rule 21HH-6.0045 exclude certain lands from being included within the OHWL?" In other words, Martinez questions whether a regulatory board for surveyors has the authority to decide, merely by passing rules for the surveying profession, that certain lands defined as public in Florida law should be excluded from boundary surveys of public lands. Martinez pointed out that, although the proposed rule was "intended to establish minimum technical standards for determination of the OHWL by the PLS," the rule actually went beyond this intent. "In my opinion, the proposed Rule does not have the authority under chapter 472, F.S., to determine title or to exclude certain lands that may be subject to sovereignty claim." An example of the board's exceeded authority, mentioned by Martinez, occurs in the section of the BPLS rule that sought to exclude certain areas outright from the water body being surveyed. These exclusions included streams, shallows, sloughs, bays, marshes, and similar bodies not themselves navigable but a part of the navigable water body. Martinez cautioned that the BPLS did not possess the authority to make rules affecting title in this way, and he observed that the exclusions in the present version of the rule would "present a problem to the public trust doctrine," that is, would be contrary to Florida law. "The proposed Rule should limit itself to establishing the procedure for use in determining the OHWL as a survey technique, subject to statutory provisions and Florida case law," he concluded, and not stray into areas over which the courts and legislature have legitimate authority.[36]

There seems to be no record of a BPLS response to Martinez's memo. Looking back over the succeeding versions of the BPLS rule, it would appear that suggestions such as Martinez's that ran counter to the original aim of the rule fell on deaf ears.

Over the months that the BPLS reviewed and expanded its rule, one board member in particular took a leading role in the project. Daniel E. Gentry, registered land surveyor, worked tirelessly on the document, enlarging its scope and refining its detail. In June 1988, he provided the BPLS a paper he had written entitled "The Ordinary High Water Mark Defined: Three Cases Examined by a Land Surveyor," in which he discussed what he saw as the modern definition of the OHWM.[37] (Gentry insists on the term "ordinary high water *mark*" in contradistinction to "ordinary high water *line*" and maintains that the boundary is not an elevation.) Gentry had some interest in history, and his writings on the OHWL clearly illustrate a commitment to elucidating the past as a means to understanding the present. But Gentry had no training in the law, and his interpretations of OHWL case law seemed more clearly aimed at providing a rationale for the property rights position than understanding Florida law.[38] A review of his reading of one case in particular, however, does shed light on why it is that Gentry referred (and continues to refer) to a *low* water boundary as the ordinary *high* water line, and it provides a possible source for this confusion of language in the contemporary debate.

As the basis for his definition of the OHWL in the BPLS rule, Gentry looked to the federal case *Howard v. Ingersoll.* It is widely acknowledged that this case, heard by the U.S. Supreme Court in 1851, raised several of the topics discussed in water boundary law today, so it is a logical place from which one might begin. The *Howard* case involved a dispute between Georgia and Alabama that turned on the question of whether the low water line, the high water line, or some other line on the western bank of the Chattahoochee River was the intended boundary between the two states. But it is precisely this question that Gentry never seems to have understood. His interpretation of the case makes clear that he believes what's at issue in the case is the location of the OHWL. Although the case takes up concepts basic to the OHWL, discovering the location of the OHWL is never the Court's purpose. The problem for the Court in *Howard* is to locate a specific boundary described in a treaty. But Gentry never seems to have grasped this point. Three opinions issuing from the case described three very different locations of the boundary, but Gentry interpreted all three as the OHWL.

In his "Three Cases" paper Gentry wrote: "Examining Howard vs. Ingersoll . . . will show that the definition arrived at by Justice Wayne, who wrote for the majority in Howard, and Justices Nelson and Curtis, who concurred, stands today as the basis for defining and establishing the OHWM in Florida. . . . Each of the Justices helped to define *the boundary*." Elsewhere, Gentry "explained" his conflation of *the boundary* with the OHWM by saying:

> The terms OHWM and OHWL were not in use in 1851 for non-tidal waterbodies; the term "boundary" was used. Nevertheless, the Court's definition of the methodology of boundary location is relevant today to OHWL location; the OHWL is "the same thing" as the boundary.[39]

Contrary to Gentry's assertion that the term *ordinary high water mark* was "not in use in 1851," the term abounds in the very case he cites. Justice Curtis, for example, stated in his (1851) opinion: "But neither the line of *ordinary high-water mark,* nor of *ordinary low-water mark,* nor of a middle stage of water, can be assumed as the line dividing the bed from the banks."[40] Further, there is no basis for imagining that when Justices Wayne, Nelson, or Curtis use the term "boundary," that they are covertly, tacitly, or implicitly describing the ordinary high water line. Although in both versions of his paper Gentry equates the terms "OHWL" and "boundary" in this way, there is no basis whatsoever in *Howard* for treating these two terms as equivalent. Nothing in the writings of any of the justices supports Gentry's claim that, whenever they use the term "boundary" in this case, they are referring to the high water line. But, following his own line of thinking, Gentry recommended that the *Howard* decision, as the "most quoted case and definitive work to describe the sovereignty/ upland boundary" be "incorporated into the rule for surveyors establishing the Ordinary High Water Mark (OHWM)."[41]

The problems with Gentry's reading of *Howard* began with his idea that each of the opinions "stands today as the basis for defining and establishing the OHWM in Florida." In actuality, the three opinions issued in the case vary substantially, most significantly in their placement of the boundary. Justice Wayne, writing the majority opinion—the only opinion that is in fact law—interpreted the treaty, in which Georgia ceded the Alabama territory to the United States, as reserving the entire river to Georgia. Wayne described the boundary using several key indicators of an ordinary high water line.[42] Justice Nelson's opinion, which Gentry mistakenly described as "concurring," is in fact a dissenting opinion. Nelson interpreted the intended boundary as a low water line, reasoning that a high water line boundary would deprive Alabama of any use of the river. Justice Curtis's opinion concurred only on a question unrelated to the boundary's location (that is, Curtis concurred with the majority that the lower court decisions should be reversed). He did not agree with either the majority opinion or Justice Nelson's dissenting opinion on the placement of the boundary. For Justice Curtis the boundary was the clearest mark on soil and vegetation—a line he failed to relate to water stage. Curtis's opinion, like Nelson's, was motivated by a desire to provide Alabama some use of the river. He wrote that the boundary was "inferable from the nature of the line, as a line or boundary of political jurisdiction as well as of proprietorship; and according to that presumed intention, we must declare it to be on that part of the bank which will best promote the convenience and advantage of both parties." [43]

It is significant that in drafting the BPLS rule Gentry took his definition of the OHWL from language in Curtis's and Nelson's opinions, citing only very brief excerpts from Wayne's opinion, excerpts which, according to Gentry, are "echoing" the opinions of the other (dissenting) justices. Gentry began by citing Justice Curtis's opinion that:

> [The boundary] should be located on the bank where the leading purpose, to have a natural boundary between the two jurisdictions, will be most effectually attained. The convenience and advantage of both parties require this. The line, therefore, is at the lowest edge of the bank, being the same natural line which divides the bank from the bed of the river. [44]

Gentry followed this quote with the comment, "Nature's clearly marked line and the avoidance of advantage to either party were Justice Curtis's criteria for establishing the boundary, or the OHWM." Notice how in this passage Gentry clearly states that Curtis is describing "criteria for establishing . . . the OHWM." In fact, Curtis nowhere says or implies this. Curtis in the quoted passage gives an unequivocal description of a low water line, the "line at the *lowest* edge of the bank" (emphasis added). Florida law directly contradicts this formulation of the water boundary, stating that, in navigable waters, sovereignty lands include the shores—those areas *above* Curtis's "lowest edge of the bank" and up to the OHWL.

In fact, contrary to his claim that Curtis is describing the OHWM, Gentry's observation that Curtis aimed to avoid "advantage to either party" makes evident that Curtis did not place the boundary at the OHWL. Any other line but the OHWL would have provided Alabama with some access to the river. The fact that the majority opinion set the boundary at something very like the OHWL (of the west bank) constituted a ruling that Georgia had reserved the entire river to itself—precluding Alabama from any "convenience" or "advantage" in the river. Thus, the one thing we can be sure of from Justice Curtis's stated criteria is that his boundary is not the OHWL. Moreover, Gentry's implication that "the avoidance of advantage to either party" is a criterion for establishing the OHWM is simply false. Florida law states, "The ordinary high water boundary on fresh waters is the ordinary or normal reach of water during the high water season." [45] The natural cycles of freshwater bodies are not affected by advantages and disadvantages to human parties.

Gentry's interpretation of these opinions as concurring in their placement of the boundary and as equally authoritative in defining Florida's

OHWL has given rise to several persistent misconceptions about Florida law. In attempting to explain how our contemporary use of the term *ordinary high water line* translates backwards to the time of the *Howard* court, Gentry conflated the term *OHWL* with the term *boundary*, a leap of logic from which his subsequent reasoning never recovered. Gentry then proceeded to read the case as if, in both majority and dissenting opinions, and in the body of each justice's argument as well as his conclusion, the term *ordinary high water line* could be substituted for the word *boundary*. This conflation of distinct terms overlooks the fact that, in *Howard*, whether or not the boundary is equivalent to the ordinary high water line—or any other line—is precisely what's at issue.[46] But in Gentry's reading, there is from the outset of the case already agreement that the boundary at issue in the treaty refers to the OHWL. Once this wholly groundless claim is allowed to stand, it follows that all of the opinions in the case, no matter where they place the boundary, are attempting to describe (some version of) the OHWL. And so, Gentry reads the opinions as though wherever they place the line, we will call it the ordinary high water line.

Thus Gentry's treatment of the three conflicting opinions as "defining the OHWM in Florida" suggests a very different conception of the ordinary high water line than that which Florida law inscribes. Indeed, it is unclear how three different locations of a boundary can constitute a coherent conception of the OHWL at all. Gentry may actually believe that the words, "ordinary *high* water line," simply *name* the public/private boundary and therefore do not differ significantly from the words "ordinary *low* water line." Understood in this way, the ordinary high water line could be placed anywhere "at the convenience of the parties." Such a treatment of language would help explain why, in apparent disregard for sense, he has come to call a low or average water line the "ordinary high water line."

So too in later years, Feagin, working together with Gentry on OHWL cases, began referring to the OHWL as a "label" as if such words as *ordinary* and *high* and *water* had neither substance nor meaning but merely named a boundary that could be located anywhere.[47] Over the next decade, it was the blurring of these important distinctions that underlay the OHWL controversy at every turn.

In conclusion, Gentry's confusion of the *Howard* case seems to have arisen from his efforts to interpret it as an OHWL case. His characterization of the *Howard* decision as the "most quoted case and definitive work to describe the sovereignty/upland boundary" implies that the case deals with the location of the OHWL, describing where that boundary between publicly owned sovereignty lands and privately owned uplands should be established.[48] But there is no description of a sovereignty/upland boundary in *Howard*. The case is a boundary issue between two states in which the language of a treaty is to be interpreted. It is not a case involving the location of an ordinary high water line boundary between a sovereign and an upland owner. Justice Wayne, writing the holding of the court, stated clearly:

> Nor do we think that the interpretation of this article is aided by any cases upon the rights of riparian proprietors. . . . In this instance, two sovereignties were dealing for a cession of country from one to the other, with a river as a boundary between them to be marked on that bank of it from which the ceded land was to commence. Now, as between them, there were no antecedent calls upon the river to raise the question of riparian rights.[49]

However, Gentry's recommendation that this case be incorporated into the BPLS rule for surveying the OHWL apparently was embraced by the board. And, to a large degree, that was to be the rule's undoing.

Accusations and Counterclaims

In the early fall of 1988, the BPLS adopted its rule describing the OHWL and how to survey it. In October, DNR's Division of State Lands moved to counter the BPLS claims with three public workshops of its own, and Attorney General Butterworth issued a legal challenge to the BPLS rule.

In November 1988, a Division of Administrative Hearings' (DOAH) officer considered the trustees' challenge of the BPLS rule. Intervening on behalf of the trustees was the Florida Game and Fresh Water Fish Commission. Intervenors for the BPLS included three mining companies, the Florida Land Council, Lykes Brothers, the Shoreline Owners and Residents Association, the Florida Forestry Association, the Florida Citrus Mutual, the Florida Sugar Cane League, the Florida Fruit and Vegetable Association, the Florida Farm Bureau, the Florida Land Title Association, and the Florida Cattlemen's Association, among others. In its challenge, the trustees specifically questioned the validity of the BPLS actions based on six allegations:

1) that the Board had materially failed to follow applicable rulemaking procedures set forth in Section 120.54, Florida Statutes;
2) that the Board had exceeded the grant of rulemaking authority;

3) that the proposed rules enlarged, modified, or contravened the specific provisions of law implemented;

4) that the proposed rules were vague, failed to establish adequate standards for agency decisions or vested unbridled discretion in the agency;

5) that the rules were arbitrary and capricious; and

6) that the rules violated Article II, Section 7, and Article X, Section 11, Florida Constitution (1968).[50]

Furthermore, the trustees asserted that the BPLS rules did not constitute minimum technical standards as the BPLS advertised, but were instead an attempt to "establish statements of legal principles pertaining to the location of an OHWL in a circumstance where this issue was unsettled in the courts, the forum ultimately responsible for resolving disputes related to the proper location of an OHWL."[51] Following the hearing, DOAH officer Charles C. Adams undertook a thorough review of the case prior to issuing his decision. With all the cards now on the table and a verdict not expected for several months, the way was paved for seemingly endless interpretations of the various points at stake.

"They're ba-a-ack," complained a *Fort Myers News-Press* article, "River Bottoms in Danger." "Just when we thought Florida's river bottoms and waterways were safe from a private landgrab, big land-owning corporations are renewing efforts to take them over," the article stated. Although people thought the submerged lands issue was settled with the Florida Supreme Court (*Coastal*) rulings affirming state ownership of waterways, the Board of Professional Land Surveyors was attempting to adopt rules that would favor the big land-owning corporations, the article said. The BPLS rule changes "would mean that only rivers and lakes which had been subject to meander surveys in the 1800s would be in public ownership," the *News-Press* explained. Only 241 of 7,000 named lakes in Florida had meander surveys. "Private ownership of other [unmeandered][52] waterways would be sealed unless navigation in 1845 could be proven by direct evidence. And that is virtually impossible—most of Florida was an uncharted wilderness then," the article pointed out. The rule change would also mean that, instead of using the OHWL as the boundary of public and private lands, the "tree line" would define the boundary. "Nearly all publicly owned aquatic forests could be lost to private owners [that is, converted into privately owned forests]," the *News-Press* noted. The article concluded by warning, "If the courts say no to this landgrab, legislators might go for it. Big landowners are already mounting a huge lobbying effort, to the point of seeking public support by creating organizations under fake names that sound like they are trying to protect the old family farm. Citizens ought to tell their lawmakers now to oppose this landgrab if the issue reaches the Legislature."[53]

On the other side various spokespersons continued to sound the alarm, claiming that the state was manipulating the boundary in order to protect environmental resources. "It is DNR that's proposing to change the rules of the game," said Les Bromwell, the Lakeland consulting engineer who worked with Feagin on the BPLS rule. "The state wants to say all wetlands are part of navigable rivers and lakes with the intent of protecting Florida's wetlands and water resources." That protection, Bromwell said, could be afforded resources without DNR holding statutory title to the land. "If the DNR rule is applied across the state it would involve literally millions of acres of land now in private ownership," Bromwell said.[54]

Florid Agriculture, the publication of the Florida Farm Bureau, reported on the situation in the Kissimmee Valley. "In an oxbow of the old Kissimmee River lies a piece of land that is home to Dozier Raulerson, his son and family, a few hundred cows and a small herd of goats," the article stated. "It is typical cattle land, covered with grass and a few stands of dog fennel, situated between the old river that sweeps in an undulating curve to the west and the straight-as-an-arrow Kissimmee River Canal, dug by the Army Corps of Engineers more than two decades ago." But, the article went on, "a cloud hangs over the Raulerson property—his title to the land is clouded by a dispute taking place in Tallahassee over where to draw the ordinary high water line for the Kissimmee River and other rivers and lakes in Florida." Raulerson has "an inch-thick abstract and title describing the land he has lived on for more than 20 years," the article said. "The state sold the land more than 100 years ago along with thousands of acres of swamp and overflowed lands. The intent was to drain the land, put it to productive use and add it to the tax base." Until recently, the article asserted, Raulerson never questioned that it was his land. "The ordinary high water line was never an issue until DNR began claiming title to lands beyond where river and lake boundaries had been established," the article said. Then the state filed claim against landowners on Lake Kissimmee, the Kissimmee River, Cypress Lake, and Lake Tohopekaliga. "It's hard for me to believe that any court would agree for the state to take your land and not give you anything for it," Raulerson told the reporter. Raulerson, a member of Farm Bureau's Kissimmee River Advisory Committee, said the Farm Bureau supported the BPLS rule for determining ordinary high water lines.[55]

But David Guest, then chief of special projects in the state attorney general's office and counsel for the trustees in their challenge of the BPLS rule, disputed the allegation that the state was claiming thousands of parcels owned by individuals. "I frankly don't expect any impairment of people's land as a result of this," Guest said. Every title, he said, sets the limit of private ownership at the OHWL. As for the OHWL, Guest said, it had not been in doubt until the BPLS stepped in where it didn't have the authority to go. "The BPLS only has authority to adopt technical standards," Guest said. "It does not have the statutory authority to deal with case law." [56]

Supporters of the BPLS rules claimed, however, that the DNR's method of determining OHWL boundaries was an unduly complicated "scientific approach" that required surveyors to understand data from fields beyond their areas of expertise. In the January 1989 issue of *ebb & FLOW*, a publication of a neighborhood association, the group president explained the problems. "The Trustees proposal has been determined by a scientific approach," he wrote. "It utilizes a process very similar to that used for purposes of wetlands regulation (vegetative species types, soil content and condition, and lastly, frequency of inundation). It is very difficult to understand," he went on, "how such a process could be undertaken by a land surveyor unless he happens also to be a botanist, hydrologist and soils engineer." Yet the trustees would require surveyors to use this process "regardless of [the surveyor's] professional evaluation that it is not the best method for determining property boundaries." Instead, the association president suggested, the trustees should allow the surveyors to establish boundaries as they saw fit. "If such a line is not acceptable to the Trustees," he said, "let them prove their case in a court of law on an individual basis, not as they are attempting to do through their statewide land grab." [57]

This suggestion that surveyors should set OHWL boundaries and let the trustees take issue with any disputed lines in a court of law describes exactly the way things had always been done—in fact, the way they are still done today. From time to time some group or other (the trustees, the BPLS, large landowners, the legislature) decides it would be a good idea to codify the criteria of the OHWL in a rule or in statute in order to provide a broader understanding of the law. Part of the impetus for these efforts is usually an idea that a clear statement of the law would resolve these disputes without the substantial cost of litigation. But it soon becomes apparent that a clear statement of the law is no solution—perhaps not even a possibility. There is no agreement between the opposing parties on what the law means, and so the disputes have to be litigated case by case. It is perhaps a measure of the profound disagreement underlying the OHWL issue that the neighborhood association president then goes on to accuse the trustees of using the *Coastal* lawsuit to claim ownership of lands adjacent to navigable lakes, rivers, and streams. The holding of the Supreme Court in *Coastal* showed that the trustees properly perceived what lands were due protection under the public trust doctrine. And this resolution of the state's dispute with the mining companies would seem to fit the format the president prefers (litigating on a case-by-case basis). But, the association president and others were still not willing to accept the outcome. "The Attorney General has stated that this issue is a 'land grab,'" the president wrote. "This is a 'land grab,' not by the private property owners but by the state of Florida."[58]

Another confusion that persisted during those months of waiting for the DOAH ruling centered on the question of who had the authority to determine an OHWL. As is often the case, this jumble seemed to turn around the conflation of two distinct but closely related questions: Who has authority to determine *an* ordinary high water line (that is, to apply the criteria of the OHWL to a particular case)? and Who has authority to determine *the* ordinary high water line (that is, to establish what the criteria of the OHWL is)?

In an op-ed piece published in the *Florida Surveyor,* the Florida Society of Professional Land Surveyors (FSPLS) president wrote, "Some time ago, the Trustees (TIIF) gave instruction to DNR to develop procedures to determine a standardized method of determining the location of the OHWL mark. . . . During the drafting of this rule the FSPLS felt there were things wrong with the proposed DNR methodology. One concern was that the surveyor, who historically was *the one determining the location of this line,* was being transformed into nothing more than *a mapper of the line as determined by others.*"[59] The president's comment hints at the difference between the authority to set the criteria of the OHWL and the authority to apply that criteria, but it does this by assuming that surveyors had always had both authorities and were now to be deprived of the first. In actuality, surveyors had never had the authority to set the criteria of—or, in the president's words, to determine—*the* OHWL. This had nothing to do with the DNR's use of scientific evidence or anything else to do with its methodology. Instead, as Dave Gibson had pointed out in the early BPLS workshop, "surveyors take their direction from the courts." The criteria establishing what the OHWL is and, therefore, where it is, are a matter of state law, not a surveyor's discretion. On the other hand, surveyors had been, were then, and are today the professionals authorized to determine *an* ordinary high water line—that is, to project the concept *ordinary high water line* into a particular situation and put the line on the ground. That line is, of course, subject to challenge, with the final arbiter being the courts—just as the neighborhood association president suggested it should be.

In his *ebb & FLOW* article analyzing the two proposed rules, the association president had also confused the issue of authority. In defending "surveyors' right to define the OHWL," he claimed that the BPLS had "historically always determined property boundaries." This comment confuses the BPLS's legitimate capacity to establish minimum technical standards for various surveying tasks with the authority to determine the criteria for the public/private boundary on navigable waters, which the BPLS did not have at any time.

Certainly it is the case that the use of hydrology, botany, and geology as evidence of the OHWL posed a threat. But the use of scientific evidence in itself did not threaten the loss of any authority surveyors had ever possessed. In providing scientific verification of the "true ordinary high water line," it did threaten anyone interested in defending a low or average water line as the sovereignty/uplands boundary. Its only real threat to surveyors came from such claims as those made by the neighborhood association president indicating that surveyors weren't capable of dealing with the complexity inherent in determining an ordinary high water line. These kinds of statements tended to create misgivings about the professional capability of surveyors to cope with the modern demands of water boundaries. As the FSPLS president said, "We are at a point in our professional careers where we need to understand the issues and be prepared to fight for our continued existence. The hearing officer has not made his decision as to who is right or wrong in the OHWL issue. When he does, we will not come out unscathed."[60]

Contrary to Florida Law

On April 17, 1989, hearing officer Charles C. Adams issued the final order in *The Board of Trustees v. Board of Professional Land Surveyors*.[61] Noting that a number of definitions in the proposed rule had been challenged, Adams examined each definition in turn. He deemed several of the definitions appropriate because they were in agreement with Florida case law; but other, key definitions he found unacceptable. The BPLS term "bank," he noted, was interpreted as "the natural feature of a water body that confines the bed and physically separates it from the adjacent lands."

This definition, Adams said, was an "attempt to paraphrase from two federal cases," *Howard* and *Oklahoma v. Texas,* both of which involved rivers with readily identifiable banks. But, he found that on the "question of whether the text set forth in the rule is a faithful adherence to the court language, the answer is in the negative. More fundamentally," he said, "the opportunity for defining the word 'bank' as it applies to the identification of OHWM in Florida is one reserved to the Florida courts. . . . The [BPLS] may only rely upon judicial precedents that have an immediate relationship to Florida case law." This reliance, Adams said, resulted from the fact that executive agencies do not possess the same authority as the courts and legislature in deciding what cases and opinions from federal law and other states may be considered and adopted to Florida law. "Finally," Adams wrote, "the rule definition by its terms is arbitrary in that it fails to provide for the numerous waterbodies in Florida that do not have well-defined banks and whose banks would not correspond to this definition." [62]

The BPLS proposed rule defined the term "bed" as "the land beneath a water body that is subject to the continued presence and action of the water in ordinary years excluding swamp and overflowed lands. The upper mark of the bed is the ordinary high water mark (OHWM)." The authority for this definition, Adams found, was *Howard, Harrison v. Fite,* and *Tilden v. Smith.* But, Adams found, the BPLS rule was "not an accurate restatement of the Florida law as found in *Tilden.* The proposed rule is an attempt to set forth an independent definition of 'bed' without legal authority." [63] Likewise, Adams found the BPLS definition of "erosion" did not accurately follow Florida courts, and so was not permissible. [64]

One of the most important sections of the proposed rule was that defining the word *navigable,* since water bodies determined to be navigable at the time of statehood comprise publicly owned sovereignty lands—not private uplands. The BPLS definition proposed that "navigable" means

> that there is direct, competent and substantial evidence that the water body or portion thereof was being used, or was susceptible to being used, in its natural and ordinary condition, as a highway for commerce, over which trade and travel was or may have been conducted in the customary modes of trade and travel on water when Florida became a state on March 3, 1845. [65]

Authority for this definition, Adams said, came from several cases in federal and Florida law. "Were it not for the fact that the proposed rule attempts to establish an evidential standard, i.e., 'direct, competent and substantial evidence . . . ' which is nowhere to be found in the cited cases, the rule would be permissible since it otherwise tracks the language of *Daniel Ball*."[66] Because of this "impermissible evidentiary standard," however, Adams found the rule invalid. In addition, Adams noted, one of the cases cited by the BPLS looked with favor on statements found in early publications (such as newspapers, memoirs, and military correspondence) as a source of evidence on the navigability question. "These historical publications correspond to indirect proof, contrary to the proposed rule," Adams declared. He concluded that the BPLS rule, by insisting on only direct proof, presented "a reasonable possibility . . . that waters over which the Trustees have a legitimate claim to ownership will be found non-navigable, depriving the state of ownership."[67]

In analyzing the BPLS definition of OHWL,[68] Adams noted that the board had cited as its authority *Tilden, Goose Creek Hunting Club, Inc., v. United States, Howard,* "The Riparian Developer's Dilemma: Locating the Boundary of Navigable Lakes and Rivers,"[69] and *State v. Florida National Properties.* "The basic meaning of OHWM in Florida, especially as it distinguishes swamp and overflowed lands," Adams said, is set out in *Tilden, Martin v. Busch,* and *State ex rel. Ellis v. Gerbing.* Citing these cases at length, Adams traced the history of the OHWL in Florida case law. "These Florida Supreme Court cases define OHWM in Florida," Adams wrote. Because the BPLS proposed rule was contrary to these opinions, Adams said, it was invalid. "The proposed rule partially relies on the Florida cases," he wrote, "but the [BPLS has] *deliberately failed to explain* in this proposed rule the appearance of OHWM in those places where the topography is low and flat, which is frequently the case in Florida" (emphasis added). In addition, he noted, the details of the OHWM set out in the board's second paragraph came from *Howard,* "and is not the standard which has been accepted in Florida by Florida courts or federal courts interpreting Florida law." Adams then concluded: "Moreover, from the evidence in this case it is not clear that the mark as a line is 'generally' discernible. It is just as possible, if not more so, that 'generally' it is not easily discernible and this rule does not make provision for what a surveyor is to do in that situation."[70]

Adams found with regard to the BPLS definition of swamp and overflowed lands[71] that the proposed rule lacked the precision of language in the controlling Florida case, *State v. Gerbing.* "As example," he wrote, "the reminder [in *Gerbing*] regarding the unavailability to the riparian owner of lands between the high and low water mark is not mentioned. The proposed rule also fails to mention lands formed by state projects through the process of reliction," Adams continued, "that do not inure to the benefit of the riparian owner which might appear to be part of swamp and overflowed land but in fact belong to the sovereign." In essence, Adams found the definition "arbitrary and not a true reflection of Florida law."[72]

One of the more complex parts of the BPLS rule contained the proposal entitled "Ordinary High Water Mark Surveys." This part of the rule attempted to establish technical standards, procedures, criteria, and general methodology to be applied by land surveyors in determining the location of an OHWL. Many of the unchallenged aspects of the proposal dealt with surveys being tied to section corners or other monumentation, approximating sinuosities, providing bearings and distances, indicating dates, and so forth. Concerning the attempts to provide legal principles mandating the methods for locating the OHWL, however, Adams found a problem. The BPLS choice as to the location of the OHWM, he wrote, "has the appearance of authority, and if these proposed rules are followed to the letter, it is an appearance that is misleading and harmful." One part of this rule, entitled "Existent Location unless Prior Date Specified," instructed the surveyors thus: "The land surveyor will determine the location of the existent OHWM, unless explicitly requested to determine the location of the OHWM as it existed on a specified prior date." But Adams held that this instruction did not comport with Florida law. "In Florida," he wrote,

> to locate the OHWM, one must understand the influences which man has had in regulating water levels. In those instances, such as the situation in *Martin*, the surveyors must depict the historical circumstance before man's activities to describe the true OHWM. . . . When man's influence is not examined, the property owner, state or private interest, stands to lose property or gain property at someone else's expense, when the proposed rule calls for no more than the identification of the existing location, absent an explicit request to locate a line on a prior date. The surveyor, not the owner, has the presumed expertise to arrive at the true OHWM, whether or not man's intervening activities have altered the natural location of OHWM. If altered, this would necessarily entail use of an earlier date for depiction of the true OHWM.[73]

Therefore, Adams said, the rule was arbitrary and contrary to Florida law.

In the part of the rule describing the steps taken to establish an OHWL, the surveyors were informed that the "banks of a water body often form a marked escarpment at the limits of its bed." The OHWL, the rule said, "is located below and on the waterward side of the natural levees." Again, Adams criticized the rule for its failure to follow applicable Florida law, which suggested that escarpments were more expected in rivers with well-defined banks but not in lakes or in rivers without well-defined banks. The rule, Adams noted, did not make this distinction. Furthermore, he wrote, "the levees that are formed . . . may or may not be indications of the OHWM." In summary, Adams said again, the rule was arbitrary and contrary to Florida law.[74]

Likewise, the instruction to surveyors that the OHWL was "to be found at that point where the presence and action of the water is so common and usual and so long continued in all ordinary years that it prevents the establishment and growth of terrestrial vegetation" failed. Florida law, Adams pointed out, referred to the wresting of vegetation destroying the land's capability to support an ordinary agricultural crop. Elsewhere in the proposed rule, "terrestrial vegetation" had been defined as "land plants, that is plants that do not require standing or flowing water for germination, support, growth, and survival, though they may tolerate periods of inundation during each year after they become established. Woody plant species, including trees, are classified as terrestrial vegetation."[75] Such a definition, Adams noted, would allow cypress trees to determine the location of the OHWL; and, as the common Florida phenomenon of "cypress lakes" amply demonstrates, cypress trees flourish in navigable waters well below the OHWL.

In a section of the proposed rule attempting to define lands landward of the OHWM, the BPLS rule listed:

1) Swamp or overflowed lands, and floodplains adjacent to a waterbody that are subject to periodic flooding when the water body overflows its banks.
2) Beds of non-navigable streams which connect with the navigable water bodies.
3) Non-navigable sloughs, arms, bays, marshes, flood channels and similar features that are connected to but are distinct from the main body or channel of a navigable water body, as distinguished from the shallow and non-navigable margin of the main body or channel of the water body.
4) Any man-made flooded area, excavation, canal, dredged area, or widened channel or border, of or connected to a non-tidal navigable water body. In such cases, the last location of the natural ordinary high water mark shall be fixed using the best evidence available so as to exclude such man-made change or feature, and shall be so noted on the drawing.[76]

Here, Adams said, the reference to the exclusion of swamp and overflowed lands from sovereignty lands was in keeping with Florida law. "The balance of the provision is not," he wrote.[77]

In discussing the "Stated Authority to Promulgate Rules: Distinction between Technical Standards and Legal Principles," Adams noted a problem of monitoring OHWM surveying. "To the extent that the proposed rules are inconsistent with the Florida decisional law," he wrote, "the Trustees and riparian owners would be forced to seek redress in court to remedy any misapprehension" concerning the true OHWL caused by the application of the proposed rules. Adams pointed out that no mechanism existed to ensure that the trustees would know of each OHWM survey, and that there was no legal obligation to notify the trustees when an OHWM survey was commissioned. "To monitor OHWM surveys and the potential activities pursuant to the survey results in areas where the Trustees might assert ownership claims is extremely onerous, if not impossible," he asserted.

Adams pointed out a persistent inclination of the BPLS rule that, contrary to Florida law, arbitrarily sought to establish a low-water boundary favored by large landowners. Noting the input of "a substantial number of suggestions from counsel for the three mining companies" as well as "extensive contribution" by counsel representing the other intervenors, Adams cautioned that "the final product that is proposed for rule adoption has an obvious connection to the views advanced by outside counsel." [78] "In summary," Adams wrote, "establishing legal principles under the guise of technical standards not only affects practicing surveyors, but property owners as well, and the result is generally adverse to the Trustees." [79] Adams explained that it was perfectly within the rights of the BPLS for the "benefit of its licensees . . . to precisely codify, restate, or recapitulate, the decisional law of Florida." But, he warned,

> To the extent that the law in Florida is less comprehensive than that desired by [the BPLS], is unfavorable to perceptions held by [the BPLS], is unclear or has correctly deviated from federal case decisions, Florida law cannot be modified by creation, mischaracterization, addition, omission, or substitution of legal principles by Board Rule. This is precisely what is done in the proposed Rules. [80]

Adams characterized the BPLS attempt to write state rules as creating "an environment of confusion. To do so is to encourage claims to land which are not legitimate," he said. [81]

Still No Meeting of the Minds

On May 23, 1989, DNR staff submitted its rule drafts to the trustees. These drafts had been in development for a year and a half and had most recently been revised to conform to points outlined in Adams's final order. The trustees instructed the staff to return on June 13 with a process to notice workshops on the rules. Meanwhile, Adams's decision was appealed by both parties. On June 13, the trustees appointed a joint BPLS/ DNR committee to develop an OHWL rule that would be acceptable to both agencies. The committee—comprised of two surveyors and a lawyer from each of the agencies—was instructed to use the DNR-proposed rule as a basic document from which to shape a final rule supported by the BPLS and bureau staff. This committee included Dan Gentry representing the BPLS and the state cadastral surveyor, Terry Wilkinson, representing DNR's Bureau of Surveying and Mapping. At the same time, notice of workshops on the DNR's proposed rule went forward, and, in August 1989, Division of State Lands staff held four public workshops.

This period of time—during which the joint OHWL committee was charged with finding common ground for a rule both agencies could support—looks, in hindsight, like one of those rare instances when a meeting of the minds concerning widely divergent views might actually have been possible. Adams's thorough analysis of the BPLS rule provided a detailed legal guide to establishing the OHWL that had not previously existed. In addition, Terry Wilkinson, chief of the Bureau of Surveying and Mapping at DNR, was entering the fray with a fresh perspective. Wilkinson had watched from the sidelines during the BPLS rule challenge, but he had listened carefully to the concerns expressed on both sides of the issue. He knew that using scientists as consultants on OHWL issues did not threaten surveyors in the way Bob Feagin had asserted at the BPLS rule workshop back in May 1988. Instead, Wilkinson thought, the threat to the surveying profession was much greater than Feagin had claimed. For Wilkinson, the BPLS stance against the use of scientific evidence oversimplified a complex issue and actually tended to make the surveying profession appear incompetent to locate the OHWL.[82]

Wilkinson had become bureau chief at a time when the bureau had recently undergone an intense examination of its own understanding of OHWL indicators. The extensive research done from the late 1970s to the late 1980s to correlate all physical indicators of the boundary was, he believed, a necessary undertaking in order to assure that the methodology the trustees used was legally and scientifically defensible as the indicator of the true ordinary high water mark. The importance of the research, Wilkinson knew, was not in its infallibility; the value of good research is as much to show what doesn't work as what does. Neither was the purpose of the research to replace the traditional method of locating the boundary. Wilkinson felt confident that scientific evidence of the line supported the method the bureau had always used—just as Feagin's own scientists had found in their studies.[83]

As a surveyor though, he was even more concerned that the BPLS involvement with the landowners' cause made surveyors look biased and unprofessional. He knew that after the *Trustees v. BPLS* hearing there was talk that it might be appropriate to find a new profession to take charge of the sovereignty boundary location and he believed such a change would be detrimental to all concerned. Perhaps most important of all, Wilkinson came into the OHWL discussions with Gentry with an open mind. In later years, he recalled, "at the time I didn't understand Dan's [Gentry's] idea, but I wasn't sure he was wrong either."[84] Thus, there existed at least the possibility that agreement might be reached. Joint committee minutes indicate a building consensus among the four surveyors in the group; but a draft rule they produced, when revised by the attorneys, was no longer satisfactory to the surveyors. On March 27, 1990, after numerous meetings and field visits, the cochairman of the joint committee sent a letter and final report to the Division of Professional Regulation secretary (BPLS's parent organization) and the DNR executive director. The report stated that the committee had developed no rule that was acceptable to all its members, and the committee had terminated its meetings.

In later years, Wilkinson recalled wanting at this point to do two things: "I felt the need to get back to what the law required me to do—mull over the Adams decision and focus on the case law pertinent to the OHWL. I also wanted to talk to surveyors and attempt to recoup our professional neutrality on these issues."[85]

On September 13, 1990, the First District Court of Appeals (DCA), having considered the appeal of administrative hearing officer Adams's order, invalidated the entire BPLS rule—*all* of the definitions of ordinary high water line and navigability that the BPLS had attempted to promulgate. The court restated Adams's conclusion that the rules were a pronouncement of the BPLS's choice among legal principles and that its rulemaking attempt did not fall within its authority. "We affirm the hearing officer to the extent that he invalidated certain of the contested rules," the court wrote, "but reverse his determination that certain other of the contested provisions were valid."[86] The court let no part of the BPLS rule stand.

One might think that this would have been the end of the Feagin-Gentry theory of the ordinary high water line. But neither the closely reasoned analysis that hearing officer Adams had made of their theory nor the ruling of the appeals court affected them. They continued in the years ahead to characterize the whole affair as a simple matter of the BPLS lacking authority to promulgate rules, refusing to acknowledge the numerous points of their theory that Adams had said were "contrary to Florida law." This response, at least on Gentry's part, seems ironic—even grievous—given that Gentry had once said his goal in shaping the BPLS rule was that it would "stand the test in the court system." During the early days of the BPLS workshops, Gentry had remarked, "I don't want us to create a document that's not going to represent what case law has told us in the past."[87] But, when it turned out that that was precisely what they had done, he was not willing to acknowledge the discrepancy.

In a subsequent use of his "Three Cases" paper issued under the letterhead of the law firm of Blain and Cone and entitled "Ordinary High Water Line in Florida: Traditional Surveying Methodology," Gentry described the conflict over the rules:

> A challenge to the [BPLS] proposed rules . . . was filed by the Attorney General. . . . The trustees claimed that the proposed rules did not conform with the OHWL methodology as established by the case law of the State of Florida, in addition to other bases of attack. The matter proceeded to hearing before a hearing officer . . . who ruled that portions of the proposed rules were valid and the Board had the authority to adopt OHWL minimum standards as rules.[88]

This characterization of Adams's ruling ("that portions of the proposed rules were valid") constitutes Gentry's entire representation of the closely reasoned, detailed analysis in which Adams declared two-thirds of the BPLS rule "contrary to Florida law."[89] Gentry then asserted that the sole issue the appeals court had ruled on was the question of whether the BPLS had authority to promulgate its rule.

> [On appeal] the court issued an opinion finding that "the determination of rights of parties to a riparian boundary dispute is . . . a matter subject ultimately to judicial resolution . . . ". In so ruling the court determined that the Board's rulemaking effort was invalid. . . .
>
> By basing its decision on the authority of the Board to adopt the OHWL rule, the Court avoided a ruling on the controversial issue of OHWL methodology.[90]

This assertion seems to stand in direct contradiction of the court's statement: "We affirm the hearing officer to the extent that he invalidated certain of the contested rules, but reverse his determination that certain other of the contested provisions were valid."[91] However one interprets the DCA ruling, Gentry's unwillingness to address the specific points on which his rule failed to represent Florida law is clear.

More important, on *every* point of Gentry's rule in which he relied on the authority of *Howard*, Adams declared that the definitions were contrary to Florida law. These points included definitions key to the placement of the OHWL, such as "banks," "bed," "swamp and overflowed lands," "terrestrial vegetation," and "lands landward of the OHWM." The proposed "steps taken in following the legal principles to establish an OHWM"—which also relied on *Howard*—Adams declared "outside Florida law" and "unacceptable." And, regarding the BPLS proposed definition of OHWM or OHWL, Adams wrote: "[T]he detailed description of the OHWM line, set forth . . . in the [BPLS] proposed rule is from *Howard*, and is not the standard which has been accepted in Florida by Florida courts or federal courts interpreting Florida law."[92]

But in the version of his "Three Cases" paper issued by Blain and Cone after the DCA ruling, Gentry claimed: "The generally accepted source of [the] modern definition of the OHWM, for non-tidal waterbodies is the case of *Howard v. Ingersoll*. The *Howard* definition of OHWM has been adopted in Florida in the cases of *Tilden v. Smith* . . . and *Martin v. Busch*." Gentry then reproduced virtually verbatim the analysis of *Howard* from his earlier "Three Cases" paper—complete with its original misconceptions about the placement of the OHWL.

Round Three

It wasn't long before another controversy came before the courts in which the parties were seeking to test the OHWL issues that had been ruled on by the Florida Supreme Court (in the *Coastal* case) and the First District Court of Appeals (in *Trustees v. BPLS*). The case was brought in 1993 by the Kissimmee River Valley Sportsmans' Association against a riparian owner, Roger MacNamara, questioning his authority to fence off a spoil island and the adjoining area in Lake Hatchineha. MacNamara claimed the area in question was his private property and said he had fenced the area to prevent boaters from camping on his property. The sportsman's association asserted that the area in question was a part of the former lake bed retained in public ownership following the ditching of the Kissimmee River and associated lakes; the Board of Trustees of the Internal Improvement Trust Fund, finding evidence to support this claim, intervened as plaintiff. Counsel for the plaintiffs included David Guest and Jonathan Glogau. For the defendants, counsel was provided by Buddy Blain of Blain and Cone, P.A. Key testimony in the case was given by two surveyors: state cadastral surveyor Terry Wilkinson for the trustees and Dan Gentry for the MacNamaras.

Early in his testimony, Wilkinson described what he looked for when locating an ordinary high water boundary. "We're looking for the water to describe the boundary during the high water season," he said. "During an ordinary or average year in the high water season the water itself describes, delineates, the boundary of a navigable water body."[93] Wilkinson went on to describe the physical indicators of this ordinary high water level: watermarks on trees, dock pilings, and other local objects that are permanent in nature; changes in vegetation and soils; on high-banked systems, wrested vegetation; on low-banked systems, the elevation where agricultural crops such as orange trees could be sustained. Using slides and pictures to familiarize the judge with the site and the issues, Wilkinson discussed watermarks on the pilings of an old boat landing adjacent to the contested property. He pointed out the changes in the character of the wood where the pilings were regularly submerged and explained that the marks correlated well with the other indicators of ordinary high water levels. "They were high water marks," he said.[94]

In his testimony, Gentry expounded his theory of the OHWL, illustrating his remarks with slides of water bodies and pointing out his placement of the boundaries. He reviewed the *Tilden* court's distinction of high-banked and low-banked water bodies, showing slides of both types of banks on the Suwannee River. Then he displayed a slide of the Chattahoochee River. "This is Columbus, Georgia," he noted. "This is the site of *Howard v. Ingersoll*, which I believe is probably the grandfather case in all ordinary high water cases. . . . This I believe is the ordinary high water mark along the Chattahoochee River as described in the court case by the three justices."[95] At another point Gentry discussed a different slide, identifying it thus: "But this is the Kissimmee River, the old ordinary channel, as I just call it. Others call it the low water channel, which I think is an incorrect way to describe it. I think this is the ordinary channel. This is a channel that's similar to the *Howard v. Ingersoll* that Justice Wayne spoke over and over again about the ordinary channel."[96] Without the benefit of the visual aids Gentry used, it is not clear what comprised his distinctions between what others called a low water channel and what he deemed the ordinary channel. What is clear is the continued reliance on *Howard* to interpret Florida water boundaries despite the outcome of *Trustees v. BPLS*.

Following the decision in the Polk County Circuit Court for the sportsmen plaintiffs, the landowner, MacNamara, appealed. Filings in the case included those from Blain, Guest, and Glogau, and amicus briefs in support of MacNamara from Michael Rosen of the Florida Legal Foundation and Stephen Parker and Joshua Kenyon of the Southeastern Legal Foundation. In his Initial Brief of Appellant Roger MacNamara, Blain argued among other points that the "trial court erred in adopting a new theory for determining the OHWL boundary of navigable fresh waters."

The language adopted by the trial court described the boundary of navigable fresh water bodies as the ordinary reach of water during the normal, annual high water season. This definition derived from an analogy to the cycle of high and low water that forms the basis for the boundary on tidal water bodies. This analogy was put forward by counsel for the plaintiffs as a means to acknowledge that the *traditional* and *original* notion of the OHWL derived not from an average water stage but from the high water stage, albeit not the flood stage, but the *ordinary* high stage—the normal reach of water during the high water season.

But Blain insisted that the trial court's analysis of OHWL law erred through its strict reliance on Florida law. In discounting federal law, Blain argued, the court ignored decisions that more accurately described "traditional tests for determining the location of the OHWL." [97] And once again citing language from *Howard* as well as other federal and state cases, Blain put forward a description of an average water line, saying the boundary was properly located where "the water usually stands." The state's definition, Blain said, would take in all the land up to the "highest point to which the stream rises"—a line Blain interpreted as synonymous with the flood line. Such a line, Blain argued, "based on the elevation reached by the rise of the waters during the annual wet season would necessarily encompass swamp and overflowed lands that were validly conveyed by the Trustees and have become vested in private ownership." [98] Thus, Blain concluded: "The OHWL test advocated by the appellees and adopted below [by the trial court] would confiscate private property without compensation and deprive riparian landowners of their constitutionally protected rights." [99]

In October 1994 the Second District Court of Appeal (DCA) upheld the lower court ruling, adopting the final order of the trial judge holding that the "evidence as to the ordinary high water boundary established that [the] area in controversy was vegetated lake bottom and that [the] spoil island was retained in public ownership." The ruling further asserted that the "owner did not establish [the] right to fence [the] lake bottom and spoil island by grant of authority or equitable estoppel." [100] Counsel for MacNamara then petitioned the Florida Supreme Court to review the Second DCA decision, but on February 1, 1995, the court declined.

In announcing the court decisions to members, the Florida Legal Foundation's Michael Rosen wrote:

> We believe the Second DCA decision . . . clearly deviates from established principles of Florida Law in several significant respects. . . . The most important change is that it redefines the "ordinary high water line" boundary between state-owned sovereignty lands and private uplands on navigable freshwater rivers and lakes. Instead of reaffirming the traditional test, which places the boundary at the visible line marked on the bank by the continuous presence and action of the water during most of the year, this decision moves the state's ownership boundary up to the invisible elevation line representing "the normal reach of water during the high water season of each year." In effect, this redefinition converts from private to public ownership the lands that are covered by water only during the few weeks or months of the rainy season—i.e., the areas historically categorized as "swamp and overflowed" lands.[101]

Here, in the face of appellate court decisions and a refusal by the Supreme Court to review, Rosen expresses one of the enduring property-rights arguments: that the current cases "redefine" the OHWL, departing from "traditional" methodologies that surveyors had always employed, and resulting in privately owned swamp and overflowed lands now being classed as publicly owned sovereignty lands. The foundation's view, Rosen went on to say, was that "such a redefinition and relocation of the OHWL boundary would amount to an unconstitutional taking of private property by judicial decision." He declared, "We have asserted this position in an effort to preserve the issue for the possibility of seeking certiorari review by the U.S. Supreme Court if the Florida state courts did not grant relief. At the same time, we have also been aware that the trial court record in this case does not provide a very strong basis for a certiorari petition, and that it might be better to wait for another OHWL case with more favorable circumstances."[102]

Rosen then wrote to the president of the Florida Society of Professional Land Surveyors, outlining the Foundation's criticism of the court ruling. He went on to say:

> I recognize that the effects of the *MacNamara* decision on the legal rights of Florida landowners may be a matter of indifference to you in light of your December 10 letter to Bob Feagin, which directed immediate withdrawal of the Society's motion for leave to file an amicus brief on the basis that surveyors "need to remain neutral in respect to litigation over land boundaries. . . ."
>
> Whether your decision to withdraw the Society's motion for leave to file an

amicus brief may have influenced the Court's ruling is impossible to determine, and it is pointless now to speculate. I understand, however, that the Society's action in reversing its position even before the Court ruled on jurisdiction was taken largely at the behest of Terry Wilkinson, Chief of DEP's Bureau of Surveying and Mapping, who charged that those opposing the State's position misrepresented the ramifications of the *MacNamara* decision to the Society's Board. In particular, Mr. Wilkinson disputed our assertion that the OHWL definition advocated by David Guest and adopted by the courts in *MacNamara* would diminish the role of surveyors by shifting primary responsibility for determining the OHWL boundary to scientists.

    . . . While only the future can reveal the full consequences of the *MacNamara* decision, the implications for the surveying profession may be discerned from the primary sources on which the opinion relies—the law review article written by David Guest, and Terry Wilkinson's own testimony at the trial.[103]

Rosen went on to cite passages from Guest's article discussing the use of scientific evidence in locating the OHWL. He then quoted Wilkinson's answer during trial to the question "Do you believe surveyors are qualified to determine the ordinary high-water mark?" to which Wilkinson responded, "I really don't know."[104] But Rosen's belief that the *MacNamara* decision would shift the authority for locating OHWL boundaries to scientific experts seems puzzling when one considers the case itself. Only two expert witnesses testified as to the location of the water boundary; both were surveyors—Wilkinson for the trustees and Gentry for the landowner.

    Indeed, if one follows up Rosen's observation that the future would reveal the real implications to surveyors of the *MacNamara* decision, one finds something quite different than what Rosen predicted. In the years since the court ruling, the most noticeable change has not been a shift toward the authority of other scientists in locating the boundary. Instead, the real change has been an increased emphasis among surveying professionals on specialized education pertaining to the location of the OHWL boundary. As the controversial nature of the boundary and the legal complexities associated with the OHWL became apparent through such cases as *MacNamara* and *Trustees v. BPLS*, surveyors realized that the boundary location requires special attention. In actuality, prior to these cases, surveyors rarely located OHWL boundaries. Surveys depicting water features generally labeled the "top of bank" or "edge of water." Indeed, it is extremely rare to find a surveyor actually claiming to locate an OHWL boundary prior to the 1990s. This simple fact is what Wilkinson acknowledges in his statement concerning whether surveyors are qualified to determine the OHWL. When he says, "I don't know [if surveyors are qualified to determine the OHWL]," he is registering the understanding that locating an OHWL boundary requires special knowledge of Florida law and experience with the physical indicators of the line under widely varying conditions. He knows surveyors do not presently receive such training as a matter of course—that in order to responsibly claim to establish an OHWL boundary, surveyors will have to educate themselves. One of the most visible outcomes of the *MacNamara* and *BPLS* cases has been the development by Wilkinson and others of OHWL seminars for the professional development of surveyors, appraisers, and other land professionals. And, whereas, prior to these controversial cases, no opportunities for such specialized education existed, hundreds of surveyors annually now avail themselves of seminars dealing specifically with these issues.[105]

And Again . . .

In 1992, during a review by the governor and cabinet of a permit challenge, the governor and cabinet (who also serve as the trustees of sovereignty lands) noted that the property involved in the permit challenge might be subject to a state claim as sovereignty land. They instructed their staff to determine what, if any, were the state's interests. As it turned out, much of the property slated for development by the riparian owner, David Smith, was below the OHWL of Lake Poinsett, a navigable water of the state. After efforts failed to negotiate a redesign of Smith's development that would be contained on his upland property, the trustees sued Smith for ejectment in 1995.

Although the case has not at the time of this writing come to trial, several components of the case are of interest to this story, most notably that Smith's counsel includes Bob Feagin and Mike Rosen, and his surveyor is Dan Gentry. These defendants have stated their opinion that the dispute between Smith and the trustees "turns first and foremost on issues of law, not on issues of fact. The most critical of these legal issues are the proper definition, interpretation, and application of the OHWL under Florida law."[106] Smith's counsel argues, "These legal issues must be decided before the location of the OHWL boundary on Lake Poinsett, between state-owned submerged lands and Smith's property, can be determined."[107] Once again Gentry has located an "ordinary high water line" boundary that falls at or below the average water level of Lake Poinsett. Once again Feagin and Rosen are urging the proposition that the trustees' method of locating the OHWL departs from the "traditional" methodology.[108] And once again we shall have to wait for the outcome of this latest rendition of the OHWL controversy.

After All

As for the Kissimmee River, the passage of the Kissimmee Restoration bill in 1976 called for completion of the restoration within five years. But landowners along the river blocked permits and mounted legal challenges to the state's sovereignty lands claims. In 1993, under petition from the district, the trustees worked out a policy concerning title to sovereignty lands that would allow the Water Management District to continue restoration efforts without further delay. Some saw this decision as a defeat of the strong protection of sovereignty lands the state had promised; and all the work to sort out the OHWL in the Kissimmee River Valley seemed to come to nothing. But, by the spring of 1999, water management agents had acquired more than 90,000 acres, most of it pasture, on which the project depended.

On June 10, 1999, contractors began work on a restoration project designed by the district and corps to return forty-three miles of the Kissimmee to its historic bed and restore 28,000 of the 35,000 acres of wetlands lost in the channelization.[109] The restoration effort, estimated to cost some $474 million and take fifteen years to complete, calls for twenty-two miles of C-38 to be filled, forcing the river's waters back into their former winding course. Modeling and testing of the restoration have been performed for two decades, and test portions have proven successful. The district reports that as the restoration effort proceeds, "some positive changes have been observed. In formerly isolated sections of the river, oxbows are flowing again. Emergent and shoreline vegetation has reappeared and is thriving. Waterfowl are returning. Water quality is improving."[110] But restoring the river means finding our way to an end never before pursued, much less accomplished. And the outcome won't be known for many years.

I do not know much about gods; but I think that the river
Is a strong brown god—sullen, untamed and intractable,
Patient to some degree, at first recognized as a frontier;
Useful, untrustworthy, as a conveyor of commerce;
Then only a problem confronting the builder of bridges.
The problem once solved, the brown god is almost forgotten
By the dwellers in cities—ever, however, implacable,
Keeping his seasons and rages, destroyer, reminder
Of what men choose to forget.
T. S. ELIOT, "The Dry Salvages," *Four Quartets*

6 A New Low for the Ordinary High Water Line: The Demand for Certainty

DISPUTES PERTAINING TO the ordinary high water line are probably as old as the law attempting to divide public lands from private. In England, the boundaries of lands adjoining the sea—lands that were granted in the sixth-century charters of Anglo-Saxon kings—were still providing the basis for litigation well into the modern age.[1] In Florida, the law and methodology establishing tidal water boundaries seem now to be well settled, but the law pertaining to freshwater boundaries continues to be challenged. For the most part, these conflicts represent the discordance of interest groups vying with one another to control the criteria of the boundary line and the method of locating it. A small group of ranchers, developers, phosphate-mining corporations, and other property-rights proponents would like to see the boundary line defined at a low water stage, allowing their use of more property in the rich margins along lakes and streams. This group tends to be well funded and able to pursue their campaign to have the boundary reflect their interests through litigation, legislation, rule making, and lobbying. Typically, this group argues that the state claims private property as sovereignty land by placing the ordinary high water line too far landward.

On the other side of the issue, a small group of air boaters, hunters, and sporting association members continually argues that the line is really much farther upland than the state has been willing to claim. This group charges that the state is allowing sovereignty lands to fall into private ownership by not asserting its claim on behalf of the public interest. This group tends to be less well organized than the landowner group, and typically makes its presence felt through letter writing to state officials and by challenging in court any trespassing arrests made on what they consider to be sovereignty lands.

Only rarely do disputes arise between the trustees (who are charged with the protection of sovereignty lands) and individual waterfront property owners. Many people move to Florida, buy waterfront property, and never understand what constitutes the water boundary of their property until some issue raises the question of its location. In an average year, the Bureau of Surveying and Mapping (as staff to the trustees) responds to hundreds of requests for waterfront boundary determinations by property owners who want to acquire permits for docks or other development plans. Generally such requests can be handled quickly and economically by determining a safe upland line instead of the ordinary high water line.

A safe upland line (SUL) is an informal term used to describe a line that is at, or above (landward of) the true OHWL. It is considered a planning and development tool—not a boundary. In most cases, riparian property owners do not need the OHWL located; instead, they need an elevation to include in a permit application (as for a dock) in order to be certain their projects are not encroaching on sovereignty lands, or to approximate areas for land transactions. Using an SUL can save the property owner the considerable cost of establishing the OHWL. A safe upland line may be mapped using aerial photography or other existing surveys and maps, thus reducing the extent and cost of a field survey. In most cases SULs are based on very limited information. For high-banked water bodies, the top of bank is considered "safe." The lower edge of mature upland vegetation or the upper limits of wetland jurisdiction are also used as good indicators of an SUL. Hydrologic data is used in many situations when the period of record is sufficient. As with the OHWL, care must be taken to assure the physical indicators and data are not influenced by artificial causes.

The data to derive an SUL may be on file with the Bureau of Surveying and Mapping, but the bureau welcomes information from those familiar with the particular site in question. The surveyor working on a project may possess significant knowledge about the water body, such as historic water levels or the type of vegetation along the shore, which could expedite the determination. The bureau also cautions surveyors that if they are surveying an SUL provided or approved by the bureau, they should keep in mind that these lines are based on limited information. If the line seems to vary greatly from the surveyor's own estimation of where the OHWL would fall, the bureau asks that the surveyor call and discuss with them what he or she is seeing in the field. Of the hundreds of requests handled each year by the bureau, less than one determination a year is contested and those rarely end in litigation.

New Strategies, Old Arguments

Today, most of the battles with the trustees over the ordinary high water line—what it is and how to locate it—still arise from the same interest groups that opposed the state in *Coastal Petroleum v. American Cyanamid, Trustees v. Board of Professional Land Surveyors*, and *MacNamara v. KRVSA*. Since the rulings in those cases, these parties have continued to work to have the boundary between sovereignty lands and private uplands defined at an average or low water line.[2] Their theory of the boundary was initially presented by Robert Feagin on behalf of Mobil Oil Corporation as a party in *Coastal* and again in 1988 when Feagin proposed it as an OHWL rule to the Board of Professional Land Surveyors (BPLS). Surveyor Dan Gentry propounded the theory in *Kissimmee River Valley Sportsmans' Association v. MacNamara*. It surfaced again in the mid-1990s, this time in conjunction with *Trustees v. David A. Smith*.

In 1995, the trustees had filed suit against Smith, charging that he had impounded (diked and drained) and illegally occupied several hundred acres of sovereignty lands in the bed of Lake Poinsett. In November 1995, Smith began lobbying the cabinet to issue him a disclaimer on the property. His rationale was based around his assertion that "State submerged lands do not include 'swamp and overflowed' lands," which, Smith pointed out, had been patented to the states for the "express purpose of encouraging their improvement" by constructing "necessary levees and drains."[3] Because this argument sounded so much like the "Mobil Theory" (as this average- or low-water theory had come to be called in legal circles), it came as no surprise to discover that Mike Rosen, Dan Gentry, and Robert Feagin were part of Smith's litigation team.

According to the Mobil Theory, swamp and overflowed lands determine the extent of sovereignty lands under criteria establishing swamp and overflowed lands as any lands that can be made useful for agriculture by diking and draining. This approach, of course, completely reverses OHWL case law that holds that shores and beds of navigable waters are sovereignty lands to the ordinary high water line. Case law defines sovereignty lands by where the water stands during high water season of an ordinary year.[4] Sovereignty lands are not defined by the uplands—for example, by the extent of lands that can be made useful to agriculture by diking and draining. Given today's technology, which makes it possible to alter entire watercourses, the Mobil Theory criteria of uplands could feasibly include large portions of the bed of any lake or river.

Smith and his team also claimed that the Division of State Lands had recently developed a new methodology that placed the OHWL more landward than the "traditional" OHWL. This claim too had been developed as part of the Mobil Theory that Feagin introduced to the BPLS when he presented a draft rule on OHWL for that board's adoption. In fact, evidence in the *Mobil Oil Corporation v. Florida* case showed that it was the Mobil Theory that radically departed from what had traditionally been seen as the OHWL boundary. In a 2001 *Florida Bar Journal* article detailing the situation of sovereignty lands, Assistant State Attorney General Monica Reimer described how the Mobil Theory came about:

> Following the Florida Supreme Court's rejection of the "I have a deed" argument in 1986, the parties in *Coastal Petroleum v. American Cyanamid* were sent to trial on the issues of navigability and the ordinary high water boundary. The cases had originally been filed because phosphate companies who owned land bordering on the Peace River were potentially liable for tens of millions of dollars worth of phosphate which allegedly had been mined from the river's bed. Because the river bed extended from the ordinary high water line on one side to the ordinary high water line on the other side, there was an extraordinary financial incentive for the phosphate companies to argue for as narrow a river as possible in order to minimize their potential liability. As a party in one of the lawsuits, Mobil Mining and Mineral invented a novel ordinary high water theory that clearly reflected this incentive.[5]

In its trial brief, Mobil argued that the boundary on all Florida water bodies was the point where the "river had wrested the bed of terrestrial vegetation."[6] Mobil then defined terrestrial vegetation as all vegetation except floating weeds such as water lilies and water hyacinths, a definition that placed the boundary line waterward of all cypress trees, including those growing in the bed of the river. "The fact that the lands might be submerged for six to nine months of an average year," Reimer wrote, "was answered by the assertion that high water which occurred during the six-month rainy season was merely an 'annual rise' which should be eliminated from the determination of ordinary high water." Mobil justified these indicators with the contention that all lands upward of this line fit the description of "swamp and overflowed lands" and could be used for "agricultural purposes" such as cypress timber operations and low water season cattle foraging. "According to the Mobil Theory," Reimer wrote, " 'if the water on the land is *not* useful for navigation and the lands *can* be made useful by agriculture (by diking and draining), then it is outside the [ordinary high water mark].' "[7]

As it turned out, the phosphate companies settled in 1987 when evidence came to light showing that "ordinary high water determinations made by Mobil itself *prior* to the commencement of the phosphate litigation (and the invention of the new ordinary high water theory) matched the state's ordinary high water line determination."[8] A series of permits for various locations on the river dating back to almost the turn of the century had required the companies to produce ordinary high water line determinations. In "some instances," Reimer reported, "the companies' new ordinary *high* water line was below prior ordinary *low* water determinations."[9] Thus it became clear that it was the Mobil Theory that had departed from traditional methods of establishing the ordinary high water boundary.

In spite of Smith's intensive lobbying, in December 1995 the cabinet declined to vote on his disclaimer, citing the pending litigation as the proper venue for settling the dispute. But this was not to be the last appearance of the Mobil Theory.

The David Smith Case

In April 1999, at a James Madison Institute fund-raiser for Smith's case, Feagin discussed the newest battleground in his longtime campaign to change the boundary between public trust sovereignty lands and privately held uplands. In his talk, "The Largest Land Swindle in the

History of Florida," Feagin told the audience about Smith's case, which he said he had taken in hopes of "settling the OHWL thing." Not surprisingly, the talk centered on key points of the Mobil Theory.

Feagin began by describing Smith's "plight" as one in which the state was seeking to eject Smith from property on Lake Poinsett that his family farmed for many years. According to Feagin, Smith's problems indicated a large-scale waterfront land grab being conducted by the Trustees of the Internal Improvement Trust Fund. "In *Trustees v. Smith,*" Feagin said, "the Trustees charge that Smith is illegally occupying public lands and planning to develop those lands into a golf course and residential suburb." Feagin claimed, however, that Smith was just one of many private landowners subject to "eviction" from their land by similar state actions. The vehicle for this "swindle," Feagin said, was the application of a new method of determining the OHWL. Using this method, Feagin asserted, some 35,000 private ownerships were subject to litigation costing $1 billion and affecting millions of acres.

This claim, however, is one that property rights proponents have made since 1986 when they lost the *Coastal* case. However, by 1999 only three cases involving OHWL methodology had arisen. Although there has been a progressive clarification of the OHWL definition by the courts—especially since the 1960s in response to increasing development of the lands around Florida's inland lakes and rivers—the state's procedure for determining the OHWL continues to follow the directives of the Florida Supreme Court, and there has been no change of procedure of the kind Feagin described.

In reviewing his own involvement in OHWL issues, Feagin recapped his participation in three key contests: the Marketable Record Title Act, *Coastal,* and *Trustees v. Board of Professional Land Surveyors.* During the 1980s, Feagin said, he represented several phosphate mining companies with mining interests in sovereignty lands. This work involved Feagin in efforts to uphold the Marketable Record Title Act (MRTA), which, he said, sought to "eliminate state claims to swamp and overflowed lands." In actuality, MRTA was created to simplify title searches and facilitate land transactions by extinguishing any claim more than thirty years old against the property being transacted. The state has no claim to privately owned swamp and overflowed lands above the OHWL, but it does have title to lands beneath navigable waters below the OHWL. Smith's title to his upland property derives from swamp and overflowed lands deeds.

Feagin went on to describe his theory that the state should not hold fee simple title to sovereignty lands. In a 1985 document called "An Analysis of the Impact of Florida's Marketable Record Title Act on Public and Private Rights," Feagin had argued that the "state does not need to have title to the land [under navigable waters] in order to protect the public rights or to regulate the use of land and water." Instead, he suggested that the beds of navigable waters should be privately owned and that "public easements" be provided to allow the public access to boating and fishing. In his talk, Feagin reiterated this theme of "navigational servitude," as it is commonly referred to in legal cases. This stance arises from a particular feature of British law, from which our version of the Public Trust Doctrine derives. This feature provides for the possibility of private ownership of lands under navigable waters but maintains public use of the water. Following out this possibility in the Public Trust Doctrine, however, is not without risks. It raises the likelihood that, with title to "public lands" in private hands, the so-called "public easements" over the waters will shrink under the constant pressure of large landowners to limit access to navigable waters adjoining their properties. It also provides the basis for "takings" claims in which title holders to "public lands" who are denied permits to develop those lands can sue the state.

Feagin argues that the "public easements" option should be endorsed in Florida. But it is difficult to imagine what the incentive to private ownership of land under navigable water bodies would be unless it includes the right to limit public access. After all, holding title to these lands entails taxes and legal liability. Dean Frank E. Maloney, professor and dean emeritus at University of Florida Law Center and principal investigator of the Water Resources Scientific Information Center of Competence in Eastern Water Law, has argued that a navigable servitude would not be enough to protect the public interest in navigable waters. In his 1978 article "The Ordinary High Water Mark: Attempts at Settling an Unsettled Boundary Line," Maloney notes: "If the bed is in private ownership the state's authority to control the taking of minerals, etc. from the bed is severely diminished. If there is any lesson to be learned from recent environmental skirmishes, it is that state ownership allows for flexibility of alternatives while private ownership does not. Clearly, it would be a mistake to irrevocably fix the interests of the public in this manner." [10] In 1968, Floridians rejected this private ownership avenue when they ratified a new constitution providing that title to lands under navigable waters be held by the state in trust for all the people.

The use of MRTA as a tool to transfer sovereignty lands into private ownership ended in 1986 when the Florida Supreme Court, in *Coastal*, held that "MRTA did not divest [the trustees] of title to state sovereignty lands below ordinary high-water mark of navigable rivers."[11] But for Feagin, this ruling was not conclusive. "This was a bad decision," Feagin told his audience, "in which the Court adopted the Notice of Navigability theory." Here, Feagin again conveyed the impression that the rules determining public and private ownership changed when the court adopted a new "theory." But what Feagin calls a "theory" is actually an established tenet of Florida law dating back to the 1927 keystone case *Martin v. Busch*.[12] In the *Coastal* case, the court merely restated the 1927 finding that grantees of swamp and overflowed lands "took with notice that such grants did not convey sovereignty lands," pointing out that grantees of swamp and overflowed lands "did not have any moral or legal claim to state sovereignty lands, nor did their successors."[13]

Not only did grantees of swamp and overflowed lands take the lands "with notice," but the court has also made clear that swamp and overflowed lands deeds cannot convey sovereignty lands. The original patent of swamp and overflowed lands from the federal government did not include sovereignty lands since they already belonged to the state. Deeds deriving from those swamp and overflowed patents cannot therefore convey any sovereignty lands, and that is why swamp and overflowed lands deeds do not entitle their holders to lands below the OHWL, even when those lands are not expressly excluded from the deed's legal description. Feagin and others have characterized these swamp and overflowed deeds as being issued "in error" by the state and claim that the state now wants to "take back" lands granted in those deeds. But from early in the twentieth century the supreme court has consistently held that a swamp deed "does not affect the title held by the state to lands under navigable waters by virtue of the sovereignty of the state"[14] and that grantees of swamp deeds were aware of this. The grantees of swamp deeds acted *with notice* "that the conveyance of Swamp and Overflowed land does not in law cover any sovereignty lands," regardless of whether the deed described lands under navigable waters as part of the lands being granted.[15]

Throughout his talk, Feagin characterized sovereignty lands conflicts as arising fairly recently as a result of radical changes made under the influence of environmental groups. "For many years there was not a controversy, there was not a dispute," he said. "The visible mark on the bank was agreed on." Prior to *Coastal*, Feagin claimed, a number of decisions "maintained the peace." In *State ex rel Ellis v. Gerbing*, he said, the court "recognized the distinction between sovereignty lands and S&O lands." This case also recognized, however, that a swamp and overflowed lands deed does not convey sovereignty lands—a point Feagin did not mention.

In *Tilden,* Feagin said, the supreme court "defined OHWL for fresh navigable waters pro-private ownership—the way we want it." But Feagin's enthusiasm for the *Tilden* definition seems puzzling, since in *Trustees v. BPLS* Feagin supported an OHWL definition that, according to the ruling, contradicted *Tilden.*

Notably missing from Feagin's list of private ownership–friendly cases is *Martin.* This is the other 1927 supreme court case that established the fundamentals of OHWL in Florida. However, because it deals with flat-banked water bodies, which do not normally have the "visible mark on the bank" on which he wishes to rely, Feagin omits it when recalling the earlier, ostensibly conflict-free time when boundaries were "agreed on." Such flat-banked water bodies are, of course, common in Florida. In the *Trustees v. BPLS* ruling, the hearing officer, Adams, cited *Martin,* saying the BPLS "deliberately failed to explain in their proposed rule the appearance of the Ordinary High Water Mark in those places where the topography is low and flat, which is frequently the case in Florida."

It was in *Coastal,* Feagin said, that "the state changed its position. They no longer used an observable mark for the OHWL, but a scientifically determined mark way up the bank," he said. This came about in the 1970s, according to Feagin, because "environmental groups believed the police power was not sufficient to protect navigable waters. . . . A new position by the state came into being." Under this "new complicated procedure of determining OHWL," Feagin said, "the phosphate companies settled the cases in order not to accept this method of OHWL." (Feagin did not mention the early permits in which the phosphate companies had placed the OHWL well above the line they later asserted in litigation.) Although the phosphate companies avoided paying fines, Feagin said, the settlement "did not resolve the question" as he hoped the David Smith case would.

Feagin's assertion that the state replaced an "observable mark" with a "scientifically determined mark" produced more than a few quizzical expressions in the audience. Some people, it seems, were puzzled by this supposed distinction, but Feagin offered no further explanation. The court, however, has not been so obscure in its instruction. Its holding is that the "best evidence attainable and the best methods available should be utilized in determining and establishing the line of true ordinary high-water mark. . . . Marks upon the ground or upon local objects that are more or less permanent may be considered in connection with competent testimony and other evidence in determining the true line of ordinary high-water mark."[16]

In fact, Feagin's characterization of the OHWL controversy does not accord with the record. A thorough reading of Florida's OHWL history and case law over the past century shows not general agreement on where the OHWL was but rather a general absence of cases in which development around inland water bodies made OHWL determinations necessary. Over the course of the last century, the court progressively clarified how the line is to be determined given the particular difficulties of Florida's topography. But prior to the 1960s, there was very little call to actually determine an OHWL, that is, to set it on the ground—primarily as a result of Florida's development patterns. Most state lands policy had until this time focused on coastal problems, since coastal areas had developed so quickly. By the mid-1960s, however, development along Florida's many inland lakes and rivers was booming. In some instances, riparian landowners along lowered lakes began fencing lake basin areas and filling exposed lands adjacent to their properties.[17] Development encroachments, not environmental groups, have spurred the need for OHWL determinations. Smith and Feagin claim that the methodology used by the Division of State Lands to determine OHWL has changed in recent years in response to the state's interest in environmental protection, but the state's OHWL determinations have been refined on the basis of court rulings, not fluctuating environmental policies.

In closing his talk, Feagin said, "To win this case is going to require a tremendous effort on David Smith's part. We face a very committed, talented foe who is well financed by all of our tax money. David Smith is seeking help from all private landowners. If we can't get this case prepared and presented it will mean a tremendous loss, not by the water of Lake Poinsett eroding the value of David Smith's property, but by government refusing its responsibility to uphold private property rights," Feagin asserted. "Are we going to have an OHWL that is determined by scientific evidence or by something observable?" Feagin asked. "The right of a person not to be ejected from his land," Feagin stated, "is what the case is about."

During the question and answer session that followed, Feagin answered queries from the audience. One attendee asked about the dikes. "The very presence of dikes tends to suggest that water is being kept out," he said. "Don't the dikes somewhat weaken the case?" Swamp and overflowed lands, Feagin claimed, "must be diked for agricultural use." That is why it's important to distinguish swamp and overflowed lands from navigable waters, he said. "Swamp and overflowed lands can be reclaimed for agricultural use. Their value is not destroyed by the long and continuous action of the water." What Feagin failed to mention is that dikes can be legitimately used only to drain swampland that is *above* the OHWL. David Smith's own engineers estimated the OHWL of Lake Poinsett at thirteen feet in 1977, and staff for the Board of Trustees concluded that the OHWL is not below the thirteen-foot contour. Smith's dikes extend below the elevation of ten feet.

The Demand for Certainty

In 2000, property rights proponents made another attempt to transfer large portions of sovereignty lands into private ownership—this time through the Florida legislature. The bill—variously dubbed the Florida Land Title Protection Act and the Sovereignty Lands Bill—purported to resolve what it described as sovereignty ownership claims against private landowners.[18] After characterizing the situation of sovereignty lands being encompassed in swamp and overflowed lands deeds descriptions as a "cloud of title" that the state was improperly asserting against landowners, the bill then proposed as the remedy that the legislature "ratify" these deeds and "make good" on what the state had conveyed in issuing the deeds. The first version of the bill sought to award to private landowners the sovereignty lands—including tidelands—encompassed in their swamp and overflowed lands deeds if the property owner had paid taxes on the land. This version would have transferred to private ownership more than 600,000 acres of lakes and rivers including most of the Peace River, the Myakka, the Manatee, the Little Manatee, and the Hillsborough River; large portions of Lake Istokpoga, Lake Harney, Lake Cypress, and the St. Johns River; and all of Lake Poinsett, Blue Cypress Lake, and the Wacissa River—the list would include any water body not meandered in the original government surveys. Florida case law is clear that the payment of taxes on sovereignty lands does not transform those public lands into private ownership. The remedy for landowners who have been charged taxes on sovereignty lands adjoining their uplands is a tax refund.

Not surprisingly, the forces behind the bill were some of the same as those who had asserted that swamp and overflowed lands deeds provided title to navigable waters during the MRTA land grab. When legislators supporting the bill were informed that the "deed question" had been asked and answered by the Florida Supreme Court in the *Coastal* case, the backers shifted gears, attempting instead to define the ordinary high water line at the low water mark. To accomplish this, the House Appropriations Committee, in a highly unusual move, passed a "strike-all" amendment to House Bill 1807 substituting "OHWL" definitions provided by the bill's sponsors in place of the original language concerning deeds. The unusual procedure was carried out over the objections of some committee members who protested that substantive changes of this scale should not be made in a fiscal committee without opportunity for analysis in a committee of substance. The major substance of the bill was now comprised of selected quotations and paraphrases of case law dealing with the OHWL, including that from other states; it also contained additions to the courts' language that had the effect of contradicting established law. Again the language and concept were identical to the low water boundary theory that failed in the *Coastal* case and in *Trustees v. Board of Professional Land Surveyors*.

The proposed definition of the "ordinary high water mark" cited selected passages from *Tilden* and *Martin*, but then proceeded to define key words from the court decisions in highly unconventional ways. For instance the bill made a fairly faithful paraphrase of *Tilden*'s statement that the OHW mark is "not the highest point to which the water rises in times of freshets or flood, but is the line which the water impresses upon the soil by covering it for sufficient periods of time to deprive it of vegetation and to destroy its value for agriculture." But it then added the following qualification: "The ordinary high water mark does not encompass lands which are temporarily covered by water during floods, including the ordinary seasonal rises caused by rains that may recur annually, but which are valuable for agriculture or capable of use as pastures during most of the year." This interpretation of "freshets or flood" as including ordinary annual rains effectively meant that the "ordinary high water line" would have to be surveyed during the dry season only—a change that would move the boundary between sovereignty lands and adjoining uplands to a low water line. It also meant that ordinary annual rises in water levels would now be considered floods.

It seemed the more the legislature tried to interpret the language of the case law, the more confused the issues became. Sponsors of the house version of the bill, Representatives Paula Dockery and Adam Putnam, in the last days of the session, held a colloquy to issue a statement of legislative intent concerning the bill. Such statements, published in the journal of the house or senate contemporaneous with passage of legislation are given great weight by the courts in subsequent cases concerning the statute. The *Journal of the House of Representatives* for May 1, 2000, noted,

On motion by Rep. Putnam, the rules were suspended and the following question(s) and answer(s) were ordered spread upon the *Journal,* in order to establish legislative intent:

Rep. Dockery: Is it the intent of the Legislature to adopt a definition of an ordinary-high-water line which uses as its methodology "the normal reach of water during the high-water season?" [This is a direct quote of language adopted by the *MacNamara* court.]

Rep. Putnam: Absolutely not. The Legislative intent is that the definition of ordinary-high-water mark is found in *Tilden v. Smith* and *Martin v. Busch*. . . . It is not the intent of the Legislature to use this definition to establish a low-water mark.

Rep. Dockery: The ordinary-high-water-mark definition contained in this bill includes the word "freshet." What is a freshet?

Rep. Putnam: This portion of the *Tilden* decision is quoted from the case authorities, all of which consistently and clearly explain that the term "freshets," as used in this context, is intended to include temporary rises of water caused by the seasonal rains that recur annually. It is the intent of the Legislature that this shall be the definition of "freshet." [19]

Of course the case authorities include no such explanations of freshets. The language attempting to extend the definition of freshet to include seasonal rains makes absolute nonsense of the phrase *ordinary high water line,* and such language originates not in case law but in theories designed to accommodate the interests of landowners and not the general public. The exclusion of the rainy season—which *is* the ordinary high water season—in determining the boundary of freshwater lakes and streams can only result in a low water boundary. Such a procedure, if adopted, would not allow for the inclusion of even well-defined banks and shores as sovereignty lands.

This example illustrates, however, one of the enduring opportunities for confusion in case law interpretation. Language in *Tilden* includes several references to durations: the high water line is to be "found by examining the bed and banks and ascertaining where the presence and action of waters are *so common and usual and so long continued in all ordinary years* as to mark upon the soil of the bed a character distinct from that of the banks"; it is the "line which the river impresses upon the soil by *covering it for sufficient periods* to deprive it of vegetation"; it is "coordinate with the limit of the bed . . . which the water *occupies sufficiently long and continuously* to wrest it from vegetation." Yet there is little comment or clarification as to how long *sufficiently long and continuously* actually is. I often feel that opposing parties in OHWL conflicts have very different ideas of this duration in their minds, but it is rarely specified. If, for example, the legislators' idea behind defining freshets to include seasonal rains was meant to exclude from OHWL determinations the sudden high and temporary rises that result from torrential downpours—the kind that flood streets and yards and overflow canals for several hours on summer afternoons—I don't think anyone would find that intention unreasonable. The state of Florida is not interested in claiming property overflowed by these downpours (freshets). In practice, the Bureau of Surveying and Mapping uses as a guideline when locating ordinary high water marks a stage duration range of 15–35 percent.[20] Bureau Chief Terry Wilkinson explains that this means that the water in a lake or river exceeds the watermarks under consideration between seven weeks and four and a half months of the year. This ensures, he notes, that the marks being used to indicate the water boundary qualify as *ordinary high water* marks—not flood marks (which generally fall in the 1–10 percent stage duration range) or average water marks (which fall around the 50 percent stage duration). The problem with the language as written in the 2000 legislative bill was that it excluded seasonal rains themselves from criteria determining the OHWL boundary. These rains are the means of recharge and the basis of life for freshwater lakes and rivers, and so excluding rain from the cycle of water bodies can't be the basis for finding their natural boundaries.

Eventually the so-called "sovereignty lands bill" raised in the 2000 legislature was defeated. The arguments made for this bill had been made before, and the court had already clarified these issues definitively; so the polemics provided little insight into the issues—even though they still threatened much of what is essential to Florida. One of the most telling words, however, that came up again and again during the legislative effort to codify the OHWL was *certainty.* Many representatives were concerned that people want certainty about their water boundaries, and they seemed to assume that the law could provide this certainty.

American philosopher Stanley Cavell has pointed out that the demand for certainty is a disease of our time. We seem unable to come to grips with situations in which we must live with perpetual shift, inexactitude, conditions beyond our control. A primary goal of much that our society undertakes is to provide stability, control, and certainty. An underlying expectation we have of our laws is that they will further this goal. As a species our history has been to control and dominate our surroundings such that they are subject to us and not vice versa. People feel vulnerable to nature, and we believe the law should be able and ready to remedy this vulnerability we feel. The same is true of the practice of surveying. Its value to society is in part its ability to establish boundaries that we regard as stable, certain, and unchanging—and that give us control over the land, transforming it from prairies, marshes, and scrub into sections, townships, and ranges.

During the final week of the 2000 legislative session, when it was still unclear whether the Sovereignty Lands Bill would pass or fail, one of the bill sponsors was interviewed on *Capitol Report,* a radio program that covers the legislative sessions. The representative was asserting that without a statute saying what the OHWL is, people have nothing to go on to determine where their water boundary is. "If we pass this bill," he said, "people can get on the internet, go to the statutes, print out a copy of the definition, go out in their back yard"—and here he paused and seemed at a loss for words before he finally said, "and look at it." During that pause all kinds of things went through my mind. What was he going to say? That people could go out in the backyard with that statute and find the line themselves? I couldn't help wondering if this was the tack this man would take if he needed to know where any of his upland property boundaries were. Would he really go to the Internet, print out a copy of the statutes governing boundary surveys, go out in the backyard, and read it? No. He would call a surveyor.[21] Why should it be any different with his water boundary, which, if anything, requires more expertise than his land boundaries? Perhaps in part the answer is because water boundaries seem so obvious. Here is land, there is water. Until we look again.

The ordinary high water line is a different kind of boundary than any other in one very important way: the OHWL is a *natural* boundary that has been adopted into law. The very nature of the line operates against certainty, and that's one of the reasons it has been difficult to satisfy the type of demand our society is so set on. The dynamic nature of the OHWL undermines the very premise of private property, which, as a commodity to be bought and sold, must be quantifiable. But the land and water were here long before we came along and began putting arbitrary, imaginary lines over the landscape. Natural boundaries of the landscape—such as a ridge or a shore—sometimes serve as calls in our legal descriptions. But these natural boundaries are in a deep way at odds with the exactitude of measured calls. Their first calling is to the dynamic forces of the world, not to the service of locating a human commodity. It may be indicative of our nervousness about approaching the land in the way we do that when we section up the land we call it *real* estate—as if it were any less real before we measured it. But, of course, what calling it *real estate* indicates is that it has been measured, quantified in a way that can be regenerated whenever necessary to establish the value of that particular parcel. But this denotation and valuation does tend to obscure the real value of the land in its state of wholeness as a functioning ecosystem that supports life.

By Any Other Name

The cavalier treatment of language, however, has become a mark of OHWL theorists working to alter the boundary to suit their purposes. The legislative bills in 2000 only provided one example of this tactic: continuing to call the boundary the "ordinary high water line" while defining the criteria so that the low or average water stage established the actual boundary. The strategy appeared again during preparations for the *Trustees v. Smith* case, months after the bill had been defeated and legislators had gone home.

In August 2000, Terry Wilkinson, chief of the Bureau of Surveying and Mapping, was deposed as the surveying expert for the trustees in the case. Robert Feagin, counsel for David Smith, conducted the questioning. In a lengthy exchange concerning the bureau's methodology for establishing the OHWL, Feagin asked Wilkinson about the language describing what he called "the condition of the water." Citing language from *Tilden*—the "presence and action of waters are so common and usual and so long continued in all ordinary years"—Feagin asked Wilkinson if this phrase would be an accurate physical description of the "condition of the water" in his OHWL methodology.

Wilkinson answered, "I think it would in a general sort of way, but again, I don't think you can [take] this alone out in the field and find an ordinary high water mark."

Feagin then questioned Wilkinson as to what provided "better clarification about the condition of the water more definitive and more authoritative than the Florida Supreme Court saying, 'so common and usual and so long continued in all ordinary years'?"

Wilkinson replied, "To be more definitive would be *Martin v. Busch,* marks on local objects."

Feagin responded, "No. Condition of the water. I want something that describes the condition of the water. . . . You talked about marks on local objects. That doesn't describe the condition of the water. What condition produced that mark?"

Wilkinson answered, "Water."

Feagin then asked, "Was it water that was so common and usual and long continued in all ordinary years? Certainly [the holding in] *Martin* didn't change that, did it? . . . That description of the condition of the water. It didn't provide any different description, any more definition to it than that. Do you agree with me?"

Wilkinson responded, "I think that that's true. When you read the whole thing and—starting with the words high water mark . . . "

Feagin interrupted, "High water mark is a label."

To which Wilkinson responded, "Well, I think it's a description of the boundary, too."[22]

Again, a few moments later, Feagin returned to the issue when questioning Wilkinson about the "agricultural crops test" in the *Tilden* case. Feagin asked Wilkinson if he would rely on the agricultural crops test today, and Wilkinson replied that it was part of what he would look at.

"And if that occurred," Feagin continued, "the fact that it was in terms of stage duration greater than 50 percent would not put the ordinary high water mark at some other place, would it?" (Feagin is asking if the agricultural crops test could be used to place the OHWL boundary more lakeward than the 50 percent stage duration—that is, where the water is at or exceeds this elevation more than half the year.)

Wilkinson replied, "It [the OHWL] would have to be above average, because high just means high. High doesn't mean average. Ordinary high means average high. Ordinary high does not mean average."

"I think this is probably what divides us," Feagin responded. "You believe that the definition is controlled by its label ordinary high and applying current statistical computations to it and not controlled by the statement about interaction between the water and the land in producing some observable marks on the land. You believe that it's the—that use of the word high from a statistical standpoint that controls."

"Well, I'm not sure about a statistical standpoint," Wilkinson answered, "since, you know, throughout Florida there aren't that many gauges in fresh waters anyhow. So you couldn't do that to begin with. But I think you have to correlate these tests: the marks on local objects—you have to look at that; the ordinary agricultural crops, which they were thinking about in *Tilden*—you have to look at that; and certain words in common usage just can't be changed. *Ordinary,* everybody knows what that means. *High,* everybody knows what that means. You can't just say, 'Here is ordinary high. It's average.' It doesn't make sense, and it won't make sense to anybody."[23]

In November 2000, surveyor Dan Gentry was deposed as an expert witness for David Smith in the *Trustees v. Smith* case. When asked if he checked the elevation of his ordinary high water marks against a stage duration curve for the water body in question, Gentry indicated that he did not trust the available data from the U.S. Geological Survey gauge (records of which are accepted by scientists and courts as official and accurate documentation of water levels). After more discussion of his practice of locating ordinary high water marks, Gentry went on to say that the range his ordinary high water marks generally fell into was "much closer to the 50 percent stage duration curve."[24]

Such arguments over the words in the concept *ordinary high water line* might indicate many things about our society today. Perhaps the one that most needs to be said is this: the meaning of the words *ordinary, high, water,* and *line* are not in dispute. These concepts are stable in the English language. The criteria for the concept *ordinary high water line* come from a long history of cases clarifying the concept in different situations. From the case law it's clear that *high* means that the boundary will be one established in the high water season—that is, somewhere above the average or low water stages—so that the shore is included as part of the water body. In *Broward v. Mabry* the court traced the origin of Florida's water boundaries: under the common law of England, the crown in its sovereign capacity held title to the beds of navigable or tide waters, including the shore or the space between high and low water marks, in trust for the people of the realm who had rights of navigation, commerce, fishing, bathing, and other easements allowed by law in the waters. This rule of the common law was applicable in the English colonies of America. After the American Revolution, title to the beds of all waters—navigable in fact, whether tidal or fresh—including their shores, was held by the states in which they were located, in trust for all the people of the states respectively.[25] In *Geiger v. Filor* the court stated that the "use of the shore (that is, of the land) that is usually overflowed by the highest tide, . . . is public in the same manner as the sea."[26]

It's clear that the concept *ordinary* means that unusually high waters such as floods or freshets do not establish the line. *Attorney General v. Chambers,* in 1854, provided perhaps the definitive discussion distinguishing the concept *ordinary high* from the *highest natural tides.* And it was on the basis of this case that our own mean high water line laws for tidewater boundaries were established. *Tilden* in 1927 considered language from several cases establishing that the highest highs did not determine the boundary. And *MacNamara v. KRVSA* in 1994 affirmed that the OHWL is the "normal reach of water during the high water season."

Water is treated in the case law as a body: "in determining what belongs to the public we have to determine what properly belongs to the river."[27] This aspect of the boundary criteria is fundamental: it is a water boundary, defined by the presence of water—not by how much land can be reclaimed for agriculture by diking and ditching. Navigable water bodies are sovereignty lands to the OHWL—even though at their margins they may be too shallow to support navigation. *Martin* in 1927 established this important concept: "In 1845 the state, by virtue of its sovereignty upon being admitted to the Union, became the owner of . . . the beds of all navigable lakes to ordinary high-water mark, however shallow the water may be at the outside lines or elsewhere, if the water is in fact a part of the particular lake that is navigable for useful purposes." But an equally important criterion of the boundary emerges from the concept *water* in the courts' acknowledgment of the boundary as an elevation. This acknowledgment is based on the physical behavior of water, its tendency to form a level surface.

The concept *line*, then, attaches to these other words (*ordinary, high, water*) the quality of being an elevation. In 1854, the British common law from which our law derives acknowledged the physics of water by the same concept: "the Crown's right did not extend landwards beyond the *line* of high water-mark of ordinary neap tides."[28] By 1994, the court in *Kissimmee River Valley Sportsman's Association v. MacNamara* declared that the method of "locating the water boundary on flat, vegetated shore lines calls for using the best evidence and methods available, including identifying the *elevation* of ordinary high water by reference to water marks on the ground or local objects."[29]

The recognition by the courts that the OHWL can be expressed as an elevation counters the claim that the boundary can be derived by determining what swamp and overflowed lands can be reclaimed for agriculture. The boundary of uplands cannot be located according to how far down into the lake bed crops can be grown when the water is excluded by diking and draining. As in the Mobil Theory, some argue that diking and ditching and using pumps to keep the water off the land should be allowable practices in determining where their uplands end. But the criteria of the ordinary high water line do not admit this interpretation. The boundary is a water line, determined not from the uplands down but from the water body up. It is a water boundary located at an actual, natural line produced by ordinary high water—not at the place where water can no longer be kept off the land sufficiently to farm it.

As for certainty about the OHWL, we need to ask ourselves under what circumstances exactitude about the line is called for. What is the limit of that exactitude? We have the capacity to divide this particle of sand from that particle of muck. But we don't need a microscope to locate the boundary between private and public lands. We have a history as a society of how these boundaries are established and preserved. We have concepts in our language and law that we can comprehend and project into new situations. What we must guard against is not uncertainty but the kind of self-assertion and private definition that marks the language of special interests and obscures the ordinary language through which we make boundaries meaningful.

Our little boat bobbed and wobbled,
and I was appalled by the sheer liquidity
of the water beneath us. If I stepped over
the side, where would my foot rest?
MARILYNNE ROBINSON, *Housekeeping*

7 Down to the Waterline:
The Nature of Our Place

IN 1994 I bought a farm adjoining a navigable lake in a rural area of north Florida. Shortly after we moved in, my husband and I took our old canoe and began exploring "the pond," as it is called by local people. Some three thousand acres of cypress swamps and intermittent open water comprise the pond, and we set out eagerly to discover the nature of this mysterious entity. We hadn't been on the water long, were barely two hundred yards from our shore, when a fellow in a boat spotted us. Making his way toward us he asked if we were lost. No, we replied, just exploring. "Well you're a long way from the landing," he said. "Are you sure you're not lost?" We were sure, we said, pointing to our cove and explaining that we had put in from our own shore. He looked perturbed as we went on our way.

The next day I received a phone call from our neighbor who owns the waterfront property just to our north. "You folks were the ones out in the canoe?" he asked. I introduced myself and gave him a brief report of our buying our farm. "Well, I own all this end of the pond," he responded. "I've sold boating rights to the people who've bought land from me, but my deed takes in the land you cross over to get to the deep-water channel."

I took a deep breath. We had moved to the country to recover a strand of our lives lost in the hectic city grind we endured for careers' sake. The last thing we wanted was to start our new lives in conflict with the neighbors, or worse, end up in litigation.

"I understand that's a state-owned lake," I said cautiously. There was a pause. "Navigable waters in Florida are state owned," I began to explain.

"My deed takes in this whole end of the pond," he said again, a little more aggressively.

"Most of the deeds around the pond derive from swamp and overflowed lands patents," I said. Another pause. "Descriptions on those deeds sometimes do include navigable waters, but the courts have ruled that those deeds don't convey navigable waters," I plunged on. "My deed is the same way."

"Oh, well," he said, "if you have a lot of frontage, you have your own access to the channel. You don't need to cross over my end."

"Look," I said, "we can get together with our deeds and maps and go over the situation with the state surveyor. I work for him and I think he would help us figure this out."

"Well, I know what you're saying," my neighbor replied, suddenly more receptive. "I've read about the state owning all the water." It was a good bet that he had, indeed, read about it, given that the local town and the county had gone on record opposing the state when the Board of Professional Land Surveyors tried to define the OHWL. "Now, does that mean anybody can come over my line?" he wanted to know.

"Anybody can use the pond up to the ordinary high water line," I said. "That's the law."

"Where exactly is that?" he asked.

I laughed. "Well," I said, "come over one day and we'll look into it."

Now at ease, he set about trying to get my donation to keep the deep-water channel open, assuring me that he always got all the permits, "by the book." I promised to do my share, and that was the last I've ever heard from my neighbor to the north.

Hanging up the phone, I couldn't help thinking of the people who argue that access to navigable waters can be adequately protected without the water bodies being state owned. I always wonder, when I hear that argument, why anyone would want to own lands reserved for public use. What is the incentive to pay taxes on, and be responsible for, property not limited to private use? I can't help but feel that placing navigable waters into private ownership is just the first step down the slippery slope to loss of public access. If I hadn't known that the law protected my access to the navigable lake adjoining my property, the phone call from my neighbor might have turned out quite differently.

But, fixing the boundary between private and public lands can elicit powerful emotions. To a large degree this response is because of our deep ties with the land we inhabit and the long traditions supporting our beliefs. Of course, flaring tempers and inflexible stands also arise from misinformation and overblown rhetoric that play on these emotional ties. Take, for example, the claim made by property rights advocates in a current OHWL controversy: "The state could then *take ownership of the land without paying any compensation.*"[1] Statements like this one are, of course, countered by pointing out that riparian owners are not due compensation when the courts find that they are encroaching on sovereignty lands. But the sheer persistence of these kinds of claims speaks of a resistance worth noting.

I suspect in much of rural America—certainly in much of rural Florida—an outlaw mentality regarding the environment lurks just beneath the surface of otherwise upstanding, law-abiding communities. A hint of this renegade culture came soon after I returned to rural life after a twenty-year hiatus in town: We were sitting outside as the sun went down, watching a burn pile we had been using that day, when a deputy sheriff came by. He had seen our fire from the road and wanted to make sure someone was tending it. We introduced ourselves, and he stood for a while and visited. He told us a lot about the neighborhood and the old fish camp that used to be on our farm; and he told us about the Torreya trees. "They're endangered," he said. "If you find out you have any of 'em on your land, cut 'em down, burn the stumps out, get rid of them. If the environmental people find out you have 'em, they'll rope 'em off and you'll never be able to use your land." Shortly after, another pillar of the community told me if I had any low areas (wetlands) to pull the trees out of them and, during a dry spell, to "get them in grass." Otherwise, he said, "they'll cordon 'em off and they won't pay you anything for 'em, even though they're as good as taking your land." I couldn't help noticing that these men were both highly respected members of our community, people who helped their neighbors and obeyed the laws. But a clear notion prevails in many rural communities that environmental laws are somehow not *the* law. "They change their minds a lot," one realtor told me when I asked him about the eighty-plus submerged acres included in the parcel he was trying to sell me. His implication was that at any moment the legislature might reverse the courts on OHWL, on MRTA, on having sovereignty lands at all. It all seemed very plastic to hear him tell it.

The idea that citizens must stand a close watch to prevent the state from "taking" land goes back to the formation of America itself. Indeed, our assertion of private property rights emerges in the very notion of democracy. In a 1970s eminent domain case involving a Florida river, the landowner's attorney cited the 1947 Florida Supreme Court:

> Over the past several centuries the general principles of our law of eminent domain have taken form from the pattern of a democratic state. At one time the state owned all the property or possessed the power to wrest it from the owner. *As our concepts of democracy have grown, greater emphasis has been placed on the rights of the citizen* among which has been the privilege to "have certain inalienable rights, among which are those of enjoying and defending life and liberty, acquiring possessing and protecting property, and pursuing happiness and obtaining safety" [Florida Constitution, sect. 1].
>
> *Our American courts have been ever alert to shield the citizen against encroachment by the sovereign* as experience has shown that where a right is extended a corresponding liberty is curtailed, seldom if ever to be restored. . . . Statutes granting such power, such as here asserted, are in contravention of the common rights of persons and should receive a strict construction.[2]

This 1947 court saw an advanced concept of democracy embodied in a greater emphasis on the rights of the citizen over against the power of the sovereign.

Yet, as the understanding of the environment deepened during the latter half of the twentieth century, ecophilosophers reasoned that the fragmenting of biological communities is part and parcel of a human problem of community.[3] The concept of democracy, itself, refers to the tension between the individual and the community. But, we have mostly interpreted the tension in "democracy" as existing between human individuals and human communities, or between minority and majority groups of people. Only recently have people begun to express a concern that the protection of biological communities now threatens the rights of the individual human or even the rights traditionally granted the human community. The methodology for determining an OHWL, which the state developed in response to case law during the 1980s, has been viewed as such a threat. In an article entitled "Lawsuit Puts Private Property Rights under Fire," the *Florid Agriculture* reported that the state had sued David Smith, a Florida citizen, for a "substantial portion of the land his family has farmed for more than 60 years." Smith's attorney, the article noted, said the case "marks a test of a new methodology for setting the ordinary high water mark along property that borders fresh water bodies in Florida." The attorney further contended that the method adopted by "state officials and several self-defined environmental advocates . . . is at variance with over a century of practice and law."[4]

Thus, one of the most difficult challenges that state environmental agencies face today is the adamant opposition of those who feel that government policies to further a healthy environment unfairly supersede private property rights. "You know government is taking away our rights," Mr. Payne told me one day. Payne is a cattle rancher, the head of a landowners' association that operates a drainage system at the north end of Florida's Fisheating Creek. He knows everything about the drainage system, but he doesn't want to talk to me. He wants to know who I work for, if my research is part of litigation, if I am a lawyer. I tell him that I research land history for the Florida Division of State Lands. I admit that we're part of the Florida Department of Environmental Protection, that litigation between the state and the Lykes Brothers is pending on the downstream stretch of Fisheating Creek. I explain that I need to understand what effect his drainage operation has on the lower portions of the creek so that we can determine what is state owned. I tell him we're not interested in his system, only in how it affects the stream in Glades County. But I don't overcome his hostility. If the state claims the creek below the county line, what's to stop it from claiming the creek in Highlands County? This phone call is, for him, a nightmare. "Most of us in the north watershed bought land here forty years ago or longer," he tells me, "and we had an understanding that the government would protect our rights. But now the government is taking away our rights." When I speak to the manager of the Highlands County Soil Conservation District, Charlotte Lee, she listens to my requests politely and then warns, "I think I should tell you that I have just a little problem with these environmentalists. You know government is trying to take away our rights. They are making it so hard for farmers, and these are the people who feed everyone. So I just think I should tell you I have a little bit of a problem with these environmentalists."

It's easy enough to understand this point of view. When Florida became a state in 1845, it was a vastly different land than it is today. Of its approximately 34 million acres, some 21 million acres were conveyed as swamp and overflowed lands. A major focus of the early state government was to attract settlers who would want to claim the land from its swampy condition—drain it, fill it, make it habitable and useful. In the early part of the twentieth century, conservation of land and resources basically meant achieving the greatest good for the greatest number of people for the longest time. Ranchers and farmers were some of the earliest settlers in Florida. Until the late 1950s, the government assisted and encouraged them to drain swamp lands, fill submerged lands, channel rivers to protect grazing lands—generally, to use the land for their own benefit. And what a job they did. If the transformation of its surroundings is the measure of a species' success, then the history of Florida's development since statehood stands as irrefutable proof of human superiority.

So farmers are a little like the firstborn child. In the beginning, they had very little competition for government favor. But now, a lot of other children have come along, so to speak, with interests of their own. Florida's booming population needs clean water to drink, and much of the state's economy now depends on its water bodies for tourists' recreation. I want to say to Mr. Payne that it's the duty of government to balance the interests of all the citizens it serves. But this is like a parent saying to the firstborn child, "This is your brother. Of course you love him." Such things may come along with time, but from the firstborn's point of view, it feels like the pie just got a whole lot smaller. And the problem is so much worse. It isn't just that there are more people who have different interests. Now it's every living thing. In the "good old days," there was no question that the land was to be used, and by and large, *use* meant farming and ranching. Today, environmentalists may debate the idea of use itself as a worthy goal for all land; and we see efforts from both private and public organizations to preserve land and regulate the use of resources for the sake of such goals as ecosystem integrity and biodiversity. In short, the twentieth century experienced a tremendous complication of the concept of nature.

In my lifetime, a startling change is occurring in our collective notions of the human relationship with the rest of the living world. As a junior in my high school English class, we read stories such as *Moby Dick* and discussed that great theme of literature and life: Man's Struggle Against Nature. Many scientific endeavors also cast themselves in this plot, as exemplified by one paper called "History of Hyacinth Control in Florida," written mid-twentieth century by a hydraulic engineer and a biologist. The paper introduced its discussion saying, "The history of man and often his survival has been one of endless battle against the forces of nature." But in the late 1960s, the idea of nature as enemy had begun to seem, to many, outdated. In that same English class, I remember writing an essay exam on Edgar Lee Masters, who specialized in elegy. The exam date corresponded with the first nationwide celebration of Earth Day, and for my essay I wrote an elegy in the fashion of Masters entitled "Forgot N. Earth." This no doubt clunky endeavor, nevertheless, marks for me how early began my sense that right relations with the world would not come easy.

When I first began studying environmental history I felt a lot of anger about the destruction of the world's abundance. The writings of early naturalists in America tell of the great bounty and variety of wildlife. William Wood, writing in Massachusetts in the early 1630s, described the "beasts that live on the land":

> The kingly lion and the strong-armed bear,
> The large-limbed mooses, with the tripping deer,
> Quill-darting porcupines, and racoons be
> Castled in the hollow of an aged tree;
> The skipping squirrel, rabbit, purblind hare,
> Immured in the selfsame castle are,
> Lest red-eyed ferrets, wily foxes should
> Them undermine, if rampired but with mold.
> The grim-faced ounce, and ravenous, howling wolf,
> Whose meagre paunch sucks like a swallowing gulf.
> Black, glistening otters and rich-coated beaver,
> The civet-scented musquash smelling ever.[5]

Wood goes on to describe the sky blackened with birds. He says the fowler would aim his gun in the general direction of up and with a single shot kill more than he could eat in a week. But he didn't fire a single shot. He fired again and again until the ground was heaped with dying geese, teal, loon, cormorant.

It was during the time I was reading these writings that I first saw the Kissimmee River, or C-38, as it was called by then. Standing by the canal, I felt impatience with and contempt for the human endeavor to control nature, for this whole subplot of Western culture. What had motivated such a war on the world? Of course, settlers arriving in America from England might well have been trigger-happy in response to the prohibitions they had experienced in England against hunting. In eighteenth-century England, shooting game was forbidden to the peasant class, and the hapless tenant caught with a bird in the hand faced hanging. One can well imagine that, for such a person, all those birds Wood describes falling to the ground might have seemed like liberty itself raining down upon the joyous shooter.

I didn't have to go far, however, to find another answer to what prompts the human war on nature. The next morning we took a skiff down the canal, exploring what remained of the Kissimmee's oxbows. As we came around a bend, I saw ahead on the bank what looked like a huge discarded tractor tire, larger than the boat we were in. But as we approached, I saw it begin to crawl toward the water, toward the boat. The physiologic response in my body was immediate and unambiguous. The hair on the back of my neck rose, my skin prickled, my heart pounded. Let anyone who imagines our combative stance toward nature demonstrates some neurotic obsession simply take the canoe onto the lake and encounter in all its natural splendor a mature bull alligator. She will quickly discover that the human fear of natural forces is neither unwarranted nor superficial. Standing in wilderness a human being feels small. Human actions seem inconsequential. Most of us today have to seek out wilderness as a kind of "experience" we rarely encounter. And we only imagine what it would be like without the map, the trail, the knowledge that the motel is "that-a-way."

Indeed it can be argued that it is our incredible success in controlling natural forces, in eradicating our natural enemies, that has afforded us the leisure we may have to reconsider our relationship with nature. In the case of the Kissimmee River, the Army Corps' unparalleled engineering feat finally accomplished what had been attempted for a hundred years: we, at long last, mastered the river. But, as with so many technological achievements, we did not anticipate all the repercussions of our victory. In our lifetime, we have seen how the human domination of the natural world can devastate not only the natural beauty of the world, but threaten the life-supporting environment on which we all depend. Now we stand at the brink of completely humanizing the world and suddenly we realize we may long for—we may need—something *not us*, something not of our making. To a great degree, I believe it is these kinds of deep currents that have brought environmental concerns to the surface. The environmental degradation created by our unparalleled success controlling nature has made the environment a government issue, not a capricious decision by the state to interfere in matters that previously had been the prerogative of the individual.

In *The Rights of Nature: A History of Environmental Ethics*, Roderick Nash offers an account of why the protection of biological communities seems to some to threaten the rights of human individuals. Nash proposes that the "rise of the science of ecology and its diffusion into a widespread popular enthusiasm" has "created a new conception of the meaning of biological community," and this, in turn, has "suggested a new basis for moral community."[6] He notes that environmentalism is frequently characterized as subversive because it seems to aim for the "disintegration of contemporary American society and culture." The "American propensity for unlimited growth, intense competition, and the domination of nature," Nash says, certainly runs "counter to ecological ideals such as stability, interdependence, and a community consciousness extended to include nonhuman beings and biophysical processes."[7]

But Nash points out that this subversive characterization overlooks the "one important intellectual foundation for protecting nature that is quintessentially American: natural-rights philosophy, the old American ideal of liberty."[8] Nash sees the rise of ecology as the latest expansion of the liberalism on which America was founded. He traces the expansion of natural rights through an evolution of ethics relating to self, family, tribe, nation, and so on, finally projecting that at some point in the future we will include animals, plants, life—in fact all of nature and the universe in our ethical considerations.[9] At present, however, we stand on the brink of a philosophical leap. Ethical problems of the past have included the issues of nationalism, racism, sexism, and other human-to-human difficulties. But ethical questions arising from our deepened understanding of biological communities require that we address our "speciesism," and in this way these problems are different than any that have arisen from past expansions of natural rights.[10] This account supports the notion that environmentalism does require a rethinking of individual rights. Nash writes, "Environmental ethics involves people extending ethics to the environment by the exercise of self-restraint."[11]

How will we reconcile our long tradition of fearing and controlling nature, our escalating power to destroy the natural world, with our need to live in the world as part of nature? We see nature, we see ourselves: we draw a black line in the sand between nature and ourselves as with public and private lands. We find out the line is not where we thought, nature is not what we thought, we are not where we thought we were. Did we think we were independent? Did we think we could, as in 1776 when we declared our independence from England, renounce nature as well?

For Earl Tulley, a Navajo activist opposing ecological destruction of Navajo lands, it is the old ways that describe the right relations of human beings to the land and other beings that share the world. In his culture, he says, "Traditional people are bound by the laws of nature. It's not written. It's just the way it is."[12] But the lessons of the Kissimmee River insist that it is not only such "traditional people" who are bound by the laws of nature. These people are simply the ones who *acknowledge* their dependence on nature. But every living thing depends on gravity, and most rely on photosynthesis, on the miracle of seeds responding to the complex cues of a living world. In Florida, we need marshes for life. All of us are bound to some degree by the laws of nature, whether we want to believe it or not.

In *Must We Mean What We Say?* American philosopher Stanley Cavell speaks of the potency of ordinary language for discovering where we are, how things stand with us. It is by searching the meanings of ordinary language, Cavell says, "that Socrates can coax the mind down from self-assertion—subjective assertion and private definition—and lead it back, through the community, home."[13] So perhaps our question must be what counts as our community, who we recognize as our relations. It seems to be a persistent question at the beginning of the twenty-first century whether any of us really belongs to a community in the way people once did unselfconsciously. We move around a lot. We change careers. We rarely see our families. Perhaps more and more what we discover is that we are members of several communities having to do with our interests as individuals: the teaching community, the adult hockey players' community, the Internet community, the cancer support community. In our day-to-day routines, we don't usually take notice of our most important relations—those organisms forming the world in which we live.

In 1993, the Florida Department of Environmental Protection (DEP), at the direction of the legislature and governor, adopted ecosystem management as its principle of stewardship of the state's air, land, and water. In a manner Socrates might have approved, the DEP developed ecosystem management around several key definitions and concepts. Ecosystem was defined as a community of organisms, including humans, that interact with one another and with the environment in which they live. "Over the last 30 years," the ecosystem management handbook stated, "we have begun to understand how the health of the planet and the welfare of our species depend upon each other. As a result, we are searching for a new balance between the ecological health of the planet and the development of human society in the broadest sense." The search for a "new balance" would be guided by the concepts of sustainability and responsibility. Connectedness and ecological integrity were identified as dominant themes of the approach. This meant a focus on the connections among natural systems with the goal of protecting and restoring "not only the native diversity, pattern, and function of ecosystems, but the processes that perpetuate diversity, pattern, and function." Humans were recognized as inseparable from nature in their influence on ecological patterns and their reliance on natural processes.[14] But perhaps the most risky aspect of the new policy involved the concept of environmental citizenship. "It isn't enough to merely change how government thinks and acts," DEP Environmental Education Director Jim Lewis wrote. "Florida's citizens and residents must change how they think. . . . One of the goals of ecosystem management is to develop a public ethic of *shared responsibility* for the environment. This is part of what we call *environmental citizenship*—all of us becoming informed about our place in the biosphere—the biological world around us—and then acting responsibly on that information. In the long run, it isn't government that will save Florida's environment. That will take concerned citizens. Government can only help."[15]

So I asked my neighbor one day what he thought government should do about wetlands. "If they're going to take away the use of them," he said, "they should pay for them."

I nodded. "Do you think there's any value to leaving them wet?" I asked.

"They say there is," he acknowledged, "but they're no good to me wet."

Then I told him about the Kissimmee River, how we channelized it, destroying all the marshes. No more fish, no birds, no good water. No protection for Lake Okeechobee against pollutants. No sponge to slow down floodwaters. No marshmallows.

"I heard they were going to fix that," he said.

"We're going to try," I said.

In Cavell's account of Socrates leading our minds away from self-assertion, we come back *through* the community, home. We come to rest neither in the isolation of self-assertion nor in the (potentially suffocating) embrace of the community. We are home. And we are home in the Heideggerian sense of having found our place, of being now able to *let things be*. In this journey to find ourselves home in the world, the concept of an ordinary high water line seems insignificant. But it is a marker, not only of the division between public and private lands, but of our relations with the world we live in. The OHWL cannot be reduced to a line we've drawn in the sand; it is an indicator we've discovered of where our rightful home is. It is a way of finding our place. The most ancient laws of civilization recognized the importance of the waters' shores to human beings. In trying to define those shores, to determine the dominion of the waters, we have had to discover what is the nature of a line in nature. For thousands of years—at least until 1851 when the Supreme Court deemed the OHWL needed "no scientific exploration to find"—the line seemed obvious enough for all practical purposes. But in the twentieth century, in Florida, we discovered that it was not necessarily obvious. We have to look more closely than anyone has done before, and we can't assume too much. This simple lesson is not one we have mastered with regard to the natural world, but the OHWL, as one of its many meditations, may help keep it before us until we do.

Notes

INTRODUCTION

1. Feynman, *The Meaning of It All*, 16–17.

CHAPTER 1: A Case of Conflict: Growth, Science, Tradition

1. This account of the incident is based on conversations with State Cadastral Surveyor Terry Wilkinson in September 1996 and on Andrew Metz's article "Hunters Hike Waist-Deep into Land Dispute."

2. *The Northwest Ordinance*, 1787, August 7, 1789, chap. 8, 1 stat. 50, 52.

3. Frank, "Forever Free," 275–76.

4. For discussions of this test see such cases as *Barney v. Keokuk* at 336; *The Genessee Chief v. Fitzhugh* at 457; *State of Florida v. Black River Phosphate Co.* at 82. See also Richard, "Tidelands and Riparian Rights in Florida," 341.

5. See *The Genessee Chief* at 457. See also Guest, "The Ordinary High Water Boundary," 206; and Houck, "Treatise," 65–77.

6. *Barney* at 336–38, held that the English common law tidal limitation was inapplicable in the United States, and found navigability to be the controlling test. See also *Shively v. Bowlby,* where Justice Horace Gray discusses the law regarding public and private ownership of the shore.

7. For a thorough discussion of Florida's sovereignty lands case law, see Reimer, "The Public Trust Doctrine," 10–20.

8. *State of Florida ex rel Ellis v. Gerbing,* 56 Fla. at 608–9, 47 So. at 355.

9. See, for example, *Attorney-General v. Chambers* at 216 for a discussion of the ordinary high water mark as the limit of the crown's right to land.

10. States with boundaries similar to Florida's include Alaska, Idaho, Illinois, North Carolina, New Hampshire, Ohio, Oregon, Pennsylvania, Washington, and Wisconsin. See Slade, *Putting the Public Trust Doctrine to Work,* 76–79.

11. Jonathan Glogau to Hon. Lawson Lamar, Orlando, January 3, 1996.

12. Metz, "Hunters Hike Waist-Deep into Land Dispute."

13. Crawford, "Lawsuit Puts Private Property Rights under Fire," 1.

14. For a discussion of Western assumptions about nature see Devall and Sessions, "The Dominant, Modern Worldview and Its Critics," 41–49.

15. Byrnes, "Are We Being Taken by Takings?" 4.

16. See, for example, Southwest Florida Water Management District, "Kuhl" and "Ensuring the Water Resource" and Central and Southern Florida Flood Control District, "Growth and Water Supply."

17. For a discussion of changing objectives in American land policy during this period, see Gates, *History of Public Land Law Development,* 765–72.

18. See Frank, "Forever Free," 275–325.

19. See, for example, Central and Southern Florida Flood Control District, *Five Years of Progress*, 14.

20. Center for Urban and Regional Studies, *The Kissimmee-Okeechobee Basin*.

21. *Howard v. Ingersoll* at 424.

22. Ibid. at 416–17.

23. Although *Howard* has been cited by some as a source for language pertaining to the ordinary high water line, a close reading of the case makes unclear what, if anything, the holdings have to do with the OHWL. See chap. 5 for an in-depth analysis of the case.

24. Guest, "The Ordinary High Water Boundary," 216.

25. Ibid., 220.

26. Richard Hamann and Jeff Wade are assistant directors at the Center for Governmental Responsibility, University of Florida College of Law.

27. Hamann and Wade, "Ordinary High Water Line Determination," 350.

28. See, for example, *United States v. Cameron,* in which a rancher diked a portion of land lying along Florida's St. Johns River. The U.S. Army Corps of Engineers claimed he had constructed the dike below OHWL without a permit. Both parties presented expert witnesses to provide an analysis of the vegetative evidence. However, according to Hamann and Wade, "neither party made any attempt to identify the relative densities of upland and submerged species," an occurrence that Hamann and Wade argue demonstrates that the courts have not yet developed the sophistication appropriate to this type of testimony. "Some courts too readily accept an expert witness's opinion although a sufficient explanation of the method used to arrive at the stated conclusion is not provided," they write. They point out that the courts have no standards for determining species dominance in reference to the vegetation test, and, because several methods for defining "dominance" exist, "any vegetative analysis should include data and discussion of each possible aspect of the definition" ("Ordinary High Water Line Determination," 350–53).

29. *The Board of Trustees of the Internal Improvement Trust Fund of the State of Florida v. Board of Professional Land Surveyors,* State of Florida Division of Administrative Hearings.

30. "SORA joins fight," 2.

31. For comprehensive discussions of navigability criteria, see W. Peyton, "Sovereignty Lands in Florida," 58–64, and Ivey, *Principals for a Navigability Assessment of Rivers and Lakes*.

32. *Board of Trustees of the Internal Improvement Trust Fund of the State of Florida v. Lykes Bros. Inc.,* June 2, 1997. Firsthand observation by the author.

33. Guest, "The Ordinary High Water Boundary," 221.

34. Ibid., 222.

35. Slade, *Putting the Public Trust Doctrine to Work,* 4.

36. Ibid.

37. *The Institutes of Justinian,* 16.

38. Slade, *Putting the Public Trust Doctrine to Work,* 5.

39. Ibid., 15.

40. See *Florida Statutes,* chap. 177.

41. Slade, *Putting the Public Trust Doctrine to Work,* 15.

42. *Cobb v. Davenport* at 378.

43. Slade, *Putting the Public Trust Doctrine to Work,* 15.

44. *The Institutes of Justinian,* 65, quoted in Slade, *Putting the Public Trust Doctrine to Work,* 58.

45. *Borax Consolidated Ltd. v. Los Angeles* at 22 quoting *Blundell v. Catterall,* 5 B.&A. 268 at 292, quoted in Slade, *Putting the Public Trust Doctrine to Work,* 58.

46. *Martin v. Waddell* at 410.

47. *Tinicum Fishing Co. v. Carter* at 30 and *Carson v. Blazer* at 477.

48. *Attorney General v. Chambers,* 43 Eng. Rep. 486 (1854). But note also *Phillips Petroleum v. Mississippi,* 469 at 475. "Some of the original states . . . recognized more private interest in tidelands than did others of the 13 — more private interests than were recognized at common law, or in the dictates of our public trust cases." See also *Oemler v. Green* for a discussion of Georgia's adoption of an upper limit to its trust shorelands based on its salt marshes, a boundary coextensive with the upper reach of the regular ebb and flow of the tide that extends above the elevation of mean high water.

49. *Borax Consolidated, Ltd.* at 25.

50. Moore, *A History of the Foreshore and the Law Relating Thereto,* 486–87. Although the argument was made for the crown that the "right extended to the highest tide, the judges decided . . . the Crown's *prima facie* title was limited to the ordinary high-water mark."

51. Slade, *Putting the Public Trust Doctrine to Work,* 17.

52. *The Northwest Ordinance,* 1787, and 14, art. 5, stat. 50, specified that any state joining the Union "shall be admitted . . . on an equal footing with the original States, in all respects whatever."

53. *Barney* at 336.

54. Slade, *Putting the Public Trust Doctrine to Work,* 20.

55. *The Genessee Chief* at 457.

56. *The Propeller Genessee Chief* at 455. Quoted in Slade, *Putting the Public Trust Doctrine to Work,* 20.

57. *The Daniel Ball* at 557.

58. Slade, *Putting the Public Trust Doctrine to Work,* 22.

59. *Barney* at 338.

60. Ibid. at 336.

61. *Illinois Central Railroad v. Illinois* at 437.

62. *Phillips Petroleum Co. v. Mississippi,* 469 at 479, citing *Barney* at 338, and *Illinois Central Railroad* at 435–36.

63. *The Daniel Ball* at 557.

64. The Supreme Court explained "a customary mode of trade or travel" in *United States v. Holt State Bank* at 56 (1926): "[N]avigability does not depend on

the particular mode in which [trade or travel on water] is or may be had—whether by steamboats, sailing vessels or flatboats—nor on an absence of occasional difficulties in navigation, but on the fact, if it be a fact, that the stream in its natural and ordinary condition affords a channel for useful commerce."

65. Ansbacher and Knetsch, "The Public Trust Doctrine and Sovereignty Lands in Florida," 342. Because the federal test of navigability for *regulation* differs significantly from the test for *title,* sorting out which criteria apply to sovereignty lands issues must be done with caution.

66. *State v. Korrer et al.* at 60.

67. Ansbacher and Knetsch, "The Public Trust Doctrine and Sovereignty Lands in Florida," 344.

68. *Bucki v. Cone* at 160–62.

69. *Broward v. Mabry* at 412.

70. The state sustained such a claim in the case of *Board of Trustees v. Lykes* (1997).

71. *Paine v. Woods* at 169.

72. See for example *State v. Cain, Haven v. Perkins, Concord Manuf'g Co. v. Robertson, State v. Strafford,* and *State v. Sunapee Dam.*

73. Slade, *Putting the Public Trust Doctrine to Work,* 24.

74. According to Slade, New Jersey (in *Cobb* at 378) and Massachusetts (in *Ingraham v. Wilkinson* at 270–72), among the thirteen original states, "continue to limit the definition of navigable waters, for title purposes, to only those waters which are subject to the ebb and flow of the tide. Mississippi, which joined the Union in 1817, does likewise" (*Putting the Public Trust Doctrine to Work,* 24). See, however, Slade's note on Massachusetts's treatment of great ponds as public waters. In a 1938 review of Mississippi's law on navigable waters (*State ex rel. Rice v. Stewart,* 184 Miss. 202), the Supreme Court stated: "Under the natural influence of precedents and established forms, a definition [of navigable waters] originally correct was adhered to and acted on, after it had ceased, from a change in circumstances, to be the true description of public waters." In a 1986 discussion of the state's "logical incongruity" in the law pertaining to navigable fresh waters (*Cinque Bambini Partnership v. State,* 491 So. 2d 508 at 517 [1986], aff'd sub nom. *Phillips Petroleum v. Mississippi*), the Supreme Court stated: "Yet, before anyone perceived that the trust extended to navigable fresh waters, Mississippi had already adopted the common law rule that riparian owners hold the bed to such waters to the center of the stream. This has placed Mississippi's trust in an anomalous position: while the lands below tidewaters may not be alienated except for high public purposes and generally only with the consent of the legislature, lands below navigable fresh waters are susceptible of wholly private ownership."

75. Butterworth, *Laws of Florida Relating to Water and Water Bodies,* 4.

76. Ibid., 8.

77. Ibid., 22.

78. See, for example, Guest, "The Ordinary High Water Line Boundary," 233–39.

79. Livingston, "Inshore Marine Habitats," 569.

80. Carter, *The Florida Experience,* 1.

81. Wallis, "The Trustees of the Internal Improvement Fund," 1.

82. Conversation with Joe Knetsch, historian, Bureau of Surveying and Mapping, Division of State Lands, Florida Department of Environmental Protection. February 18, 1997.

83. Butterworth, *Laws of Florida Relating to Water and Water Bodies,* 35.

84. Ibid., 59.

85. Florida Constitution of 1838, quoted from Turner, "The Trustees of the Internal Improvement Fund," 1–2.

86. "Whitfield's Notes," 232.

87. Sect. 8, chap. 16, act, September 4, 1841, 5 U.S. Stats. 455, and chap. 94, acts, 1847.

88. Gates, *History of Public Land Law Development,* 298.

89. Knetsch, "The Meaning of the Swamp Lands Act of 1850."

90. Wallis, "The Trustees of the Internal Improvement Fund," 3.

91. Ibid.

92. *Laws of Florida,* chap. 791 (1856) 25.

93. Wallis and Landrum, "The Management of Florida's Sovereignty Lands," 2.

94. *Laws of Florida,* chap. 791. Emphasis added.

95. Gay, "The High Water Mark," 563.

96. Guest, "The Ordinary High Water Boundary," 233–34.

97. Gay, "The High Water Mark," 563.

98. *State v. Black River Phosphate Co.* at 654, 655, quoted in Gay, "The High Water Mark," 564.

99. Gay, "The High Water Mark," 564.

100. Guest, "The Ordinary High Water Boundary," 234.

101. *State v. Black River Phosphate Co.* at 648.

102. *State v. Black River Phosphate Co.* at 649, quoted in Gay, "The High Water Mark," 564.

103. Guest, "The Ordinary High Water Boundary," 234.

104. Wallis, "The Trustees of the Internal Improvement Fund," 4.

105. Derr, *Some Kind of Paradise,* 86–87.

106. Tebeau and Carson, *Florida from Indian Trail to Space Age,* 250.

107. Ibid., 251.

108. Derr, *Some Kind of Paradise,* 87.

109. Wallis and Landrum, "The Management of Florida's Sovereignty Lands," 2.

110. Wallis, "The Trustees of the Internal Improvement Fund," 4. Some Florida land contracts, such as the Bolles and Chambers contracts, offer evidence counter to Wallis's view.

111. Ibid., 3.

112. "Whitfield's Notes," 235.

113. *Gerbing* at 356–57.

114. *Broward* at 831.

115. *Laws of Florida*, chap. 6451 (1913).

116. Gay, "The High Water Mark," 566.

117. Ibid., 564.

118. Ibid., 565.

119. See for example Wallis and Landrum, "The Management of Florida's Sovereignty Lands," 3, where the authors make the assumption that the 1856 law had divested the state of "title to all sovereignty land lying between privately owned upland and the nearest navigable channel."

120. *Laws of Florida*, chap. 8537, sect. 1 (1921).

121. See Wallis and Landrum, "The Management of Florida's Sovereignty Lands," 4.

122. Ibid.

123. Ibid.

124. Also contributing to the decline in residential bay fills was the conveyance by the trustees of extensive submerged tracts to cities or counties, usually for public purposes. Wallis and Landrum, "The Management of Florida's Sovereignty Lands," 5.

125. *State ex rel. Buford v. City of Tampa* at 337.

126. Ibid. at 340.

127. Ibid. Emphasis added.

128. Ibid.

129. Ibid. at 341.

130. Ibid. at 343.

131. Ibid. Emphasis added.

132. See, for example, *Laws of Florida*, chap. 6769 (1913), chap. 6961 (1915), chap. 15749 (1931), chap. 16296 (1933), chap. 18401 (1937), chap. 21130 (1941), chap. 21345 (1941), and chap. 21169 (1941).

133. Wallis and Landrum, "The Management of Florida's Sovereignty Lands," 5.

134. *Martin v. Busch* at 284.

135. Ibid. at 283.

136. *Howard* at 419. The case involved a treaty dispute between Georgia and Alabama over what line on the western bank of the Chattahoochee River formed the boundary between the two states.

137. Ibid. at 416.

138. *Tilden v. Smith* at 711.

139. Ibid.

140. Ibid. at 712.

141. Ibid., quoted in *Minnetonka Lake Improvement*.

142. *Tilden* at 708.

143. University of Florida Dean Emeritus Frank E. Maloney notes that, in the 1937 Iowa Supreme Court case *State v. Sorenson*, the court relied on the testimony of a botany expert that "large trees may sometimes continue to grow although covered with water at their bottoms for some period." According to the testimony,

"trees of the size and character involved could easily have gained a foothold and grown below the OHWL notwithstanding the fact that small vegetation could not grow there." Maloney cites this case to support his conclusion that "it would be impractical and unrealistic to strictly apply the OHWL definition where the situation calls for some departure." Maloney interprets the case as exemplifying that the "presence or absence of vegetation is not always conclusive" of a "realistic OHWL." I find the case exemplary of the finer distinctions about natural indicators that have in the later half of the twentieth century increasingly come under the courts' consideration in determining the OHWL. *Sorenson*'s botanist is not testifying about whether vegetation is present or absent, but about the varieties of plant life found at the margins of water bodies and what can be told about the water regimes based on those plants' tolerance for inundation. See Maloney, "The Ordinary High Water Mark," 475.

144. *Florida Statutes,* chap. 253 (1941).

145. Wallis and Landrum, "The Management of Florida's Sovereignty Lands," 5.

146. Ibid., 9, 11. Emphasis added.

147. Ibid., 12.

148. Ibid., 14.

149. *Zabel v. Pinellas County Water & Navigation Control Authority,* 387.

150. Aldo Leopold, *Sand County Almanac,* 224–25.

151. For a discussion of the then-emerging environmental movement, see Drengson's "Foreword," ix–xiv.

152. Gay, "The High Water Mark," 574.

153. Ibid., 574–75.

154. Ibid., 575–76.

155. Guest, "The Ordinary High Water Boundary," 238.

CHAPTER 2: The Kissimmee River Story: Empire and Ecology

1. Patton and Sanford, *Interim Report,* 31, citing Parker, "Hydrology of the Pre-drainage System of the Everglades" and Carter et al., *Ecosystem Analysis.*

2. Ibid.

3. Carter et al., *Ecosystem Analysis,* 5.

4. Parker et al., *Water Resources of Southeastern Florida,* 4.

5. Carter et al., *Ecosystem Analysis,* 6.

6. This watershed, comprising 3,013 square miles, is located in the center of the state and includes most of Osceola and Okeechobee and parts of Orange, Polk, and Highlands Counties; it is bounded on the north by the lakes of the Orlando area, on the west by the Peace River watershed, on the south by Lake Okeechobee, and on the east by the upper St. Johns River basin.

7. Patton and Sanford, *Interim Report,* 10.

8. Hartwell, "Hydrology," 8.

9. Parker, "Hydrology of the Pre-drainage System of the Everglades," 2.

10. Toth, "The Ecological Basis of the Kissimmee River Restoration Plan," 32.

11. Ibid., 28–29.

12. Merchant, *The Death of Nature*.

13. Derr, *Some Kind of Paradise*, 359.

14. Blake, *Land into Water—Water into Land*, 75.

15. Tebeau and Carson, *Florida from Indian Trail to Space Age*, 251.

16. Derr, *Some Kind of Paradise*, 87.

17. Ibid., 89.

18. Quoted in Morris, *The Florida Handbook*, 436.

19. Ibid., 89.

20. The Disston contracts, however, provide evidence to the contrary.

21. Blake, *Land into Water—Water into Land*, 80.

22. Johnson, *Beyond the Fourth Generation*, 75–76.

23. Ibid.

24. Morris, *The Florida Handbook*, 436.

25. U.S. Congress, House, "Examination and Survey of Kissimmee River, Florida, Etc., Letter from the Secretary of War," 4.

26. Morris, *The Florida Handbook*, 436.

27. See the *Florida Times-Union*, May 1, 1896; Chandler, *Land Title Origins*, 396–97; and Knetsch, *Sunland Tribune* 24 (1998): 5–19.

28. Devall and Sessions, "The Dominant, Modern Worldview and Its Critics," 21.

29. Tebeau and Carson, *Florida from Indian Trail to Space Age*, 253.

30. G. Tyler Miller, *Living in the Environment*, 100.

31. Patton and Sanford, *Interim Report*, 10.

32. South Florida Water Management District, "Kissimmee River Restoration," 1.

33. Derr, *Some Kind of Paradise*, 93.

34. Central and Southern Florida Flood Control District, *Five Years of Progress: 1949–1954*, 8.

35. Ibid., 8–9.

36. Ibid., 9.

37. Ibid., 10.

38. Ibid., 12. Emphasis added.

39. More on the "sins" of modernity may be found in the debates between Jurgen Habermas, who characterizes modernity as an "unfinished project," and Jean-Francois Lyotard, who sees modernity as a crisis of Western culture.

40. CSFFCD, *Five Years of Progress*, 12–14.

41. Ibid.

42. Ibid., 17.

43. Derr, *Some Kind of Paradise*, 333.

44. Barada, "Restoring the Kissimmee River."

45. Ibid., 3.

46. Florida Game and Fresh Water Fish Commission, *Recommended Program for Kissimmee River Basin by Florida Game and Fresh Water Fish Commission,* 2.

47. Ibid.

48. Ibid.

49. Barada, "Restoring the Kissimmee River," 3.

50. *Recommended Program for Kissimmee River Basin,* 2.

51. Toth, "The Ecological Basis of the Kissimmee River Restoration Plan," 30.

52. Trumbull, *Miami Herald.*

53. Ibid., 31.

54. Barada, "Restoring the Kissimmee River," 4.

55. Toth, "The Ecological Basis of the Kissimmee River Restoration Plan," 31.

56. Ibid., 32.

57. Ibid., 32–33.

58. Center for Urban and Regional Studies, *The Kissimmee-Okeechobee Basin,* 55–56. Boldface emphasis added.

59. Bellinger, "Dredging, Filling, and the Inalienable Public Trust," 11.

60. Ibid., 12.

61. Ibid., 13.

62. Ibid., 17.

63. Ira A. Parks to Fred Vidzes, Land Management Division, Winter Haven, Florida, May 24, 1971.

64. Florida Constitution, art. 10, sect. 11 (1968).

65. Florida Constitution, art. 10, sect. 11 (1970).

66. Attorney General Earl Faircloth, memorandum to Trustees of the Internal Improvement Trust Fund, January 20, 1967.

67. Jacobson, "Graduate Education in Conservation Biology," 431–40.

68. Lubchenco, "The Sustainable Biosphere Initiative," 371.

69. In 1972, Reubin Askew was serving as governor of Florida. The cabinet was comprised of Richard Stone, secretary of state; Robert L. Shevin, attorney general; Floyd T. Christian, commissioner of education; Doyle Conner, commissioner of agriculture; Fred O. Dikinson, Jr., comptroller; and Thomas D. O'Malley, treasurer.

70. Arthur R. Marshall, introduction, in Center for Urban and Regional Studies, *The Kissimmee-Okeechobee Basin,* 1. Lake Apopka had already suffered eutrophication, a condition caused by overenrichment from sewage, citrus wastes, storm runoff, and so forth, in which excessive plant growth deprives the aquatic environment of the oxygen necessary to support aquatic life.

71. Ibid., 2.

72. Ibid., 3.

73. David S. Anthony, "Eutrophication: Process," in Center for Urban and Regional Studies, *The Kissimmee-Okeechobee Basin,* 18.

74. John V. Betz, "Eutrophication: Hazard," Center for Urban and Regional Studies, *The Kissimmee-Okeechobee Basin,* 24–26.

75. Aerial Lugo, "Marsh Ecology," Center for Urban and Regional Studies, *The Kissimmee-Okeechobee Basin,* 29.

76. Ibid., 29–30.

77. Ibid., 33.

78. *City of Tampa* at 337. Emphasis added.

79. Lugo, "Marsh Ecology," 35.

80. South Florida Water Management District, "Kissimmee River Restoration," 5–6.

CHAPTER 3: Custom, Criteria, and Community: Clarifying the OHWL Concept

1. Guest, "The Ordinary High Water Boundary," 213.

2. Conversation with Florida's chief cadastral surveyor, Terry Wilkinson, May 13, 2000. Other markers cited in bulkhead line determinations included the waterward edge of the mangrove swamps.

3. Board of Trustees of the Internal Improvement Trust Fund, *Minutes,* January 31, 1956; April 24, 1956; July 7, 1957.

4. Earl Faircloth, memorandum to trustees, January 20, 1967.

5. Board of Trustees of the Internal Improvement Trust Fund, *Minutes,* September 17, 1968.

6. "Information Concerning Submerged or Sovereignty Lands in the State of Florida," Board of Trustees policy statement, October 8, 1970, 7.

7. *Florida Statutes,* chap. 69-308, 253.12(1).

8. Board of Trustees of the Internal Improvement Trust Fund, *Minutes,* vol. 37, 48.

9. Tom Adams, memorandum to trustees, June 17, 1969.

10. *Laws of Florida,* chap. 75-22 (3): "All bulkhead lines heretofore established pursuant to section 253.122, *Florida Statutes,* are hereby established at the line of mean high water or ordinary high water. There shall be no filling waterward of the line of mean high water or ordinary high water except upon compliance with chapter 253, Florida Statutes."

11. Guest, "The Ordinary High Water Boundary," 229. Guest cites *Martin v. Busch,* 93 Fla. 535, 112 So. 274 (1927) at 574, and *Bryant v. Peppe,* 238 So. 2nd 836, 838 (Fla. 1970.)

12. Florida Society of Professional Land Surveyors, Ordinary High Water Line Seminar manual, December 1993, records of the Bureau of Surveying and Mapping, Tallahassee, Fla., 16.

13. *Laws of Florida,* chap. 7891 (1919) codified at *Florida Statutes,* sect. 253.36 (1989).

14. Guest, "The Ordinary High Water Boundary," 229.

15. James W. Apthorp, memorandum to trustees, November 12, 1969. Emphasis added.

16. Ibid.

17. Although the trustees' counsel seemed not to have noticed any problem with the idea of locating the *original* OHWL, the counsel was concerned with a problem in the Apthorp plan centered on the definition of reclaimed lake bottom as the permanent lowering of a water body by a "legally constituted authority." With that phrase controlling the definition of reclaimed lake bottoms, the status of lakes that had been lowered by someone other than a "legally constituted authority" would have to be determined. As it turned out, the number of water bodies falling into this category would be considerable, since, as Fred Vidzes observed, the "prime example of such circumstance [is] the reclamation works undertaken by Hamilton Disston during the 1890s" (Vidzes to trustees memo, January 15, 1970, DEP vault, Tallahassee, Fla.). That the trustees did not consider Disston to be some version of a legally constituted authority when he was under contract from the trustees to drain land and lower lakes is somewhat surprising. Vidzes went on to say: "Agreements and contracts were executed by the Trustees and Disston for the express purpose of lowering lakes and reclaiming swamp and overflowed lands for purposes of agricultural development. Many lakes in the central part of the State were affected by the works of Disston with the consequence that a significant amount of reclaimed lake bottom land, which was created by someone other than *a legally constituted authority*, is available for disposition."

Perhaps the trustees' stance took into account that until 1969 the legislature had not specifically vested in the trustees title to Florida's freshwater sovereignty lands, making it somewhat unclear whether the trustees' contract with Disston constituted the legal authority to lower those waters. Whatever the case, the final version of the plan retained this language but included a directive for dealing with the Disston-type cases: "Until such time as those lakes and lands that were subject to reclamation by someone other than a legally constituted authority have been identified and inventoried, only those bodies of water under the jurisdiction of legally constituted authorities having the power, as granted by the Legislature, to regulate, control, manage, conserve and administer such bodies of water lying within the lawfully established boundaries of such authorities, shall be subject to disposition by the Trustees." The idea, then, was that these types of cases would be "identified and inventoried" before being subject to disposition. Yet, it remained unclear exactly how this operation would proceed. Presumably, the process would take place in somewhat the same fashion as for the "normal" cases—those falling under the category of "lowered by a legally constituted authority." That is, the identification and inventory would be accomplished by the trustees' staff, which would then determine the "original" OHWL and the new "acceptable boundary line."

18. Board of Trustees of the Internal Improvement Trust Fund, *Minutes*, January 20, 1970.

19. Breed, *Surveying*, 118–20, 198.

20. Davis, Foote, and Kelley, *Surveying*, 619.

21. In his November 6, 1951, correspondence to the chief drainage engineer, F. C. Elliot, Attorney General Richard Ervin spelled out his view concerning the evidence of meandering: "The fact that Hillsborough river or Mosquito South Inlet was meandered by the government surveyors raises the presumption that the waters were at that time navigable waters. . . . Such waters are prima facie navigable by reason of such meandering, although the question of actual navigation may be rebutted."

22. Joe Knetsch, presentation at Florida Society of Professional Land Surveyors Ordinary High Water Line Seminar, February 4, 1994, Tallahassee, Fla. Knetsch is historian to the Bureau of Surveying and Mapping, State Lands Division, Department of Environmental Protection.

23. Ibid.

24. In *Trustees v. Lykes* for example, counsel for the plaintiff presented the jury with expert testimony concerning the significance of the meandering—or lack thereof—of a water body. Judge Carlton instructed the jury that meandering presented a rebuttable presumption of navigability and that the absence of meandering presented a rebuttable presumption of non-navigability. The jury, finding for the plaintiff that Fisheating Creek was navigable at the time of statehood, presumably felt that the state had convincingly rebutted the presumption of non-navigability: only a portion of Fisheating Creek was meandered—and only on one bank.

25. Knetsch, "Summary of Instructions," 1; citing "Instructions to the Principal Deputy Surveyor of the Land District East of Island of New Orleans," 1819.

26. Knetsch, "Summary of Instructions," 1; citing "Instructions to the Principal Deputy Surveyor of the Land District East of Island of New Orleans," 1819, 13.

27. Knetsch, "Summary of Instructions," 2; citing "Letters from Commissioner," vol. 1. 518–19.

28. *Bucki v. Cone* at 160.

29. Knetsch, "Summary of Instructions," 3; citing General Land Office circular, September 23, 1831.

30. Knetsch, "Summary of Instructions," 3.

31. Knetsch, "Summary of Instructions," 4; citing General Land Office instructions, 1845.

32. Knetsch, "Summary of Instructions," 5; citing General Land Office, November 21, 1850.

33. Ibid.

34. Knetsch, "Summary of Instructions," 6; citing General Land Office, May 3, 1881.

35. *Broward v. Mabry* at 830.

36. *Broward* at 831.

37. Knetsch, "Summary of Instructions," 7; citing *Manual of Surveying Instructions for the Survey of the Public Lands of the United States* (1894), U.S. Department of the Interior, 56. Emphasis added.

38. *Barney v. Keokuk* at 324.

39. *Manual of Surveying Instructions for the Survey of the Public Lands of the United States* (1902), 62.

40. See also Guest's critique of the 1902 manual's characterization of the cases cited; "Ordinary High Water," 218–19.

41. *Manual of Surveying Instructions for the Survey of the Public Lands* (1902), 62.

42. Ibid.

43. *Manual of Surveying Instructions for the Survey of the Public Lands* (1930), 217. Emphasis added.

44. *Tilden v. Smith,* 113 So. 708 at 712. Emphasis added.

45. Ibid.

46. Ibid.

47. American philosopher Stanley Cavell, following Wittgenstein, says, "Knowing something is ineluctably a matter of aligning concepts with the world" (*The Claim of Reason,* 157).

48. Trustees' Correspondence 1949–1952. Emphasis added.

49. James W. Apthorp, memorandum to trustees, November 12, 1969. Emphasis added.

50. Richard Ervin to W. Turner Wallis, July 18, 1957. Emphasis added.

51. Van H. Ferguson, January 6, 1960, trustees policies—Lakes file. Emphasis added.

52. Executive order, February 3, 1970, trustees policies—Lakes file.

53. E. W. Bishop, *Florida Lakes, Part 1, A Study of the High Water Lines of Some Florida Lakes,* 1.

54. Ibid.

55. Ibid.

56. The committee to "recommend original ordinary high water levels in the subject lakes" was comprised of: Fred Vidzes, Director, Division of Land Management, Trustees Chairman; Colonel J. V. Sollohub, Director, Division of Interior Resources, Department of Natural Resources; Dr. William H. Morgan, University of Florida; Myron Gibbons, Attorney at Law; William R. Kidd, Professional Engineer; A. O. Patterson, Director, Florida Water Resources Research Center; Robert Taylor, Hydrologist, Central and Southern Florida Flood Control District; William C. Hart, President, Florida Society Professional Land Surveyors; H. E. Wallace, Biologist, Florida Game and Fresh Water Fish Division. Board of Trustees of the Internal Improvement Trust Fund, *Minutes,* March 10, 1970. The trustees later appointed Mr. Frank Andrews, Consulting Geologist, to the committee in lieu of Patterson, who had retired. *Minutes,* June 16, 1970.

57. Board of Trustees of the Internal Improvement Trust Fund, *Minutes,* June 16, 1970.

58. Ibid.

59. Chap. 70-97, Acts of 1970, amending *Florida Statutes,* chap. 253.

60. Ibid.

61. Board of Trustees of the Internal Improvement Trust Fund, *Minutes,* February 23, 1971.

62. Lake Kissimmee, Lake Tohopekaliga, East Lake Tohopekaliga, Alligator Lake, and Lake Lizzie.

63. Board of Trustees of the Internal Improvement Trust Fund, *Minutes,* February 23, 1971.

64. Public Hearing concerning establishment of the boundary line of Lake Kissimmee, Lake Tohopekaliga, East Lake Tohopekaliga, Alligator Lake, and Lake Lizzie, June 22, 1971, Jones and Jones Court Reporters, West Palm Beach, Fla., 2–5.

65. Ibid., 7–8.

66. Ibid., 10.

67. Ibid., 16.

68. Ibid.

69. Ibid., 17.

70. Ibid., 22.

71. Ibid., 23–24.

72. Ibid., 27.

73. Ibid., 41–42.

74. Ibid., 35.

75. Ibid., 44.

76. Ibid., 51.

77. Ibid., 54.

78. Ibid., 57–58.

79. Cavell, *The Claim of Reason,* 31. American philosopher Stanley Cavell has written extensively on the problem of skepticism in modernity.

80. Ibid.

81. Public hearing, 59–60.

82. McVety, "Column confused issues."

83. Ibid.

84. Ibid., 67.

85. Ibid., 68.

86. *State of Florida and Board of Trustees of the Internal Improvement Trust Fund v. Florida National Properties, Inc.* at 16.

87. Ibid. at 17.

88. Ibid. at 18–19.

89. Winesett, "Legal Standards for Determining the Ordinary High Water Mark," 30.

90. Ibid., 22–23.

91. Ibid., 15. Emphasis added.

92. Ibid., 26.

93. *Howard v. Ingersoll* at 413.

94. Schneider and Busen, "Ordinary High Water Elevations of Four Major Lakes of the Kissimmee Chain."

95. See for example *Martin v. Busch,* no. 27 and 28, at 276.

96. Schneider and Busen, "Ordinary High Water Elevations of Four Major Lakes of the Kissimmee Chain," summary and recommendation.

97. Schneider and Bishop, "Pre-Regulation Ordinary High Water Elevations along the Kissimmee River," 1.

98. Ibid., 2.

99. Ibid., 4.

100. Ibid., 5.

101. Robert Shevin, October 27, 1978.

102. Cole, "Proposed Water Boundaries Legislation," part 4, 177.602.

103. Ibid.

104. See, for example, *Trustees v. Lykes,* in which the court held that commerce conducted in dugout canoes typical of the day was sufficient to prove navigability at the time of statehood on Fisheating Creek.

105. Cole, "Proposed Water Boundaries Legislation," part 4, 177.603.

106. Ibid.

107. Means, *Developing a Methodology for Surveying the Ordinary High Water Line,* 14.

108. Ibid., 15.

109. Ibid., 16.

110. *Paradise Fruit Company, Inc., v. Board of Trustees of the Internal Improvement Fund and State of Florida, Department of Natural Resources.* Summary final judgment, March 3, 1981, Circuit Court for Brevard County, Tom Waddell, Jr., judge.

111. Means, *Developing a Methodology for Surveying the Ordinary High Water Line,* 17.

112. Ibid.

CHAPTER 4: Drawing the Line: The Changing Status
of the Natural World

1. For a discussion of early water control policy in Florida, see chap. 2.

2. Louis A. Toth, senior environmental scientist with the South Florida Water Management District, and William R. Barada, editor of *ENFO,* have provided some of the most detailed descriptions of the devastation resulting from the channelization of the Kissimmee River. See, for example, Toth's "The Ecological Basis of the Kissimmee River Restoration Plan" and Barada's "The Kissimmee Chain of Lakes." Original film footage of the dredges at work can be seen on WFTV's documentary, "The Kissimmee . . . Fighting for Life."

3. Interview with Boland in WFTV, "The Kissimmee . . . Fighting for Life."

4. Interview with Louis Toth in WFTV, "The Kissimmee . . . Fighting for Life."

5. Barada, "The Kissimmee Chain of Lakes," 3.

6. Interview with Coffee in WFTV, "The Kissimmee . . . Fighting for Life."

7. Interview with Dunnick in WFTV, "The Kissimmee . . . Fighting for Life."

8. Ibid.

9. Interview with J. C. Bass in WFTV, "The Kissimmee . . . Fighting for Life."

10. Brownell, *Lake Kissimmee, Florida Ordinary High Water Study,* October 1983, 4–11.

11. Brownell, *Lake Kissimmee, Florida Ordinary High Water Study,* 4–19.

12. Division of State Lands, "The Kissimmee Dilemma," notes for a talk, records of the Bureau Chief, KR-OHW-82-001e.

13. Ibid. Boldface emphasis added.

14. Ibid.

15. Ibid. The notes do not indicate what book was attached.

16. Division of State Lands, letter, August 30, 1982, KR-OHW-82-001e.

17. *Howard v. Ingersoll.* For an explanation, see chap. 1.

18. Division of State Lands, Rohe to Douglas A. Thompson, memorandum, September 7, 1982, KR-OHW-82-001e.

19. Division of State Lands, letter, December 12, 1982, KR-OHW-82-006b.

20. Ibid.

21. Brownell, *Lake Kissimmee, Florida Ordinary High Water Study,* October 1983, 1–2.

22. Abernethy, "Cabinet Survey Team Setting High Water Line for Kissimmee."

23. Ibid.

24. Luther Holloway, Ph.D., served as the botanist on the DNR surveying team.

25. Kilsheimer, "State to Hold Meetings on Lake Boundary Issue."

26. Ibid.

27. The law firm was Holland and Knight; the engineering firm was Bromwell Engineers.

28. The presentation was by William Morris.

29. Division of State Lands, correspondence, KR-OHW-82-001e.

30. Division of State Lands, correspondence, KR-OHW-82-001e.

31. Smith, "Chronology of Events Re David Smith Matter."

32. A phenomenon Roderick Nash refers to as the expansion of natural rights in *The Rights of Nature.*

33. Division of State Lands, Lake Kissimmee Public Hearing.

34. The team consisted of E. R. Brownell, P.L.S., project manager, historian, and surveyor in charge; Thomas H. Patton, Ph.D., J.D., geologist; Luther F. Holloway, Ph.D., botanist; Daniel R. Sistrunk, Ph.D., dendrochronologist; Raul S. McQuivey, Ph.D., P.E., hydrologist; Thomas P. Brownell, P.L.S., coordinator of control surveys; and John W. Myers, P.L.S., transect surveyor.

35. Division of State Lands, Lake Kissimmee Public Hearing.

36. Ibid.

37. Ibid.

38. Ibid.

39. Ibid.

40. Ibid.

41. Although Dr. Holloway was present at the hearing, his presentation was not preserved in the recordings of the proceedings. The botanical aspects of the study have been summarized from his written report in "Lake Kissimmee, Florida: Ordinary High Water Study," prepared by E. R. Brownell and Associates.

42. Holloway, "Lake Kissimmee, Florida: Ordinary High Water Study," III 1– III 4 and III 19–III 20.

43. Division of State Lands, Lake Kissimmee Public Hearing.

44. Ibid.

45. Ibid.

46. Ibid.

47. Ibid.

48. Ibid.

49. Ibid. Quinn misspoke, confusing the two agencies dealing with environmental issues. He should have said DNR instead of DER.

50. Coordinating Council on the Restoration of the Kissimmee River Valley, "Kissimmee River Restoration," August 1983.

51. Loftis, "Water Managers Want Massive Floodplain Purchase."

52. Ibid.

53. Ibid.

54. Ibid.

55. Division of State Lands, correspondence of the executive director, KR-OHW-82-001e.

56. Ibid.

57. Ibid.

58. Division of State Lands, deposition exhibit 19, Save Our Rivers file.

59. Division of State Lands, Save Our Rivers file.

60. Division of State Lands, deposition exhibit 19, Save Our Rivers file.

61. Division of State Lands, Save Our Rivers file.

62. Division of State Lands, correspondence of executive director.

63. Ibid.

64. Marketable Record Title Act, *Florida Statutes,* sect. 712.04 (1963).

65. *Florida Statutes,* sect. 712.03(7) (1979).

66. *Board of Trustees of the Internal Improvement Trust Fund of the State of Florida v. Paradise Fruit Company, Inc.,* opinion of Justice Cowart, filed April 28, 1982, 3.

67. Cook, "Submerged Land Changes in Rules Stir up Opposition."

68. Florida Forestry Association, *Pines and Needles,* February 1985.

69. Ibid.

70. Ibid.

71. Ibid.

72. "Farm Bureau Protects Private Property Rights," *Graceville News,* July 4, 1985.

73. Ibid.

74. Ibid.

75. Ibid.

76. Moses, "Land Dispute Pits State against Private Interests."

77. Ibid.

78. Pendleton, "Panel Dives into Submerged-Land Fray."

79. Thomas, "Group May Take Fight over Title Act to Court."

80. Pendleton, "Panel Dives into Submerged-Land Fray."

81. Burgess, "Government's Land Act Could Cost Them Millions," and "County Undecided on Title Search Law."

82. Ibid.

83. Foister, "Underwater Land Ownership Debated."

84. Ibid.

85. Ibid.

86. Ibid.

87. 454 So. 2d 6, 7 (Fla. 2d D.C.A. 1984).

88. Many details of this case summary come from Hamann and Wade, "Ordinary High Water Line Determination," 325–26.

89. Figures attributed to Attorney General Butterworth, "The Mobil Land Grab Is on Again."

90. *Coastal Petroleum v. American Cyanamid,* 454 So. 2d 6 and 455 So. 2d 412.

91. *Coastal Petroleum v. American Cyanamid,* 492 So. 2d 339 (Fla. 1986).

CHAPTER 5: Lawyers, Landowners, Surveyors, and the State: The OHWL Language Wars

1. *Coastal Petroleum v. American Cyanamid,* 492 So. 2d 339 (Fla. 1986).

2. *Coastal* at 343.

3. Feagin, "The Largest Land Swindle in the History of Florida," a fund-raising address on behalf of David Smith at the James Madison Institute.

4. The Bureau of Surveying and Mapping operated in 1985 under the Division of State Lands, Florida Department of Natural Resources.

5. Board of Trustees, agenda, November 3, 1987.

6. The safe upland line (SUL) was developed as a means to provide the public with an economical way of determining a line that can be used for development planning and other purposes on freshwater lakes and rivers. It does not replace the OHWL as the true boundary of the water body. The SUL is upland of the OHWL and its location is generally based on the presence of mature upland vegetation. Hydrological data and soils may also be used to determine the location of the SUL. Division of State Lands, "Safe Upland Line Methodology," August 29, 1988.

7. Dartland, "Chronology of Events."

8. Dartland to Smith, May 17, 1988.

9. Ibid.

10. Gomia and Associates, workshop on rule chap. 21HH-6.0045 FAC. The BPLS on that date was comprised of H. Bruce Durden, chair; Gus A. Sliger, Buell H. Harper, Jr., Daniel E. Gentry, and Wilbur M. Christiansen, Jr.

11. Feagin, "The Largest Land Swindle in the History of Florida."

12. Ibid., 5–8. Emphasis added.

13. Ibid., 8–9.

14. Ibid., 11–12.

15. Ibid.

16. Gomia and Associates, workshop on rule chap. 21HH-6.0045 FAC, 17.

17. See chap. 3, "By the Distinctive Appearances They Present."

18. See chap. 3, "Freshwaters."

19. See for example, *Borough of Ford City v. United States*. See also Winesett, "Legal Standards for Determining the Ordinary High Water Mark." For a short discussion, see chap. 3, "By the Distinctive Appearances They Present," in this book.

20. Gomia and Associates, workshop on rule chap. 21HH-6.0045 FAC, 29–37.

21. Ibid., 48.

22. Ibid., 51–52.

23. Ibid., 3–4.

24. Ibid., 4–5.

25. Blain and Manson, "Memorandum of Law."

26. Ibid., 2–3.

27. Ibid., 9.

28. Robert A. Butterworth to Tom Gardner, June 1, 1988.

29. Percy W. Mallison, Jr., to David Heffner, December 14, 1988.

30. Michael S. Davis to Bruce Durden, May 5, 1988. Emphasis added.

31. Conversation with Doug Woodward, March 15, 1999.

32. Bob O'Brien, Jr., to Governor Bob Martinez, May 12, 1988.

33. John S. Thornton, Jr., to Allen R. Smith, Jr., May 4, 1988.

34. Conversation with Rod Maddox, professional land surveyor, October 16, 2000.

35. See, for example, *Martin v. Busch*, which deals with the flat-banked topography of Florida water bodies for which determining the line of ordinary high water mark can be "difficult of accurate ascertainment."

36. Vince Martinez, memorandum to the Board of Professional Land Surveyors, May 6, 1988.

37. Gentry, "Ordinary High Water Line in Florida."

38. See Gentry's testimony in *Board of Trustees of the Internal Improvement Trust Fund v. Lykes Bros., Inc.*, in which he testified that he did not accept the holdings of the *Coastal* court as being consistent with Florida law.

39. Gentry, "Ordinary High Water Line in Florida," 3.

40. *Howard* at 427. Emphasis added.

41. Gentry to Allen Rex Smith, Jr., June 16, 1988.

42. *Howard* at 416. Wayne described the boundary as the western bank of the river, the "fast land which confines the water of the river in its channel or bed in its whole width." Wayne explained that the phrase "along the bank thereof" was the "controlling call in the interpretation of the cession." He insisted that the court "reject, altogether, the attempt to trace the line by either ordinary low water or low water," saying that water was "not a call in the description of the boundary, though the river is, and that, . . . does not mean water alone, but banks, shores, water, and the bed of the river." Wayne then described the boundary in terms that unmistakably take in the (ordinary) high stages of the river: "The bank or the slope from the bluff or perpendicular of the bank may not be reached by the water for two thirds of the year, still the water line impressed upon the bank above the slope is the line required . . . and the shore of the river, though left dry for any time, and but occasionally covered by water in any stage of it to the bank, was retained by Georgia as the river up to that line."

43. *Howard* at 427.

44. Ibid., 427–28.

45. *MacNamara v. Kissimmee River Valley Association* at 159.

46. Justice Wayne begins his opinion saying, "The point for decision in these cases is one of boundary, between the States of Georgia and Alabama."

47. See, for example, Wilkinson, deposition, 294.

48. Gentry, "The Ordinary High Water Mark Defined," 2.

49. *Howard* at 416.

50. *The Board of Trustees of the Internal Improvement Trust Fund of the State of Florida v. Board of Professional Land Surveyors, Department of Professional Regulation of the State of Florida.*

51. Ibid.

52. The *News-Press* incorrectly inserted the word "unmeandered." The correct term is *nonmeandered.*

53. "River Bottoms in Danger," *Fort Myers News-Press*, March 8, 1989.

54. Bush, "Where Do You Draw the Line?"

55. Ibid.

56. Ibid.

57. SORA, "SORA Joins Fight to Defend Surveyors' Right to Define Lines."

58. Ibid.

59. Vrabel, "Can You Practice without a License?" Emphasis added.

60. Ibid.

61. *Trustees v. BPLS*, final order.

62. Ibid., 9–10.

63. Ibid., 10–12.

64. Ibid., 12–13.

65. Ibid., 13.

66. *The Daniel Ball v. United States.*

67. *Trustees v. BPLS*, final order, 13–14.

68. The BPLS rule defined the OHWL: "the natural boundary that separates the bed of a non-tidal water body from its banks; for navigable water bodies the OHWM is the title boundary between sovereignty submerged lands and riparian land; it is the actual, observable, physical mark impressed on the bank of a water body by the long continued presence and action of the water during normal years, and reflects the point to which the water has exerted dominance over the bed so as to wrest the bed from terrestrial vegetation and destroy its value for agricultural purposes.

Generally, the OHWM is a visible mark in which parties providing for a water boundary between them would naturally have in their minds. In all cases the OHWM is a natural object, and is to be sought for as other natural objects are sought for and found by the distinctive appearances they present. Generally, this natural boundary is capable, not only of being ascertained upon inquiring but also, of being seen and recognized in the common practical affairs of life. It neither takes in overflowed land beyond the bank, nor includes swamps or low grounds liable to be overflowed, but reclaimable for meadows or agriculture, or which being too low for reclamation though not always covered with water, may be used for cattle to range upon as natural unenclosed pasture.

The OHWM is an ambulatory boundary and is subject to gradual and imperceptible change due to erosion, accretion, reliction or submergence" (*Trustees v. BPLS*, final order, 14–15).

69. Washburn, *Real Property, Probate and Trust Journal*, 547. Washburn, a California attorney, represented land developers in litigation with the state of California. His article makes no mention of the key Florida cases *Gerbing* and *Martin*.

70. *Trustees v. BPLS*, final order, 19–20.

71. The BPLS rule stated "Swamp and Overflowed Lands shall mean lands that lie on the landward side of the ordinary high water line but that are so subject to inundation during the normal planting, growing or harvesting season of the region that they are not useful for normal agricultural purposes unless they are drained to remove excess water or diked to prevent flooding" (*Trustees v. BPLS*, final order, 11 FALR 2467).

72. Ibid., 22.

73. Ibid., 27.

74. Ibid., 28–30.

75. Ibid., 22–23.

76. Ibid., 31.

77. Ibid., 32.

78. Ibid., 7–8.

79. Ibid., 49.

80. Ibid., 51.

81. Ibid.

82. Wilkinson, interview, January 23, 2001.

83. Ibid.

84. Ibid.

85. Ibid.

86. *The Board of Trustees of the Internal Improvement Trust Fund and Florida Audubon Society v. Board of Professional Land Surveyors,* et. al., District Court of Appeal, First District, State of Florida, Case Nos. 89-1293, 89-1294, opinion filed September 13, 1990.

87. Gomia and Associates, workshop on rule chap. 21HH-6.0045 FAC, 51.

88. Gentry, "Ordinary High Water Line in Florida." The paper is undated but refers to the district court of appeal's decision in September 1990. The paper was probably updated as part of Gentry's reliance on *MacNamara v. Kissimmee River Valley Association* in 1993, which Blain and Cone litigated on behalf of MacNamara.

89. On twenty-three contested points of the BPLS rule, Adams found eight acceptable, fifteen not acceptable under Florida law.

90. Ibid.

91. *Trustees v. BPLS,* First District Court of Appeals (1990).

92. *Trustees v. BPLS,* DOAH, Final Order, Case No. 88-4710R, 19.

93. *Kissimmee River Valley Sportsmans' Association v. Roger MacNamara* at 72–73.

94. Ibid. at 92.

95. Ibid. at 228.

96. Ibid. at 246.

97. "Initial Brief of Appellant Roger MacNamara," L. M. Blain, attorney for appellants, Second District Court of Appeals, case no. 93-2494, 27.

98. Ibid., 36.

99. Ibid., 42.

100. *MacNamara v. Kissimmee River Valley Sportsmans' Association and Board of Trustees of the Internal Improvement Trust Fund.*

101. Michael Rosen to all foundation members, February 2, 1995.

102. Ibid.

103. Michael Rosen to Kent Green, February 7, 1995.

104. Ibid.

105. Conversations with Rod Maddox, Land Management Survey section, Bureau of Surveying and Mapping, Florida Department of Environmental Protection; Doug Woodward, professional land surveyor; Dave Kealy, professional land surveyor; and research of the announcements of the FSPLS.

106. *Trustees v. Smith,* case no. 95-19896-CA-S; defendant's affirmative defenses.

107. Ibid.

108. See, for example, Rosen, "The Significance of the David Smith Case."

109. Tampa Bay Online, "Construction Begins on Kissimmee River Restoration Project."

110. Kissimmee River Restoration Web Site, February 10, 2003, http://www
.sfwmd.gov/org/erd/krr/.

CHAPTER 6: A New Low for the Ordinary High Water Line: The Demand for Certainty

1. See for example the 1854 case of *Attorney-General v. Chambers,* in which the debate over the location of the ordinary high water mark turned in part on the issue of what was to be considered *ordinary* high tides.

2. The most notable of these are Mike Rosen of the Florida Legal Foundation; Dan Gentry, the surveyor who helped author the BPLS rule; and Robert Feagin, the attorney who presented the draft rule to the BPLS and served as counsel for Coastal Petroleum.

3. "David Smith Fact Sheet."

4. *MacNamara v. Kissimmee River Valley Association* at 159.

5. Reimer, "The Public Trust Doctrine," 15.

6. Mobil Oil Corporation's Trial Brief Regarding the Ordinary High Water Mark, *Mobil Oil Corporation v. The State of Florida,* case no. GC-G-82-1089, 10th Judicial Circuit, Polk County, Florida, October 12, 1987, at 14–15.

7. Reimer, "The Public Trust Doctrine," 15.

8. Ibid., 16.

9. Ibid., n. 85.

10. Maloney, "The Ordinary High Water Mark," 485.

11. *Coastal Petroleum v. American Cyanamid* at 340.

12. *Martin v. Busch* at 285–86.

13. *Coastal* at 340.

14. *State ex rel. Ellis v. Gerbing.*

15. *Martin v. Busch* at 285–86.

16. Ibid. at 283.

17. Board of Trustees of the Internal Improvement Trust Fund, *Minutes,* January 31, 1956; April 24, 1956; July 7, 1957.

18. HR 1807, Relating to Land Conveyances.

19. *House Journal,* May 1, 2000, 1341–42.

20. Wilkinson, "Developing a Methodology."

21. In addition, for any degree of certainty with regard to the OHWL, you not only need a survey, you need a court. Richard Hamann at the University of Florida College of Law has pointed out no surveyor should expect to be able to use any methodology to establish unequivocally the OHWL because only the courts can establish an uncontestable boundary.

22. Wilkinson, deposition, 287–89.

23. Ibid., 294–95.

24. Gentry, deposition, 35.

25. *Broward v. Mabry.*

26. *Geiger v. Filor,* quoting Angell, *A Treatise on Tidewaters,* 18, 68. Thomas Jefferson explained that the purpose of the high water boundary was to facilitate public use of the shores and beaches. *Land in New Orleans Called the Batture, American State Papers,* 17, Public Lands 2:2, 91 (1810).

27. *Houghton v. The C., D. & M. R. Co.*

28. *Attorney-General v. Chambers* at 206.

29. *Kissimmee River Valley Sportsmans' Association v. MacNamara,* 648 So. 2d 155 at 160.

CHAPTER 7: Down to the Waterline: The Nature of Our Place

1. "Lawsuit Puts Private Property Rights under Fire," 1.

2. Richard H. Miller to Judge Roger F. Dykes, correspondence in the matter of *Central and Southern Florida Flood Control District v. Saffan,* et al., May 3, 1973, citing *Peavy-Wilson Lumber Co. v. Brevard County.* Emphasis added.

3. See, for example, Tuan, *Segmented Worlds and Self;* Sessions, "Ecological Consciousness and Paradigm Change"; Tobias, Introduction to *Deep Ecology;* and Devall and Sessions, *Deep Ecology, Living as if Nature Mattered.*

4. "Lawsuit Puts Private Property Rights under Fire," 1.

5. Wood, "Of the Beasts That Live on the Land," 95–96. An ounce is a "wildcat" or bobcat; a musquash is a muskrat.

6. Nash, *The Rights of Nature,* 9.

7. Ibid., 11.

8. Ibid.

9. Ibid., 5.

10. Ibid. Nash points out that the term was coined by Richard Ryder in his essay, "Experiments on Animals," in Stanley and Rosalind Godlovitch and John Harris, eds., *Animals, Men and Morals* (New York, 1972), 81.

11. Ibid., 10.

12. Rudner, "Sacred Geographies," 16.

13. Cavell, *Must We Mean What We Say?* 43.

14. Lewis, "Ecosystem Management, It's in Our Hands!" 1–3.

15. Ibid., 8.

Glossary

Accretion The gradual and imperceptible accumulation of land along the shore or bank of a water body.

Avulsion The sudden or perceptible loss of or addition to land by the action of water or a sudden change in the bed of a lake or the course of a stream.

Bank The elevation of land that confines the waters of a stream in their natural channel at their highest flow.

Board of Trustees The Board of Trustees of the Internal Improvement Trust Fund, which consists of the governor, secretary of state, attorney general, comptroller, state treasurer, commissioner of agriculture, and commissioner of education; created by *Florida Statutes,* chap. 253.

Erosion The gradual and imperceptible wearing away of lands due to natural causes.

Excedence frequency The duration of time the water level is at or above a certain elevation.

Eutrophication An enrichment of lakes by nutrients received from their watersheds.

Hydrograph A graph of water-level elevation plotted against time.

Meander line A line established during the public lands surveys conducted by the federal government. The water body was traversed and its sinuosities described so that the quantities of land in fractional sections could be estimated. In most cases, a meander line is not a boundary line.

MHWL Mean high water line; the boundary between tidal waters and the adjoining uplands.

Navigable A permanent water body in its ordinary, natural condition that was used or susceptible of being used for navigation for useful purposes and purposes common to the public in the locality is deemed "navigable." In determining the status of water bodies as sovereignty lands, this test is applied to the water body at the time of statehood (March 3, 1845).

OHWL The ordinary high water line; the boundary between publicly owned sovereignty lands and the adjacent uplands that are subject to private ownership. The OHWL approximates the elevation to which the water rises during the high water season of an ordinary year. The OHWL excludes exceptionally high water events caused by floods or freshets. The OHWL establishes the boundary of a navigable water body however shallow the water may be at the outer margins or elsewhere, as long as the water is in fact a part of the navigable water body. It is an ambulatory line that shifts in response to long-term, gradual, natural changes in water levels or in the shoreline. In general, accretion, erosion, reliction, and submergence shift the OHWL, while avulsion and artificial (man-made) changes do not shift the OHWL.

OHWM   Ordinary high water mark; a mark, or other indicator of the OHWL.

Reliction   An increase of the land by the gradual and imperceptible lowering of any body of water.

Riparian lands   Lands bordering nontidal navigable water bodies.

Stage duration curve   A graph showing the percent of time water levels exceed a certain elevation during a given period of time at a specific location on a water body.

Submergence   The gradual and imperceptible covering of formerly riparian lands by waters whose levels are slowly rising as a result of natural processes.

Trustees   Board of Trustees of the Internal Improvement Trust Fund (see Board of Trustees).

Bibliography

Abbreviations

BSM   Bureau of Surveying and Mapping
DEP   Florida Department of Environmental Protection
DSL   Division of State Lands
TIITF   Trustees of the Internal Improvement Trust Fund

Books, Articles, and Correspondence

Abernethy, Arch. "Cabinet Survey Team Setting High Water Line for Kissimmee." *Daily Highlander,* July 21, 1983.

Adams, Tom. Memorandum to TIITF, June 17, 1969. Trustees' Policy file, DEP vault, Tallahassee, Fla.

Ansbacher, Sidney F., and Joe Knetsch. "The Public Trust Doctrine and Sovereignty Lands in Florida: A Legal and Historical Analysis." *Journal of Land Use and Environmental Law* 4, no. 2 (1989).

Apthorp, James W. Memorandum to TIITF, Nov. 12, 1969. Trustees policies—lake files, DEP vault, Tallahassee, Fla.

Barada, William R. "The Kissimmee Chain of Lakes: A Mismanaged Tourist Bonanza." *ENFO.* Winter Park: Florida Conservation Foundation.

———. "Restoring the Kissimmee River May Be Florida's Environmental Armageddon." *ENFO,* March 1977. Winter Park: Florida Conservation Foundation.

Bellinger, John W. "Dredging, Filling, and the Inalienable Public Trust: The Future of Florida's Submerged Environment." Paper presented at the 24th annual conference of the Southeastern Association of Game and Fish Commissioners, Atlanta, Ga., 1970. Florida Archives Series 86, Carton 7, Tallahassee, Fla.

Bishop, E. W. *Florida Lakes, Part I, A Study of the High Water Lines of Some Florida Lakes.* Florida Board of Conservation, Tallahassee: 1967.

Blain, L. M. "Initial Brief of Appellant Roger MacNamara." 2nd D.C.A. Case no. 93-2494.

Blain, L. M., and Douglas P. Manson. "Memorandum of Law." January 4, 1988, revised April 7, 1988. BSM Records, Tallahassee, Fla.

Blake, Nelson Manfred. *Land into Water—Water into Land: A History of Water Management in Florida.* Tallahassee: Florida State Univ. Press, 1980.

Board of TIITF. Agenda, November 3, 1987. Records of the DSL, Tallahassee, Fla.

———. "Information Concerning Submerged or Sovereignty Lands in the State of Florida." Policy statement, October 8, 1970.

———. Minutes of the TIITF, January 31, 1956; April 24, 1956; July 7, 1957.

———. Minutes of the TIITF, vol. 37, no. 48 (1968).

———. Minutes of the TIITF, September 17, 1968.

———. Minutes of the TIITF, January 20, 1970.

———. Minutes of the TIITF, June 16, 1970.

———. Minutes of the TIITF, February 23, 1971.

Breed, C. *Surveying.* 2nd ed. Rev. with the assistance of Alexander J. Bone. New York: Wiley, 1957.

Brownell, E. R., and Associates. *Lake Kissimmee, Florida Ordinary High Water Study.* October 1983. DSL, BSM Records, Tallahassee, Fla.

Burgess, Susan. "County Undecided on Title Search Law." *News-Tribune,* September 18, 1985.

———. "Government's Land Act Could Cost Them Millions." *News-Tribune,* September 17, 1985.

Bush, Rick. "Where Do You Draw the Line?" *FloridAgriculture,* February 1, 1989.

Butterworth, Robert A. *Laws of Florida Relating to Water and Water Bodies, 1822– 1941.* 1991.

———. Letter to Tom Gardner, June 1, 1988.

———. "The Mobil Land Grab Is on Again." *St. Petersburg Times,* February 23, 1987.

Byrnes, Patricia. "Are We Being Taken by Takings?" *Wilderness* (spring 1995).

Carter, Luther J. *The Florida Experience: Land and Water Policy in a Growth State.* Baltimore: Johns Hopkins Univ. Press, 1974.

Carter, Michael R., et. al. *Ecosystem Analysis of the Big Cypress Swamp and Estuaries.* Atlanta, Ga.: U.S. Environmental Protection Agency, 1973.

Cavell, Stanley. *The Claim of Reason.* New York: Oxford Univ. Press, 1979.

———. *Must We Mean What We Say?* Cambridge: Cambridge Univ. Press, 1969.

Center for Conservation Biology Network. Introduction to "Academic Programs in Conservation Biology." http://conbio.rice.edu/programs:1997.

Center for Urban and Regional Studies, Division of Applied Ecology, Univ. of Miami. *The Kissimmee-Okeechobee Basin: A Report to the Florida Cabinet.* December 12, 1972.

Central and Southern Florida Flood Control District. *Five Years of Progress: 1949– 1954.* West Palm Beach: November 1954.

———. "Growth and Water Supply: More People, More Problems." 24th Annual Report, 1972.

Chandler, Alfred N. *Land Title Origins: A Tale of Force and Fraud.* New York: Robert Schalkenbach Foundation, 1945.

Cole, George M. "Proposed Water Boundaries Legislation." Part 4, 177.602. BSM Records, Tallahassee, Fla.

Cook, Bruce. "Submerged Land Changes in Rules Stir up Opposition." *Press Journal,* September 22, 1985.

Coordinating Council on the Restoration of the Kissimmee River Valley and Taylor Creek–Nubbin Slough Basin. *First Annual Report to the Florida Legislature.* April 1977.

———. "Kissimmee River Restoration: Public Hearing Discussion Paper Public Meetings." August 1983, KR-OHW-82-001e, BSM Records, Tallahassee, Fla.

Crawford, G. B. "Lawsuit Puts Private Property Rights under Fire." *FloridAgriculture* 55, no. 1 (January 1997).

Dartland, Diana. "Chronology of Events," report to David Heffner, Senate Economic, Community, and Consumer Affairs Committee. November 1, 1988.

———. Letter to Allen "Rex" Smith, Jr., May 17, 1988.

Davis, Michael S. Letter to Bruce Durden, May 5, 1988.

Davis, Raymond E., Francis S. Foote, and Joe W. Kelley. *Surveying: Theory and Practice*. New York: McGraw-Hill, 1966.

Derr, Mark. *Some Kind of Paradise*. New York: William Morrow, 1989.

Devall, Bill, and George Sessions. "The Dominant, Modern Worldview and Its Critics." *Deep Ecology: Living as if Nature Mattered*. Layton, Utah: Gibbs M. Smith, 1985.

DSL. Correspondence. KR-OHW-82-006b, BSM Records, Tallahassee, Fla.

———. Correspondence of the executive director. KR-OHW-82-001e, BSM Records, Tallahassee, Fla.

———. "The Kissimmee Dilemma." KR-OHW-82-001e, BSM Records, Tallahassee, Fla.

———. Lake Kissimmee Public Hearing. Audiotapes, KR-OHW-82-001e, BSM Records, Tallahassee, Fla.

———. "Safe Upland Line Methodology." August 29, 1988, BSM Records, Tallahassee, Fla.

———. Save Our Rivers file. KR-OHW-82-014, BSM Records, Tallahassee, Fla.

Drengson, Alan R. Foreword to *Ecophilosophy: A Field Guide to the Literature*. Ed. Donald Edward Davis. San Pedro: R. and E. Miles, 1989.

Ervin, Richard. Letter to Chief Drainage Engineer F. C. Elliot, Nov. 6, 1951. DEP records, vault, Tallahassee, Fla.

———. Letter to W. Turner Wallis, July 18, 1957. DEP vault, Tallahassee, Fla.

Faircloth, Earl. Memorandum to TIITF, Jan. 20, 1967. Trustees' Policy file, DEP vault, Tallahassee, Fla.

"Farm Bureau Protects Private Property Rights." *Graceville News*, July 4, 1985.

Feagin, Robert. "The Largest Land Swindle in the History of Florida." Presentation at the James Madison Institute, April 1999, Tallahassee, Fla.

Ferguson, Van H. January 6, 1960. Trustees policies—Lakes file, DEP vault, Tallahassee, Fla.

Feynman, Richard. *The Meaning of It All*. Reading, Mass.: Perseus, 1998.

Florida Forestry Association. *Pines and Needles*, February 1985.

Florida Game and Fresh Water Fish Commission. *Recommended Program for Kissimmee River Basin by Florida Game and Fresh Water Fish Commission*. August 1957. Federal Aid Projects F-8-R, W-19-R, and W-39-R.

Florida. *Journal of the House of Representatives*. May 1, 2000, 1341–42.

Florida Times-Union, May 1, 1896.

Foister, Cecil. "Underwater Land Ownership Debated." *Daytona Beach Journal,* September 18, 1985.

Frank, Richard M. "Forever Free: Navigability, Inland Waterways, and the Expanding Public Interest." *The Public Land and Resources Law Digest* 20, no. 2 (1983).

Gates, Paul W. *History of Public Land Law Development.* New York: Arno Press, 1979.

Gay, Norwood. "The High Water Mark: Boundary between Public and Private Lands." *University of Florida Law Review* 18, no. 4 (spring 1966).

Gelzer, Sonya. "Area Realtors Upset over State's Attempted Takeover." *Jackson County Floridan,* September 20, 1985.

Gentry, Daniel. Cover letter to Allen Rex Smith, Jr., June 16, 1988.

———. Deposition. *Board of Trustees of the Internal Improvement Trust Fund of the State of Florida v. David A. Smith.* Case No. 97-6341. November 29, 2000. Vol. 1.

———. "Ordinary High Water Line in Florida: Traditional Surveying Methodology," unpublished paper distributed under the letterhead of attorneys Blain and Cone, Tampa, Fla., provided to Board of Professional Land Surveyors June 16, 1988.

———. "The Ordinary High Water Mark Defined: Three Cases Examined by a Land Surveyor," unpublished paper distributed to the Board of Professional Land Surveyors on June 16, 1988.

———. Testimony in *Board of Trustees of the Internal Improvement Trust Fund v. Lykes Bros., Inc.* Transcript of the record, Premier Reporting. Case No. CA93-136. Vol. 29.

Glogau, Jonathan A. Letter to Hon. Lawson Lamar, Orlando. Sovereignty lands correspondence, January 3, 1996, BSM Records, Tallahassee, Fla.

Gomia and Associates. Board of Professional Land Surveyors, Workshop on Rule Chapter 21HH-6.0045 FAC Ordinary High Water Line Surveys, May 11, 1988, Tallahassee, Fla.

Guest, David. "The Ordinary High Water Boundary on Freshwater Lakes and Streams: Origin, Theory, and Constitutional Restrictions." *Journal of Land Use and Environmental Law* 6, no. 2.

Hamann, Richard, and Jeff Wade. "Ordinary High Water Line Determination: Legal Issues." *Florida Law Review* 42, no. 2 (April 1990).

Hartwell, James H. "Hydrology." *The Kissimmee-Okeechobee Basin: A Report to the Florida Cabinet.* Miami: Center for Urban and Regional Studies, Univ. of Miami, 1972.

Houck, L. "A Treatise on the Law of Navigable Rivers." 1868.

Institutes of Justinian, Liber 2, Tract 1, Section 1. Reprinted in J. K. Angell, *A Treatise on Tide Waters.* 1826.

Ivey, Steven. *Principals for a Navigability Assessment of Rivers and Lakes.* Washington Department of Natural Resources, 2001.

Jacobson, S. K. "Graduate Education in Conservation Biology." *Conservation Biology* 4 (1990).

Johnson, Lamar. *Beyond the Fourth Generation.* Gainesville: Univ. Presses of Florida, 1974.

Kilsheimer, Joe. "State to Hold Meetings on Lake Boundary Issue." *Orlando Sentinel,* February 1984.

Kirk, Claude. Executive Order, February 3, 1970. Trustees policies—Lakes file, DEP vault, Tallahassee, Fla.

Knetsch, Joe. "The Meaning of the Swamp Lands Act of 1850." 1997, BSM Records, Tallahassee, Fla.

——. Presentation at Florida Society of Professional Land Surveyors Ordinary High Water Line Seminar, February 4, 1994, Tallahassee, Fla.

——. "Summary of Instructions Concerning the Meandering of Florida Waterbodies." 1993 report, BSM Records; citing "Instructions to the Principal Deputy Surveyor of the Land District East of Island of New Orleans," 1819, and *Manual of Surveying Instructions for the Survey of the Public Lands of the United States* (1894) 56, U.S. Dept. of the Interior, Bureau of Land Management, microfilm 1964.

——. *Sunland Tribune* 24 (1998).

Land and Water Law Review 13, no. 2 (1978): 485.

"Lawsuit Puts Private Property Rights under Fire." *FloridAgriculture* 55, no. 1 (January 1997).

Leopold, Aldo. *Sand County Almanac.* New York: Oxford Univ. Press, 1949.

Lewis, Jim. "Ecosystem Management, It's in Our Hands!" DEP Ecosystem Management handbook, 1993.

Livingston, Robert J. "Inshore Marine Habitats." *Ecosystems of Florida.* Ed. Ronald L. Myers and John J. Ewel. Orlando: Univ. of Central Florida Press, 1990.

Loftis, Randy. "Water Managers Want Massive Floodplain Purchase." *Miami Herald,* March 16, 1984.

Lubchenco, J., et al. "The Sustainable Biosphere Initiative: An Ecological Research Agenda." *Ecology* 72 (1991).

Maddox, Rod. Conversation, October 16, 2000.

Mallison, Percy W., Jr. Letter to David Heffner, December 14, 1988.

Maloney, Frank E. "The Ordinary High Water Mark: Attempts at Settling an Unsettled Boundary Line." *Land and Water Law Review* 13, no. 2 (1978).

Martinez, Vince. Memorandum to the Board of Professional Land Surveyors, May 6, 1988.

McVety, Pam. "Column Confused Issues of Ecosystem Management." *Tallahassee Democrat,* August 3, 1998.

Means, D. Bruce. *Developing a Methodology for Surveying the Ordinary High Water Line: Is It Feasible?* A report to the Florida Department of Natural Resources, February 1986. BSM Records, Tallahassee, Fla.

Merchant, Carolyn. *The Death of Nature: Women, Ecology, and the Scientific Revolution.* San Francisco: Harper and Row, 1980.

Metz, Andrew. "Hunters Hike Waist-Deep into Land Dispute." *Palm Beach Post,* July 21, 1996.

Miller, G. Tyler, Jr. *Living in the Environment.* Belmont, Calif.: Wadsworth, 1990.

Miller, Richard H. Letter to Judge Roger F. Dykes, in the matter of *Central and Southern Florida Flood Control District v. Saffan,* et al. May 3, 1973.

Mobil Oil Corporation. Motion for Pre-Trial Ruling and for Order in Limine Regarding the Ordinary High Water Mark. *Mobil Oil Corp. v. The State of Florida.* Case No. GC-G-82-1089, 10th Judicial Circuit (October 19, 1987).

———. Trial Brief Regarding the Ordinary High Water Mark. *Mobil Oil Corporation v. The State of Florida.* Case No. GC-G-82-1089, 10th Judicial Circuit, Polk County, Fla. (October 12, 1987).

Moore, Stuart A. *A History of the Foreshore and the Law Relating Thereto.* London: Stevens and Haynes, 1888; repr., Holmes Beach, Fla.: Gaunt and Sons, 1993.

Morris, Allen, comp. *The Florida Handbook, 1987–1988.* Tallahassee: Peninsular, 1987.

Moses, Galen. "Land Dispute Pits State against Private Interests." *Gainesville Sun,* July 14, 1985.

Nash, Roderick. *The Rights of Nature: A History of Environmental Ethics.* Madison: Univ. of Wisconsin Press, 1989.

Northwest Territory Ordinance to Grant State's Rights. July 13, 1787. Chap. 8, 1, stat. 50, 52.

O'Brien, Bob, Jr. Letter to Governor Bob Martinez, May 12, 1988.

Parker, Gerald G. "Hydrology of the Pre-drainage System of the Everglades in Southern Florida." *Environments of South Florida.* Miami: Miami Geological Society, 1974.

Parker, Gerald G., et al. *Water Resources of Southeastern Florida with Special Reference to the Geology and Ground Water of the Miami Area.* U.S. Geological Survey Water-Supply paper 1255, 1955.

Parks, Ira A. Letter to Fred Vidzes, Land Management Division, May 24, 1971. Department of Air and Water Pollution records, microfiche group: Polk Co., Submerged Lands Division, Tallahassee, Fla.

Patton, Donald, and Bruce Sanford, eds. *Interim Report on the Special Project to Prevent Eutrophication of Lake Okeechobee.* Tallahassee: Department of Administration, Division of State Planning, Bureau of Comprehensive Planning, 1975.

Pendleton, Randolph. "Panel Dives into Submerged-Land Fray." *Florida Times-Union,* July 15, 1985.

Peyton, Daniel W. "Sovereignty Lands in Florida: It's All about Navigability." *Florida Bar Journal,* January 2002.

Public Hearing concerning establishment of the boundary line of Lake Kissimmee, Lake Tohopekaliga, East Lake Tohopekaliga, Alligator Lake, and Lake Lizzie, June 22, 1971. Jones and Jones Court Reporters, West Palm Beach, Fla.

Reimer, Monica K. "The Public Trust Doctrine: Historic Protection for Florida's Navigable Rivers and Lakes." *Florida Bar Journal,* April 2001.

Richard, Melvin J. "Tidelands and Riparian Rights in Florida." *Miami Law Quarterly* 3, no. 3 (April 1949).

"River Bottoms in Danger." *Fort Myers News-Press,* March 8, 1989.

Rosen, Michael. Letter to all Florida Legal Foundation members, February 2, 1995.

———. Letter to Kent Green, February 7, 1995.

———. "The Significance of the David Smith Case as a Last Line of Defense for Florida Landowners against State Sovereignty Ownership Claims." *State Sovereignty Ownership Claims: The Private Landowner's Perspective.* The Florida Legal Foundation.

Rudner, Ruth. "Sacred Geographies." *Wilderness* 58, no. 206 (1994).

Ryder, Richard. "Experiments on Animals." *Animals, Men and Morals.* Ed. Stanley and Rosalind Godlovitch and John Harris. New York, 1972.

Schneider, Douglas L., and Ernest W. Bishop. "Pre-Regulation Ordinary High Water Elevations along the Kissimmee River: A Preliminary Investigation." December 14, 1976. BSM Records, Tallahassee, Fla.

Schneider, Douglas L., and Karen L. Busen. "Ordinary High Water Elevations of Four Major Lakes of the Kissimmee Chain: East Tohopekaliga, Tohopekaliga, Hatchineha and Kissimmee." Boundary Determination Section, Bureau of Coastal and Land Boundaries, August 25, 1976. BSM Records, Tallahassee, Fla.

Sessions, George. "Ecological Consciousness and Paradigm Change." *Deep Ecology.* Ed. Michael Tobias. San Marcos, Calif.: Avant Books, 1984.

Shevin, Robert. Letter, October 27, 1978. OHWL 1978 file, BSM Records, Tallahassee, Fla.

Slade, David C. *Putting the Public Trust Doctrine to Work.* The Connecticut Department of Environmental Protection, Coastal Resources Management Division, 1990.

Smith, David. "Chronology of Events Re David Smith Matter." Circulated to the Florida cabinet members in November 1995. DSL, BSM Records, Tallahassee, Fla.

———. "David Smith Fact Sheet." Circulated to the Florida cabinet members in November 1995. BSM Records, Tallahassee, Fla.

SORA, the Shoreline Owners and Residents Association. "SORA Joins Fight to Defend Surveyors' Right to Define Lines." *ebb & FLOW* 1, no. 2 (January 1989).

South Florida Water Management District. "Kissimmee River Restoration." West Palm Beach, [n.d.].

Southwest Florida Water Management District. "Ensuring the Water Resource until 2050 and Beyond." *Hydroscope.* Summer 1988.

———. "Kuhl: Challenges Brought by Growth." *Hydroscope.* Quarter 4 (1983).

Tampa Bay Online. "Construction Begins on Kissimmee River Restoration Project." June 11, 1999. http://www.tbo.com.

Tebeau, Charlton W., and Ruby Leach Carson. *Florida from Indian Trail to Space Age.* Vol. 1. Delray Beach, Fla.: Southern Publishing, 1965.

Thomas, Gina. "Group May Take Fight over Title Act to Court." *Orlando Sentinel,* July 26, 1985.

Thornton, John S., Jr. Letter to Allen R. Smith, Jr., Florida Board of Professional Land Surveyors, May 4, 1988.

Tobias, Michael. Introduction to *Deep Ecology.* Ed. Michael Tobias. San Marcos, Calif.: Avant Books, 1984.

Toth, Louis A. "The Ecological Basis of the Kissimmee River Restoration Plan." *Florida Scientist* 1 (1993).

Trumbull, Steven. *Miami Herald,* October 3, 1965.

Trustees' Correspondence 1949–1952. File, DEP vault, Tallahassee, Fla.

Tuan, Yi-Fu. *Segmented Worlds and Self: Group Life and Individual Consciousness.* Minneapolis: Univ. of Minnesota Press, 1982.

U.S. Congress. House of Representatives. "Examination and Survey of Kissimmee River, Florida, Etc., Letter from the Secretary of War." 57th Cong., 1st sess., 1902. Document no. 176.

U.S. Department of the Interior, Bureau of Land Management. *Manual of Surveying Instructions for the Survey of the Public Lands of the United States* (1894). Microfilm 1964.

————. *Manual of Surveying Instructions for the Survey of the Public Lands of the United States* (1902). Microfilm 1964.

————. *Manual of Surveying Instructions for the Survey of the Public Lands of the United States* (1930). Microfilm 1964.

Vrabel, Steve. "Can You Practice without a License?" *Florida Surveyor,* January 1989.

Wallis, W. Turner. "The Trustees of the Internal Improvement Fund: An Analysis and Discussion of Florida's Public Land Management Agency." December 1, 1960. DSL records, Tallahassee, Fla.

Wallis, W. Turner, and Ney C. Landrum. "The Management of Florida's Sovereignty Lands and Its Implication for the Engineering and Surveying Professions." April 22, 1958. Office of the TIITF of the State of Florida, State Lands records, Tallahassee, Fla.

Washburn, Edgar B. *Real Property, Probate and Trust Journal* 18 (fall 1983).

WFTV. "The Kissimmee . . . Fighting for Life." 1997.

"Whitfield's Notes: Governmental, Legal, and Political History of Florida," *Florida Statutes* (1941).

Wilkinson, Terry. Conversation with Florida's Chief Cadastral Surveyor, May 13, 2000.

————. Deposition. *Board of Trustees of the Internal Improvement Trust Fund of the State of Florida v. David A. Smith.* Case no. 97-6341. August 8, 2000. Vol. 3.

————. "Developing a Methodology." *Florida's Non-Tidal Water Boundaries.* Seminar presentation, April 2002.

————. Interview, January 23, 2001.

————. Interview, June 12, 2002.

Wilkinson, Terry, Joe Knetsch, and David Guest. "Florida Society of Professional Land Surveyors Ordinary High Water Line Seminar." December 1993. BSM Records, Tallahassee, Fla.

Winesett, Richard Warner. "Legal Standards for Determining the Ordinary High Water Mark." 1972. Paper submitted to Dean Frank Maloney, Water Law Seminar, Florida State Univ. BSM Records, Tallahassee, Fla.

Wood, William. "Of the Beasts That Live on the Land." *This Incomperable Lande.* Ed. Thomas J. Lyon. Boston: Houghton Mifflin, 1989.

Woodward, Doug. Conversation, March 15, 1999.

Cases Cited

Alden v. Pinney, 12 Fla. 348 (1868).

Attorney-General v. Chambers, 4 DE G. M. & G. 216, 43 Eng. Rep. 486 (1854).

Barney v. Keokuk, 94 U.S. 324 (1876).

The Board of Trustees of the Internal Improvement Trust Fund and Florida Audubon Society v. Board of Professional Land Surveyors, et al. (Fla. 1st D.C.A. Case Nos. 89-1293, 89-1294. Opinion filed September 13, 1990.

The Board of Trustees of the Internal Improvement Trust Fund of the State of Florida v. Board of Professional Land Surveyors, Department of Professional Regulation of the State of Florida. Case No. 88-4710R. Charles C. Adams, hearing officer, April 17, 1989. Final Order, 11 FALR 2467.

Board of Trustees of the Internal Improvement Trust Fund of the State of Florida v. Lykes Bros., Inc., June 2, 1997.

Board of Trustees of the Internal Improvement Trust Fund of the State of Florida v. Paradise Fruit Company, Inc., 414 So. 2d 10 (Fla. 5th D.C.A. 1982).

Borax Consolidated Ltd. v. Los Angeles, 296 U.S. 10 (1935).

Brickell v. Trammel, 77 Fla. 544, 82 So. 221 (1919).

Broward v. Mabry, 58 Fla. 398, 50 So. 826 (1909).

Bucki v. Cone, 25 Fla. 1, 6 So. 160–62 (1889).

Carson v. Blazer, 2 Binn. 475 (Pa. 1810).

Coastal Petroleum v. American Cyanamid, 454 So. 2d 6, 7 (Fla. 2d. D.C.A. 1984).

Coastal Petroleum v. American Cyanamid, 492 So. 2d 339 (Fla. 1986).

Cobb v. Davenport, 32 N.J.L. 369, 378 (Sup. Ct. 1867).

Concord Manuf'g Co. v. Robertson, 66 N.H. 1, 425 A. 718 (1889).

The Daniel Ball v. United States, 77 U.S. (10 Wall.) 557 (1870).

Geiger v. Filor, 8 Fla. 325, 335 (1859).

The Genessee Chief v. Fitzhugh, 53 U.S. 443 (1851).

Goose Creek Hunting Club Inc. v. United States, 518 F.2d. 579 (Ct. Cl. 1975).

Harrison v. Fite, 148 F.2d 781 (8th Cir. 1906).

Haven v. Perkins, 92 Vt. 414, 105 A. 249, 251 (1918).

Houghton v. The C., D. & M. R. Co., 47 Iowa 370, 373–74 (1877).

Howard v. Ingersoll, 54 U.S. 381 (1851).

Illinois Central Railroad v. Illinois, 146 U.S. 387 (1892).

Ingraham v. Wilkinson, 21 Mass. (4 Pick.) 268, 270–72 (1826).

Kissimmee River Valley Sportsmans' Association v. Roger MacNamara, Circuit Court of the Tenth Judicial Circuit of Florida, Polk County. Case no. GCG 92-644, Transcript of Proceedings, Vol. 3.

MacNamara v. Kissimmee River Valley Sportsmans' Association and Board of Trustees of the Internal Improvement Trust Fund, 648 So. 2d 155 (Fla. App. 2 Dist. 1994).

Martin v. Busch, 93 Fla. 535, 112 So. 274 (1927).

Martin v. Waddell, 41 U.S. 367, 410 (1842).

Minnetonka Lake Improvement, 56 Minn. 513, 58 N.W. 295, 45 Am. St. Rep. 494.

Oemler v. Green, 134 Ga. 198, 67 S.E. 433 (1910).

Oklahoma v. Texas, 260 U.S. 606 (1923).

Paine v. Woods, 108 Mass. 160 (1871).

Paradise Fruit Company, Inc., v. Board of Trustees of the Internal Improvement Fund and State of Florida, Department of Natural Resources. Summary final judgment, March 3, 1981, Circuit Court for Brevard County, Tom Waddell, Jr., Judge.

Peavy-Wilson Lumber Co. v. Brevard County, 31 So. 2d 483.

Phillips Petroleum Co. v. Mississippi, 484 U.S. 469, 108 S. Ct. 791 (1988).

The Propeller Genessee Chief, 53 U.S. 443 (1851).

Rivas v. Solary, 18 Fla. 122 (1881).

Shively v. Bowlby, 152 U.S. 1 (1893).

State of Florida and Board of Trustees of the Internal Improvement Trust Fund v. Florida National Properties, Inc., 338 So. 2d 13, 16 (Fla. 1976).

State of Florida v. Black River Phosphate Co., 32 Fla. 82, 13 So. 640 (1893).

State of Florida ex rel. Buford v. City of Tampa, 88 Fla. 196, 102 So. 336 (1924).

State of Florida ex rel. Ellis v. Gerbing, 56 Fla. 603, 47 So. 353 (1908).

Sullivan of Florida v. Moreno, 19 Fla. 200 (1882).

State v. Cain, 126 Vt. 463 (1867).

State v. Korrer et al., 127 Minn. 60 (1914).

State v. Strafford, 99 N.H. 92, A.2d 569 (1954).

State v. Sunapee Dam, 70 N.H. 458, (1900).

Symmes v. Prairie Pebble Phosphate Co., 64 Fla. 480, 60 So. 223 (1912).

Tilden v. Smith, 94 Fla. 502, 113 So. 708 (1927).

Tinicum Fishing Co. v. Carter, 61 Pa. 21 (1869).

United States v. Holt State Bank, 270 U.S. 56 (1926).

Utah v. U.S., 403 U.S. (1971).

Zabel v. Pinellas County Water & Navigation Control Authority, 171 So. 2d 376 (Fla. 1965).

Index

accretion, 86, 90, 107, 243n68, 247
agricultural crops test, 36, 207
Alden v. Pinney, 24
Attorney General v. Chambers, 14, 208, 223n9, 225n48
average water line, 14, 169, 175, 186
avulsion, 76, 247

Barada, William R., 60–61, 64–65, 117, 237n2
Barney v. Keokuk, 16, 85, 223n4
bay fills, 37–39, 75, 228n124
Bishop, E. W., 92–93, 106, 110–11
Board of Professional Land Surveyors (BPLS) 10, 212
Board of Professional Land Surveyors (BPLS) rule, 153–56, 161, 165, 170, 194; BPLS/DNR rule, 181–82; and definitions pertaining to OHWL, 161, 163, 175–79, 184, 212; DNR objections to, 162; *Howard v. Ingersoll* and, 166–70, 176–77, 184; and methodology, 163; Mobil Theory and, 194–96; perceptions of, 171–75
Board of Trustees of the Internal Improvement Trust Fund: bulkhead lines and, 78; defined, 247; *Florida National Properties* and, 107; Kissimmee River and, 68, 120, 184; *MacNamara* and, 184; and moratorium on sale of submerged lands, 69; *Trustees v. Smith*, 196
Board of Trustees of the Internal Improvement Trust Fund and Florida Audubon Society v. Board of Professional Land Surveyors, Department of Professional Regulation of the State of Florida, 175, 193, 196, 202

Board of Trustees of the Internal Improvement Trust Fund of the State of Florida v. Lykes Bros., Inc., 11, 224n32, 226n70, 234n24, 237n104, 241n38
Board of Trustees of the Internal Improvement Trust Fund of the State of Florida v. Paradise Fruit Co., Inc., 142, 237n110, 239n66
Borax Consolidated Ltd. v. Los Angeles, 225n45
Brickell v. Trammel, 30
Broward v. Mabry, 17, 28, 32, 84, 208
Bucki v. Cone, 17, 82
bulkhead law, 38–40, 74–75
bulkhead line, 38–40, 74–78, 92, 232n2, 232n10
Butler Act, 30
Butterworth, Robert A., 150, 161, 170

Carson v. Blazer, 18
Cavell, Stanley, 103, 204, 220–21, 235n47, 236n79
Coastal Petroleum v. American Cyanamid, 150, 193, 194
Cobb v. Davenport, 13
common law, English, 2, 13, 15–16, 18–19, 223n6
conflict/controversy over the OHWL, xiii, 6–12, 189, 198–99; and issues of authority and methodology, 128, 156, 158, 191, 203; in judicial opinions, 169; in Kissimmee River channelization, 41, 137, 141; between private and public interests, 3; in public input, 125; and public lands protection v. disposal, 20; between ranchers and city dwellers, 136; and the understanding of nature, 4
criteria, 6, 74, 191, 204, 206–9;

and, 28, 37–38; beds and shores of navigable waters and, 2, 168; boundary of, 2, 7, 23–24, 33, 128, 169, 187, 193, 195; in BPLS rule, 10, 153, 161, 176; defined, 247; estimation of, 145; exposed, 76, 77–78; Florida Constitution and, 41, 68–69, 148; "great ponds" and, 18; inventory of, 6; Kissimmee River restoration and, 52, 73, 190; Lake Kissimmee and, 119, 129, 134; loss of, 142, 146, 162; and meander lines, 81; Mobil Theory and, 194; navigability tests and, 10–11, 17, 226n65; navigable waters not mapped or identified as, 6, 142; "original" OHWL and, 86, 89–90; and policy on freshwaters, 74, 76, 94, 126, 233n17; private property/landowner claims to, 3–4; protection of, 7, 20, 21, 28, 37, 39, 106, 112–14, 144; public trust/nature of, 2, 12, 19, 23, 78; swamp and overflowed lands and, 22, 28, 152, 179, 198. See also Florida case law pertaining to sovereignty lands; legislation affecting sovereignty lands; shore— as sovereignty lands

spring tides, 14–15

State of Florida and Board of Trustees of the Internal Improvement Trust Fund v. Florida National Properties, Inc., 107, 177

State of Florida ex rel. Ellis v. Gerbing, 28, 177, 198, 243n69

State of Florida v. Black River Phosphate Co., 25, 30

Sullivan of Florida v. Moreno, 25

Swamp and Overflowed Lands Act of 1850, 22, 49, 200–201, 216; BPLS rule and, 176–79, 184, 243n71; Coastal Petroleum v. American Cyanamid and, 149–50, 198; deeds

and, 101; Disston drainage contract and, 27; Internal Improvement Fund and, 22–23; Lake Tohopekaliga patent and, 97; MacNamara and, 186; Martin v. Busch and, 33–34; Mobil Theory and, 194–95; MRTA and, 141–42, 196; navigable waters and, 28–29, 142, 151–52, 198; property rights and, 187; "Sovereignty Lands Bill" and, 201; surveying and, 83; Trustees v. David A. Smith and, 193, 196

Symmes v. Prairie Pebble Phosphate Co., 29

tidal, 2; in American law, 15–16, 25, 208, 223n6; as boundary criterion, 15, 186, 191; bulkhead lines and, 39; in English common law, 2, 13; in Florida Statutes, 94; MHWL and, 13, 74–75, 247; navigable and, 15; OHWL and, 26

tidelands, 22, 31, 33–34, 72, 201, 225n48

tides: neap, 14–15, 209; spring, 14–15

Tilden v. Smith, 206–8; agricultural crops test and, 36–37, 108, 207; BPLS rule and, 176–77, 199; flat-banked waterbodies and, 87; Gentry theory and, 184–5; and OHWL, 33, 87; and "ordinary," concept of, 35; and physical-fact method, 129; and scientific exploration, 37; and "Sovereignty Lands Bill," 202–3; and vegetation indicators, 35–36

title test, 18

Toth, Louis, 45, 64–65, 237n2

United States Supreme Court, 9, 15–17, 85–86, 166, 187, 221, 225n64, 226n74

Utah v. United States, 17

Wade, Jeff, 9, 224n26, 224n28
Wallis, W. Turner, 22, 24, 26–27, 31, 37–39, 101–2
water line. *See* average water line; low water line; Mean High Water Line (MHWL); Ordinary High Water Line (OHWL)
Whitfield, J. B., Chief Justice, 26, 28–30, 32–33

Wilkinson, Terry E., 181–82, 185, 188–89, 204, 206–7

Zabel v. Pinellas County Water & Navigation Control Authority, 67
Zabel v. Russell, 67